J. Z. Tyler

Kinship to Christ

And other sermons

J. Z. Tyler

Kinship to Christ
And other sermons

ISBN/EAN: 9783743355361

Manufactured in Europe, USA, Canada, Australia, Japa

Cover: Foto ©Lupo / pixelio.de

Manufactured and distributed by brebook publishing software (www.brebook.com)

J. Z. Tyler

Kinship to Christ

KINSHIP TO CHRIST

AND OTHER SERMONS.

By J. Z. TYLER.

"He is not ashamed to call them brethren."

ST. LOUIS:
JOHN BURNS, Publisher,
717 and 719 Olive Street.

TO THE MEMBERS

OF THE

SEVENTH STREET CHRISTIAN CHURCH,

OF

RICHMOND, VIRGINIA,

THIS SELECTION OF SERMONS IS AFFECTIONATELY

DEDICATED,

IN GRATEFUL RECOGNITION OF THEIR CONSTANT KINDNESS TO ME

DURING MY MINISTRY AMONG THEM,

FROM

OCTOBER 1, 1872, TO FEBRUARY 1, 1883.

CONTENTS.

I. KINSHIP TO CHRIST 7–17

There came then his brethren and his mother, and, standing without, sent unto him, calling him. And the multitude sat about him, and they said unto him, Behold, thy mother and thy brethren without seek for thee. And he answered them, saying, Who is my mother, or my brethren? And he looked round about on them which sat about him, and said, Behold my mother and my brethren! For whosoever shall do the will of God, the same is my brother, and my sister, and mother. Mark iii: 31–35. — *Preached second Lord's Day, in February, 1882.*

II. INCREASING IN THE KNOWLEDGE OF GOD . . . 18–29

For this cause we also, since the day we heard it, do not cease to pray for you, and to desire that ye might be filled with a knowledge of His will in all wisdom and spiritual understanding; that ye might walk worthy of the Lord unto all pleasing, being fruitful in every good work, and increasing in the knowledge of God. Col. 1: 9–10. — *Preached third Lord's Day, in October, 1880.*

III. THE CENTRAL FACT IN THE CHRISTIAN SYSTEM . . 30–46

And many other signs truly did Jesus in the presence of his disciples, which are not written in this book; but these are written, that ye might believe that Jesus is the Christ, the Son of God; and that believing ye might have life through his name. John xx: 30–31. — *Preached first Lord's Day, in January, 1877.*

(i)

IV. THE GLORIOUS GOSPEL 47–57

But if our gospel be hid, it is hid to them that are lost; in whom the God of this world hath blinded the minds of them that believe not, lest the light of the glorious gospel of Christ, who is the image of God, should shine unto them. II Cor. iv: 3–4. — *Preached fourth Lord's Day, in July, 1876.*

V. SPECIAL INFLUENCE IN CONVERSION 58–65

And a certain woman named Lydia, a seller of purple, of the city of Thyatira, which worshipped God, heard us; whose heart the Lord opened, that she attended unto the things which were spoken by Paul. Acts xvi: 14. — *Preached first Lord's Day, in October, 1882.*

VI. YOUR OWN SALVATION 66–80

Wherefore, my beloved, as ye have always obeyed, not as in my presence only, but now much more in my absence, work out your own salvation, with fear and trembling; for it is God which worketh in you both to will and to do of his good pleasure. Phil. ii: 12–13. — *Preached March 22d, 1882.*

VII. ORDINANCES OF THE LORD 81–89

And they were both righteous before God, walking in all the commandments and ordinances of the Lord blameless. Luke i: 6. — *Preached second Lord's Day, in October, 1882.*

VIII. SAFETY IN SHIPWRECK 90–96

Paul said to the centurion and to the soldiers, Except these abide in the ship ye cannot be saved. Acts xxvii: 31. — *Preached third Lord's Day, in September, 1882.*

IX. THE MANIFESTATION OF FAITH 97–111

What doth it profit, my brethren, though a man say he hath faith, and have not works? Can faith save him? If a brother or sister be naked, and destitute of daily food, and one of you say unto them, Depart in peace, be ye warmed and filled; notwithstanding ye give them not those things which are needful to the body; what doth it profit; Even so faith, if it hath not works, is dead, being alone. Yea, a man may say, Thou hast faith, and I have works: show me thy faith without thy works, and I will show my faith by my works. James ii: 14–18.—*Preached first Lord's Day, in December, 1876.*

X. THE EXTERIOR AND THE INTERIOR OF OUR DEEDS . 112–119
And though I give all my goods to feed the poor, * * * and have not charity, it profiteth me nothing. I Cor. xiii: 3.
For whosoever shall give you a cup of water to drink in my name, because ye belong to Christ, verily I say unto you, he shall not lose his reward. Mark ix: 41.—*Preached third Lord's Day, in September, 1882.*

XI. THE UNIFYING POWER OF THE CROSS 120–130
And I, if I be lifted up from the earth, will draw all men unto me. This he said, signifying what death he should die. John xii: 32-33.—*Preached fourth Lord's Day, in August, 1876.*

XII. PAUL'S CHAPTER ON CHARITY 131–143
Though I speak with the tongues of men and of angels, and have not charity, I am become as sounding brass, or a tinkling cymbal And though I have the gift of prophecy, and understand all mysteries, and all knowledge; and though I have all faith, so that I could remove mountains, and have not charity, I am nothing. * * * And now abideth faith, hope, charity, these three; but the greatest of these is charity. I Cor. xiii: 1-13.—*Preached first Lord's Day, in February, 1882.*

XIII. THE GROUND OF OUR HOPE 144–153
Be ready always to give an answer to every man that asketh you a reason of the hope that is in you, with meekness and fear. I Peter iii: 15.—*Preached second Lord's Day, in June, 1882.*

CONTENTS.

XIV. DRIFTING FROM GOD 154–164

Take heed, brethren, lest there be in any of you an evil heart of unbelief, in departing from the living God. Heb. iii:12. — *Preached third Lord's Day, in October, 1882.*

XV. CHRIST AS A TEACHER 165–172

Rabbi, we know thou art a teacher come from God: for no man can do these miracles that thou doest, except God be with him. John iii: 2. — *Preached third Lord's Day, in September, 1876.*

XVI. THE WAY, THE TRUTH AND THE LIFE . . . 173–178

Jesus saith unto him, I am the way, the truth, and the life; no man cometh unto the Father, but by me. John xiv: 6. — *Preached fifth Lord's Day, in January, 1882.*

XVII. OUR SINS AND OUR SAVIOR 179–188

And she shall bring forth a son, and thou shalt call his name Jesus: for he shall save his people from their sins. Matt. i: 21. — *Preached third Lord's Day, in February, 1882.*

XVIII. CHRIST'S PURPOSES IN OUR CONVERSION . . 189–199

But I follow after, if that I may apprehend that for which also I am apprehended of Christ Jesus. Phil. iii:12. — *Preached second Lord's Day, in August, 1882.*

XIX. CHRISTLESS REFORMATION 200–209

When a strong man armed keepeth his palace, his goods are in peace; but when a stronger than he shall come upon him, and overcome him, he taketh from him all his armor wherein he trusted, and divideth his spoils. * * * When the unclean spirit is gone out of a man, he walketh through dry places, seeking rest; and finding none, he saith, I will return unto my house whence I came out. And when he cometh he findeth it swept and garnished. Then goeth he, and taketh to him seven other spirits more wicked than himself; and they enter in and dwell there: and the last state of that man is worse than the first. Luke xi: 21-26. — *Preached second Lord's Day, in February, 1881.*

XX. THE FRUIT OF THE SPIRIT 210–221

But the fruit of the Spirit is love, joy, peace, long-suffering, gentleness, goodness, faith, meekness, temperance; against such there is no law. Gal. v: 22-23. — *Preached third Lord's Day, in May, 1874.*

XXI. CHRIST'S LESSONS FROM THE VINEYARD . . . 222–231

I am the true wine, and my Father is the husbandman. Every branch in me that beareth not fruit he taketh away; and every branch that beareth fruit he purgeth it, that it may bring forth more fruit, etc., etc. John xv: 1-6. — *Preached second Lord's Day, in September, 1876.*

XXII. HINDERANCES 232–239

Ye did run well; who did hinder you that ye should not obey the truth? Gal. v: 7. — *Preached second Lord's Day, in September, 1880.*

XXIII. OBEDIENCE TO HEAVENLY VISIONS 240–249

Whereupon, O King Agrippa, I was not disobedient to the heavenly vision. Acts xxvi: 19. — *Preached fourth Lord's Day, in October, 1877.*

XXIV. THE DIVINE ESTIMATE OF MAN 250–258

When I consider thy heavens, the work of thy fingers, the moon and the stars, which thou hast ordained; what is man, that thou art mindful of him? and the son of man, that thou visitest him? Psalm viii: 3-4. — *Preached second Lord's Day, in December, 1881.*

CONTENTS.

XXV. MUTUAL HELPFULNESS 259–270

We then that are strong ought to bear the infirmities of the weak, and not to please ourselves. Rom. xv:1.
Bear ye one another's burdens, and so fulfil the law of Christ. Gal. vi: 2. — *Preached fourth Lord's Day, in August, 1877.*

XXVI. SERVICE AND HONOR 271–280

If any man serve me, let him follow me; and where I am, there shall also my servant be; if any man serve me him will my Father honor. John xii: 26. — *Preached third Lord's Day, in June, 1875.*

XXVII. HERE AND HEREAFTER 281–291

Be not deceived; God is not mocked: for whatsoever a man soweth that shall he also reap. For he that soweth to his flesh, shall of the flesh reap corruption; but he that soweth to the spirit shall of the spirit reap life everlasting. And let us not be weary in well doing: for in due season we shall reap, if we faint not. Gal. vi: 7–9. — *Preached second Lord's Day, in October, 1877.*

XXVIII. IDLERS INTERVIEWED 292–304

And about the eleventh hour he went out, and found others standing idle, and said unto them, Why stand ye here all the day idle? Mat. xx: 6. — *Preached fourth Lord's Day, in December, 1879.*

XXIX. DISTINCTIVE PECULIARITIES OF THE DISCIPLES . 305–332

But we desire to hear of thee what thou thinkest, for as concerning this sect, we know that everywhere it is spoken against. Acts xxviii: 22. — *Preached first Lord's Day, in March, 1882.*

KINSHIP TO CHRIST,

AND OTHER SERMONS.

KINSHIP TO CHRIST.

There came then his brethren and his mother, and standing without, sent unto him calling him. And the multitude sat about him, and they said unto him, Behold, thy mother and thy brethren without seek for thee. And he answered them saying: Who is my mother, or who my brethren? And he looked round about him, and said, Behold my mother and my brethren! For whosoever shall do the will of God, the same is my brother, and my sister and mother. — Mark iii: 31-35.

I feel that it is difficult for us to realize how widespread and intense was the enthusiasm awakened by the ministry of Christ. His works were so wonderful and so philanthropic, while his teaching in its freshness, its tenderness, and its adaptation to human wants, was so unlike anything they had ever heard, that the people gathered about him from every part of the land. The incident recorded in the text occurred at a time when a wave of popular enthusiasm was rapidly rising about him. Mark tells us, in an earlier part of this chapter, that from Galilee, and from Judea, and from Jerusalem, and from over in Idumæa, and from about Tyre and Sidon down by the sea, there came great multitudes. It was such an uprising of the people as we have never witnessed, and it is difficult for us even to imagine.

In the midst of such surroundings the answer which Jesus made to the request of his mother and his brethren seems peculiarly hard. He appears to ignore them in the hour of his popularity. It looks, at first glance, as if he undervalued the tender ties of the family. And, there are opposers of his religion who fancy they find in this incident, and others in his life, not only an undervaluation of family ties, but a positive disregard of their obligation. And, not only that *he* contemptuously set aside these claims, but that his teaching would produce the same sad results among his followers. They make the startling statement that, "under the full sway of Christianity as taught by Christ and his apostles, the natural ties of the family would be dissolved and the household would go down under religious fanaticism."

This scarcely deserves consideration in the presence of those who know the facts of his personal life and are in any measure familiar with the development of the history of the religion established in his name. As a child he was obedient to his parents; and even in the pain and agony of the dying hour, he affectionately remembered his widowed mother and provided for her a hospitable home. We know that wherever his teachings have been received family ties have been elevated and sanctified. The New Testament, in the wide sweep of its instruction, touches every possible relation, — husbands to wives, wives to husbands; parents to children, children to parents; brother to brother; sister to sister; masters to servants, and servants to masters, — its instructions extend to every point in the circle of home with the magic touch of love and purity and make it a type of the holiest spiritual relationships and a symbol of the fellowship of Heaven. The religious delusion of the Shaker, the morbid fanaticism of the monastery and the nunnery, the celebacy of the clergy, and similar social monstrosities find no sanction from Christ or elsewhere in the Word of God. The Scriptures sanction and sanctify the marriage tie, teach reverent regard for parents, make the relation between master and servant less rigorous, and fill the home with the fragrance and melody of love.

When, therefore, our Savior answers the request from his mother and his brethren as he does in the text, we cannot suppose that he means to ignore the relationship they sustained to him, but he finds in the occasion a fitting opportunity to teach them of a higher and holier relationship based upon other conditions. It is as if he had said, "While the family according to the flesh, has in it the dearest ties of nature, I am come to establish among the divided and discordant elements of society a family in which will be found stronger and holier ties, arising from a new birth and binding the children of God into an eternal brotherhood." He makes this fact stand out prominently by the contrast. "Who is my mother or my brethren? * * * * Whosoever shall do the will of God, the same is my brother, and my sister and mother."

The first thought, lying upon the very surface of the event, is the marvellous fact that the *Son of God has kindred among the children of men.* That is a fact; not a poetic fancy. And this fact so wonderful to every one who pauses to consider it, marks a new era in the history of our race.

It was this coming brotherhood that formed the burden of the prophetic preaching of John, the harbinger of Christ. In the wilderness he cried, "Behold, the kingdom of Heaven is at hand." And when Christ entered upon his public ministry he took up the same prophetic cry. The Twelve were sent upon their limited mission, and the seventy, to make the same announcement in the villages and cities and towns of that land. The Kingdom is at hand! The kingdom of Heaven is at hand!

What was the meaning of this? Certainly, that a new era in the world's history was ready to open. But what was meant by the kingdom of which they spoke? Was it that some heaven-sent and heaven-crowned king was about to establish a throne like that of the Cæsars, and rule over an empire like that of Rome? A kingdom of force and imperial authority? A kingdom not united by an inward unity, but by outward compulsion? I fear too many take this prophetic announcement and interpret it by the lowest and most earthly features of an earthly kingdom. But remember that Christ said, "My kingdom is not of this world." In its origin, its nature, its principles, its purposes, its methods, and its outward appearance it is not of this world. It is a reign rather than a kingdom. It is the sway of divine love over the hearts of men, filling and flooding them with goodness, as the moon sways the tides, and floods the estuaries and inlets along our coast. It is the reign of grace over fallen human nature as the sun reigns over the barren grounds of the fields in spring, quickening the hidden seed and nourishing it into a full harvest. Let us do away with crude mechanical, earthly notions of God's kingdom among men. Let us not think of the church of Christ as a combination of men and women, subscribing to a creed, supplied with grades of officers, and governed by police regulations.

The prominent feature of the church is brotherhood. It is Christ's spiritual family. He gathered around him chosen men and taught them fresh lessons of God. He led them up in thought. He breathed into them something of his own spirit. He poured upon them, out of his heart, warm, quickening love. There was found in his work nothing of the cold manipulations of the ritualistic Rabbi. He gave them liberty by giving them life. As he unfolded God's will they saw love in it, goodness in it, grace in it, fatherhood in it, and with the spirit of sons rather than of slaves they bowed before that will and sought to do it. Upon this group he looked, over these he waved his hand, as he said, "Behold my brethren." Here was the church in embryo. It was a brotherhood.

But, as a stone cast into the pool makes first a small circle immediately about itself, and then others beyond, wider and wider, until they touch the margin, so this fraternal circle would be enlarged. Not these only but "whosoever shall do the will of God." The circle sweeps out. It goes beyond national boundaries, it sweeps away social barriers, it uproots prejudices, it melts selfishness, it drowns bigotry, it overturns whatever stands in its way until Greek and Jew, circumcision and uncircumcision, barbarian, Scythian, bond and free stand within the circle of this Scriptural brotherhood. This was the church in its primitive simplicity. It was a spiritual family. Its members are akin to each other, because each is akin to Christ.

Without this thought of kinship we cannot have the right idea of the church. Men may form themselves into partnerships for the conduct of business; they are bound together by a business contract. This is not a type of the church. Nations are made by the conquest of provinces and are held together by force, yet though they all yield obedience to the same laws and are governed from the same throne the type of the church is not found in the nation. Armies are gathered of scattered individuals and are bound into a body by the force of military authority. There is unity in an army. But it is not the unity which forms the members of the church into one body. The unity of the family is the unity of the church, as the family itself is the best type of the church. Our Father is the king; Christ's spiritual brotherhood the kingdom.

The second point to which I turn is this — *The ground upon which this kingdom rests.* "Whoever shall do the will of God." This, it seems to me, cuts up, by the very roots, two theories held upon this point. The first is, that the position of any one of our race in this family depends wholly and absolutely upon the sovereign choice of God. As is stated in one of the creeds, — "By the decree of God, for the manifestation of his glory, some men and angels are predestinated unto everlasting life," — and more, — that this choice and decree was " out of His mere free grace and love, without any foresight of faith or good works, or perseverance in either of them, or *anything in the creature, as conditions,* or causes moving him thereunto." Yet Jesus says that entrance into this family is conditioned upon doing the will of God. I suppose it will not be claimed by any, in answer to this, that men may enter into everlasting life without entering into spiritual kinship with Christ. Life itself is dependent upon this kinship, and the kinship rests upon doing. Life, therefore, depends upon doing. If it depends upon doing it cannot depend wholly upon arbitrary choice and decree.

The second theory is that fleshy birth of Christian parents gives the child a place in this spiritual family. The creed from which I have just quoted says, in its definition of the church, that it "consists of all throughout the world who profess the true religion, *together with their children.*" Now, while it is true that a position in the great Jewish family or nation depended upon the birth of the flesh, it is also true, that this is one of the points of sharp contrast between that people and the spiritual Israel of God. The birth of flesh has absolutely nothing to do with this. How godly soever your parents may be it gives to you no claim to any position or privilege. "Think not to say within yourselves, we have

Abraham to our Father." It will not profit. The ground now is, "whosoever shall do the will of God."

But let us guard against the danger of giving to this statement a narrow and slavish application. The doing of which Christ speaks is born of love and faith. It is not the careful observance of any number of specific commandments. Here is where the Pharisee made his mistake. He selected and classified commands. He gave a slavish observance to them. He was diligently doing commandments, and yet he was not in any worthy sense doing the will of God. Suppose your child should treat you in a similar way. If you are such a father as you should be your will should govern your household. Your will is good-will and its benign and gentle sway over your home fills it with joy. But your child responds to your will as a slave to the tyranny of a task-master. You ask it to do something and, in a servile spirit, it does the specific thing named and in the exact manner, but there it stops. You kindly bid it do something else, and it is done. And so, day after day, without the inspiration of filial devotion, without the sympathetic spirit that can interpret your will and read your pleasure even where specific commands for the detail of each duty are not given, day after day, in such a servile spirit, your child goes about your home *doing your commandments!* What a child! What a home where such a spirit rules or serves! Save me from such a home, and save me from such a church!

It is true that a commandment is a revelation of will, and because it is, it should be cheerfully obeyed. But doing the will rises above the thought of doing any number of specific commandments. Whatever, in any degree, indicates the divine will is a light upon the path of Christian life. The spirit of his promises, the nature of his threatenings, the objects of his benedictions, the general tone of his message, the earth-life of his Son, the character of those who live most with him, all these and many more blend their light in a revelation of his will. To be a Christian, then, is to have the will of the Supreme, the Supreme will in us. It is to be under its gentle sway and guidance.

Then, too, there is this feature in God's will never wanting — it is always good-will. If you show me that which is cruel and selfish and malign I know that it is not God's will. Nor can he be under the sway of God's will in whom such elements are found. Take no narrow view of God's gracious will. Do not think you can give full expression to it in three commandments, or ten commandments, or a hundred commandments, or any number of specific commandments. Do not for one moment suppose that because you have exercised faith and made the good confession of Christ, because you have sorrowed over sin and been baptized, that therefore you have met the full meaning of the condition given in the text.

It was my purpose to mention and to make prominent the thought that *this condition commends itself by its very reasonableness.* I can give only a few points, and leave them, without elaboration. First, it is reasonable that we should be received back to God through submission to his will, because we fell through casting it off. It is reasonable, in the second place, because it requires conformity to the image of Christ, his Eternal Son. And, finally, because it opens the way to all alike, — "*Whosoever,*" etc.

I have spoken of the wonderful fact that the Son of God has kindred among men, and shown from that, what seems to me to have been his idea of the church — a spiritual brotherhood or family; I have pointed out the ground upon which this brotherhood is based, and have contrasted it with theories, and have sought to elevate and enlarge our conceptions of what is meant by doing the will of God. One point remains. It is *the superiority of spiritual to carnal kinship* Christ puts this before us very strikingly in the incident recorded in the text. "These about me are more truly my kindred than those who stand without desiring to see me," is his conduct framed into words. Spiritual kinship is superior to carnal

It is more comprehensive. If I am a Christian, —if Christ is my brother,—then I can stand here and under the shield of Christ's words in the text say that whosoever, in the whole world, is doing the will of God is my brother, my sister, my mother. Let sectarian walls tumble down, let party lines be blotted out, let selfish conceits perish. This brotherhood is not fully enrolled on the church books of any one denomination. It is larger than any ecclesiastical organization, whatever its name or its pretensions. Its circle embraces all social classes, all nations, all tongues. Yea, it reaches beyond this earth. It is the one unbroken family, whether in heaven or in earth.

It is more lasting. We know but little of what we shall find beyond the gate of death, but the Scriptures indicate that carnal ties, family bonds, will be, in a great measure, obscured and forgotten. But the hidden ties by which we have been bound together in this spiritual brotherhood will only begin to reveal their full strength when we reach Home. The fellowship will be sweeter. Death cannot break it. On forever and forever, without rupture, without discord, without end, shall go this spiritual family of Christ.

It brings superior blessings. What may come to us from family connection, — what social standing, what natural gifts, what inheritance! How great the honor of being of the family to which Christ belonged, according to the flesh. Once, as Jesus was teaching, " a certain woman out of the multitude lifted up her voice, and said unto him, "Blessed is the womb that bare thee and the breasts which thou didst suck. But he said, Yea rather, blessed are they that hear the word of God, and keep it." Many thousands to-day reverently worship Mary because she was his mother. But greater blessing comes of doing God's will, freely and lovingly, than comes of simple motherhood to Jesus. He is my brother. With a brother's love he loves me. God is my Father. Not in theory — not in a word only — but in blessed reality. The Spirit is my helper and my comforter. Heaven is my home. I am made an heir of God — a joint-heir with Jesus Christ.

It is more binding in its obligation. For, while the Scriptures inculcate obedience to parents, should a conflict arise by which your obligations to your parents come in conflict with your obligation to your Heavenly Father you are solemnly to renounce all for his will. Christ says, "If you love father or mother more than me ye cannot be my disciple." Such a conflict can scarcely arise in the life of any one here, but should it — should parental ties stand in the way of doing God's will, rise above these ties and choose to do God's will. How many have in early times left all for this? How many have faced death to do God's will? Yet we hesitate when but the smallest obstacle presents itself. What hinders you to-day from becoming a Christian? Is the excuse one you would dare to present to God?

I conclude with this thought, that *Christ is not ashamed of his kinship.* Paul says, "For both he that sanctifieth and they who are sanctified are all of one; for which cause he is not ashamed to call them brethren." Christ himself said, "Whoso shall confess me before men, him will I confess before my Father and the holy angels."

I open at the twenty-fifth chapter of Matthew, and a scene

of awful significance and grandeur rises before me. A throne — a judge — the sound of trumpets — the gathering of nations — multitudes, multitudes, multitudes which no man can number. It is the end of time. It is the day of judgment. It is the assemblage of the universe. Christ will own them then. He will identify the humblest one of them with himself, saying, "Inasmuch as ye have done it unto one of the least of these my brethren, ye have done it unto me." The king goes down if he is not akin to Christ; the sage is unhonored if he did not learn God's will and do it; the warrior is not acknowledged if he has not in life taken Christ as the captain of his salvation. It is the time for the family gathering. His kindred hear him say come, and the great doors to his Father's house, with its many mansions, are thronged. Here they are coming up out of every nation, and kindred, and people and tongue, under the whole heavens. I cannot count them. No man can number them. Come, narrow bigot, and try to count them. Come, you who are dealing out God's grace to men and fencing in the elect, come and number these multitudes. It will do you good to try? Who are they? Ask Christ, and he answers, these are my kindred coming home, for "whosoever shall do the will of God, the same is my brother, and my sister and mother."

INCREASING IN THE KNOWLEDGE OF GOD.

> For this cause we also, since the day we heard of it, do not cease to pray for you, and to desire that ye might be filled with the knowledge of his will in all wisdom and spiritual understanding; that ye might walk worthy of the Lord unto all pleasing, being fruitful in every good work, and increasing in the knowledge of God. Col. i: 9, 10.

The thought which runs through this entire passage comes out most clearly in its last clause — "increasing in the knowledge of God." The passage is part of a prayer. Paul's nature was so finely strung — his sympathies were so responsive and he was so conscious of the divine presence that thoughts of his brethren moved his heart to prayer. And so we frequently meet with mention of these prayers: sometimes, as in this case, he gives a summary statement of their substance.

He had heard of their faith in Christ Jesus, of their love for all the saints, and of the fruit they had brought forth since the day they had known the grace of God in truth. For all this he was thankful, and knowing that in all these things they would continue to grow, and that their joy in them would be deepened should they increase in the knowledge of God, the fountain of all good, he prayed for this increase. In addition to this, he esteemed personal, heart-knowledge of God of the greatest intrinsic value. It is not only the spring of spiritual excellence, but the ultimate aim of all revelation.

In the lesson for this morning [1] you may have observed

---

[1] Rom. i: 19–32.

how Paul traces the moral degradation of the Gentiles to their loss of the knowledge of God. They did not like to retain a true and pure conception of Him. When they knew Him they glorified Him not as God, neither were thankful. They changed the glory of the uncorruptible God into an image made like to corruptible man, and to birds, and to four-footed beasts, and to creeping things. Then, in the strong language of Paul, God gave them up to uncleanness, and to vile affections, and over to reprobate minds. With the skill of a master he sketches this frightful picture of moral degradation, and then with the insight of a profound philosopher he lays his finger upon that out of which it all came.

Since, then, moral degradation comes of the loss of the true knowledge of God, moral elevation and sanctification must find their main spring in this knowledge. It is a vain thing to attempt to purify and to adorn with moral beauty that which carries degraded and degrading conceptions of God within. Whether we will it or not, theology, in its strict sense, lies at the basis of right living.

What, then, are our conceptions of God? While I recognize the sacredness which rightly belongs to the hidden thoughts of our hearts in these matters of our holy religion, I venture to press this as a personal question, — What is your conception of God? When you bow down to pray; when you withdraw to meditate; when you read the Holy Scriptures " alone with your beating heart and your God;" when thoughts of the great change come and the meeting which must be beyond, what image of the Eternal One rises before you? In your best moments, when you are lifted into the region of clear and vigorous thinking, what are your visions of God? Or, is God only a name? Does it stand simply for vastness and the majesty of vagueness? You recognize the fact that the Bible uniformly teaches that He is a person, but is he really personal to you, and, if so, what is the character of that personality?

I do not hold that any one may know the Almighty to perfection. He is infinite. We can know only in part. Not until our senses are multiplied so that channels lie open along which all knowledge may flow, and not until our nature is so enlarged that it can comprehend the infinite, will it be possible for us to know God in the fullness of that knowledge. He lies above us and beyond, and is far greater than all human thought. Yet it is important that our part-knowledge be correct, so far as it goes, and we should recognize the possibility of its increase beyond all past growth. Let us not delude ourselves by supposing that because we are Christians, because we already know something of him, that there is no need for enlarged views of his character. Those for whom this prayer was offered were not unbelievers, they were not skeptics, but they were believers in Christ and had learned of the grace of God in truth. They were Christians, yet Paul prayed that they might be filled with a knowledge of His will, in all wisdom and spiritual understanding and that they might, beyond all present attainments, increase in the knowledge of Him. So pray I for ourselves. I pray that there may be awakened within us a longing for fuller knowledge, a deeper crying out after Him, a hungering and a thirsting for this feast and fountain of the soul.

This knowledge is not an intuition, nor does it come to us as an inspiration. We are to seek for it. It comes to reverent hearts as a reward of earnest search. The light which reflects the divine character falls upon us from various quarters; we are to combine the instructions of many teachers.

1. I mention, first of all, *a devout study of his works.*

"For the invisible things of Him since the creation of the world are clearly seen, being perceived through the things that are made, even His everlasting power and divinity." So says Paul. Nor is a profound scientific knowledge of these works most needed ; a reverent spirit is their best interpreter. In the Roman letter the Gentiles are said to have been without excuse for their ignorance and immorality. Creation was a revelation of the Creator so simple that they might have known Him. It was their Bible.

I have somewhere seen the story of a king who employed an architect to erect a very extensive and magnificent building, and in order that he might have all the glory of it he decreed that the name of the architect should nowhere appear in the building. But the ingenious architect so designed it that should you stand at a certain point, the beams and pillars and cross bars would form the letters of his name. So has the Great Architect framed this material universe. But we must occupy the right position. We must stand in the proper place. David knew but few of the lessons of our modern sciences, and they were the simplest, yet as he looked up with a reverent heart he exclaimed, "The heavens declare the glory of God, and the firmament showeth his handiwork."

Much of the teaching of Christ rests upon the hypothesis that nature is a revelation of the divine character. Many of his lessons concerning God were drawn from this source. He walked forth under the blue skies and into the fragrant fields and said, "Behold the fowls of the air," and, "Consider the lilies of the field," and, "The Kingdom of Heaven is like seed cast into the ground." All things about him were redolent of the thoughts of God. To him the material universe was a Bible, full of suggestive texts. And this is one reason why his teaching had such a wonderful freedom about it — it was fresh as the early dew, and fell upon waiting hearts like rain upon the dry and thirsty ground.

As the still waters below reflect from their depths the quiet stars above, so is the Maker of all things reflected from all things He has made. And He is greater than all. As the watchmaker's genius and skill are shown by the watch he has made, and as he is greater than the watch, so of God. Creation is crystallized thought. It is, in the strict sense, an evolution. Wisdom, power, beauty, goodness, — all there is in it,— was first in Him who is the author of it. It feebly represents Him. The canvas breathes with life and glows with beauty under the magic touch of the artist's pencil, but more beautiful than the picture upon the canvas is the picture resting upon his soul. The richest melody that rises from the singer is but an echo of the richer that still rolls in sweet cadences within. The artist is more than his picture; the singer is more than his song.

How strange that any should think that the Maker of all is less than all He has made! If there is harmony, melody, music and beauty; if there is wisdom and honor and forethought and goodness all about us and above us what must God be! Go forth under the stars and ask — what must their Maker be; standing upon the beach and looking out upon the wide ocean ask — what must the great God be; pause by the beautiful fragrant flower with your question — what must their Father be? Walk to and fro in this great house He has built and ask what must the builder of it be. Let your thoughts ascend the stairway of the material universe, let fancy go on free wing among the things of God, in the spirit of earnest inquiry and reverent worship, and you must increase in your knowledge of God.

2. But, even better than this is *a devout study of* **His** *written word.* Character comes out in what one says. Out

of the heart, the mouth speaketh. And for this was the word of God given. It is a revelation of Himself. It speaks of many other persons and things, but all in subordination to this chief purpose. When it tells of Adam and Enoch and Abram and of the patriarchs, it is that by means of these we may learn of Him. All history, all prophecy, all law, all ceremony, all poetry, in short, all things found within the volume of this book are placed there that they may enrich our knowledge of its author. These form the scenery — the setting of the picture — and the picture is of God.

Nor is this picture flashed upon the canvas in a moment. It appears slowly. Events are strokes of the brush. Power, wisdom, justice, holiness, love, fatherhood are brought out through centuries. Nor are all the parts of this picture grouped together and brought out fully at any one place. They extend through the entire book and lie half concealed under incidents, are enfolded in laws, appear in promises, shine out of ceremony and form the soul of sacred history.

If we would find God we must *search* the Scriptures. Ransack them. That is what Christ meant when he said search. Carefully examine every part — look diligently into every nook and corner.

I take this book into my hands to learn all I possibly can concerning its author. I approach it reverently. I do not handle it just as I would any other book. This is God's book — not only that He gave it, but because it reveals Him. From first to last it is about the Invisible One. I enter upon my search, I read many things, but I search among them all for fuller, clearer knowledge of God. I pause and think; I lift my heart in prayer. Events pass in review before me with rapid, solemn tread, and I eagerly listen for the footfall of God, for I know He is in their midst directing their march. I walk with Enoch in his walk with God; I follow Abram in his wanderings from his native land, knowing the divine presence blesses and guides him; I rest with Jacob on his stony pillow and look with upward gaze along the ladder of vision into the opened heavens; I go with Moses into the holy mount and tremble at the display of divine majesty and the voice of the Omnipotent; I frequent the school of the prophets; I ponder the mystery of the Urim and Thummim; I linger in the temple, hanging upon the notes of its inspired song, and studying its divinely appointed ritual; I become a companion of Elijah and Elisha, and follow the Baptist into the wilderness; I become a disciple in the school of Christ, and attend apostles and evangelists on their holy missions, until amid the heavenly splendors of that memorable Lord's day, I rest with the beloved disciple on the isle of Patmos. All the while I have been a searcher after God. At each step I have added something to my store of knowledge and blessed experience. I have gathered sheaves from the field of revelation as I have wandered from Eden to Patmos. This is the way to read the Bible. It is God's book revealing Himself. Search it. Search with a reverent purpose, search with a diligent heart, search in all its parts for a larger, better knowledge of him.

3. The third means of this increase is *a careful study of that which is best in man.* Christ used this method. You remember how he said, in the Sermon on the Mount, "What man is there of you, whom if his son ask bread, will he give him a stone? or if he ask a fish will he give him a scorpion? If ye then, being evil, know how to give good gifts to your children, how much more shall your Father who is in heaven give good gifts to them that ask him?" That is as if he had said, you can understand heavenly fatherhood through earthly fatherhood. If you in your imperfection, your selfishness can so care for yours, will not the perfect and un-

selfish and infinitely benevolent Father do far better for all who call upon him? Paul also adopts this same method when he would lift us up into an understanding of the fullness of the divine heart, "For scarcely for a righteous man will one die," says he, "yet peradventure for a good man some would even dare to die. But God commended his love toward us, in that, while we were yet sinners Christ died for us." This is as if he had said, love is the same both in heaven and in earth. If you desire to understand the greatness of God's love, call up the cases of strongest love among men and say God's love for man — sinful man — is far greater than that. The best there is in man is a reflection of what there is in God.

The possibility of a revelation of the divine character rests upon the supposition that elements in that character find their correspondence in man. If fidelity, and mercy, and love, and patience, and all moral qualities in God in no way resemble the qualities in man which bear these names, how can we know what they are in him? Should you come to me and say, "I have just returned from Australia and I saw there birds of most gorgeous plumage," and then proceed to describe them, using names of colors with which I am familiar, but in a sense radically different from that in which I am accustomed to use them, so far from your giving me a just idea, your description would be misleading. When you say blue, or red, or orange you do not mean the colors we see in these windows and designate by these names. You mean something wholly different. Red does not mean red; blue does no mean blue. So it must be with reference to names for moral qualities when they are applied to God. If they do not mean in that case substantially the same as when applied to man, then, so far as any revelation to us is concerned, they mean worse than nothing. They are misleading.

You may take that which is purest and best in man and say, this is like God, only God is infinitely purer and better. Gather the most exalted elements from different persons and harmoniously combine these into a single character and you can say, God is infinitely above this. Take love out of motherhood, providence and affectionate government out of fatherhood, take sweet sympathies out of sisterhood, and fidelity out of brotherhood and unite them all into one, and God is infinitely better than that. Justice, mercy, fidelity, purity, patience, benevolence, love — all moral qualities in man — reflect these qualities in the Divine One.

Since I have learned this simple lesson how much nearer, how much more personal and helpful God seems to me. There was a time when he seemed so remote, so vague, so vast, so cold, that thoughts of him brought no delight to my heart; no inspiration to my fainting spirit. He seemed the combination of intelligence and law and force. And are there not some among you who still think of him thus? You have troubles and you long for your mother, and for dear friends of other days, saying, "If my dear trusted ones were only here so I could unbosom myself to them and be soothed by their sympathies, but they have been taken away! To whom can I go?" But why not go to God? Is it not because you have never felt that he really cares for you? So of all human wants, of all heartaches, of all weariness, of all sorrow, when you come to know God better you will carry all to him as to a sympathetic, helpful one. We can never fully know him, but we may know him for comfort, for guidance, for salvation.

4. But better than a study of that which is best in man, I place *a devout study of the character of Christ as shown in his earth-life.* He was a revelation of the Father. You remember that Philip, on a certain occasion, said to him, "Lord

show us the Father and it sufficeth us," and that Jesus replied, "Have I been so long time with you, and yet hast thou not known me, Philip? He that hath seen me hath seen the Father." Paul says, "In him dwelleth all the fulness of the Godhead bodily." Nowhere can we find God so fully manifested as in Christ. He shows us his character; he reveals his great loving heart. God was in Christ. The gospel records possess a matchless interest, when we remember that the incidents contained within them reflect the character of our Father by reflecting the character of his only-begotten and well-beloved Son.

But in our study of the memoirs of Jesus we must look upon these wonderful works and gracious words to find what he was in the essential features of his character. We may be familiar with the incidents of his life, and be able to repeat his words without, in any worthy sense, being familiar with him. We may know that he was born in Bethlehem, and that he fled into Egypt, and grew up in Nazareth, and went up to Jerusalem when twelve years of age, and was baptized in the Jordan, and dwelt in Capernaum, and made frequent circuits of Galilee, and passed through every part of Palestine fulfilling his ministry, and that he healed the sick, and opened the eyes of the blind, and fed the hungry, and raised the dead, and was crucified, and buried and raised to life again, and that he ascended to heaven — we may be familiar with every incident and be able to picture it all in our imaginations — and yet not know him. What he did showed what he was. The story of his life is an empty, idle story, unless we use it.

The older I grow the greater is the charm for me in the gospels. I cannot weary in my study of Christ. His nature is a great deep, and I feel more than ever that I cannot fathom it. New beauties continually appear. He is the fairest among ten thousand and the one altogether lovely. His unselfishness shines forth everywhere; his benevolence was soft and serene, with the chaste beauty of a morning in spring, when the air is full of life and peace. He was full of helpfulness. The people soon perceived this and gathered about him as thirsty ones about a refreshing fountain, and hungry ones to a feast. They brought their sick and afflicted and he healed them. His miracles proclaim his divinity more by their benevolence than by their marvellous power. He was tender towards the penitent, yet terrible in His denunciations of hypocrisy. The most timid might approach him. A child could take him by the hand. He was infinitely tender toward all that was sincere — it was a tenderness that warmed and softened and saved. He was merciful, yet just in judgment. His long-suffering, his forbearance, his patience surpass a mother's. His goodness took upon itself the form of self-denial. He loved sinning, struggling men and women with a love stronger than death, and the offering of Himself upon the cross for the sins of the race was a fitting close to his personal ministry. Not so much the demands of law and justice — not so much the solution of some great problem in moral government — led him to that cross. It was love. "God commendeth his love toward us in that while we were yet sinners Christ died for us." Christ reveals the Father's heart. What he was, he still is; what he was, the Father is.

5. In the last place, we may learn of God *by walking in fellowship with him.* This is a condition rather than a means. We can understand and interpret the divine nature more and more as we become more completely conformed to it, and this conformation gradually comes of fellowship with him.

It is a fundamental principle that revelation is limited by our ability to understand. A dog may understand his master in a few things, and these the lowest and simplest.

But suppose the master undertakes to make a full revelation of himself to his dog. You say it would be impossible. Why? Because there is not that in the dog which can receive such a revelation. Your child understands you in a measure. But suppose you undertake to reveal yourself fully to that child — you speak to it out of your higher nature, you tell of your most profound experiences, and of the deep spiritual yearnings of your heart — and the little child in your arms understands nothing of all you say. It must grow before it can comprehend such things. What can a rude savage know of the finer feelings of a Christian? There is not in him that which can interpret such feelings. So we must grow into divine likeness and divine sympathy, if we would increase in our knowledge of God. There must be developed within us, that which can grasp his revelation of himself.

Do not you who have been long in his school, feel that you know far more of him than you knew when you entered — yea, more than you could have known then? He does not seem just the same to me he did when I became a Christian. He is far more to me than he was when I entered the ministry. He is more personal, more precious, and nearer. But what must he have been to Enoch? What must he have been to John? And yet John did not feel that he knew him to perfection. After many years of blessed experience he was still looking forward joyfully to the time when he should "see him as he is." And when that glorious vision shall burst upon us we will not be able to comprehend it at once. The central joy of Heaven will be perpetual progress in this delightful study. No longer through material works, and written words, and reflected light, but face to face, we shall see as we are seen, we shall know as we are known.

THE CENTRAL FACT IN THE CHRISTIAN SYSTEM.

And many other signs truly did Jesus in the presence of his disciples which are not written in this book; but these are written that ye might believe that Jesus is the Christ, the son of God; and that believing ye might have life through his name.—John xx: 30-31.

John does not claim to have written a full and complete history of the life of Jesus. Many things were done by him in the presence of his disciples which find no place in this record. And while the other evangelists give us many facts omitted by John, yet were we to combine the four inspired and authorized accounts of the earth-life of our blessed Lord, the history thus compiled would be fragmentary and incomplete. John in speaking of that wonderful life has said, "There are also many other things which Jesus did, the which, if they should be written every one, I suppose even the world itself could not contain the books that should be written." Out of the many things, then, which Jesus said and did each one made a selection and placed it upon record. But what governed in making the selections? And why did they select different materials? We should remember when reading the gospels that they are not histories simply, but that they are primarily and avowedly argumentative works, based upon the history of a wonderful life. Each writer was constructing an argument, and whatever best suited this purpose was placed in his book. Two reasons, very apparent, will account for the variety in their selections. First of all, the differences between the persons for whom they wrote. Evidently the facts best suited to carry conviction to the Jew would not always be the most effective with the Gentile. As their readers differed, in character and condition, so should the material out of which their arguments were constructed. Then, too, the writers differed, each from the others, in their mental organizations. Inspiration, whatever that may have been, did not destroy one's individuality. John, inspired, was none the less John, for in his inspired writings we may see some characteristics peculiar to him. And so of all the others. Their personality was not destroyed by their inspiration. The differences in both the readers and the writers then will account for the difference in the material selected. Their purpose, however, appears to have been substantially the same. Each one wrote that men might believe that Jesus is the Christ, the Son of God. In examining the text it seems best to notice these points: —

I. *The proposition submitted.*

II. *The proof offered.*

III. *The importance of the fact thus demonstrated.*

I. *The proposition submitted.* I desire to unfold in a simple manner the meaning of the statement that *Jesus is the Christ, the Son of God.* Jesus was his proper name, divinely given; Christ, a significant title. In many places when we read Jesus Christ it should undoubtedly read Jesus *the* Christ. The distinction is important. Let me illustrate. George King is a man's name. George, *the* King, is much more. It indicates that he holds the position of ruler over a kingdom, and in that we say *the* king we indicate that he is king over some particular people or nation already mentioned, or that he is above other kings — pre-eminent. So when we say that Jesus is the Christ, we mean that he is the anointed, and in that we say that he is *the* Christ we indicate that he is pre-eminent over all anointed — for Christ means simply anointed. Now, among the chosen people, the Jews, three classes of officers were installed by holy anointing — prophets, priests, and kings. You remember that God sent the prophet Elijah to anoint Elisha, the son of Shaphat, to be prophet in his room. (I Kings xix: 16.) In referring to such anointing the Psalmist, speaking in the name of God, says, "Touch not mine anointed and do my prophets no harm." (Ps. cv: 15.) Prophets are here called God's anointed. In Exodus xl: 13-15, we have an account of the anointing of Aaron and his sons as priests. Afterwards, however, anointing seems not to have been repeated at the consecration of ordinary priests, but to have been specially reserved for the high-priest. (Ex. xxix: 29; Lev. xvi: 32.) So that "the priest that is anointed" (Lev. iv: 3), is generally thought to mean the high-priest. The high-priest differed chiefly from the ordinary priest in that he only was permitted to enter the holy of holies in the sacred temple. Kings were also anointed. You remember of Samuel's anointing Saul, and many years after that of his anointing David the son of Jesse to reign in his stead. The theocratic king is often called "the Lord's anointed." Anointing with oil was a rite of inauguration into each of the three typical offices of the Jewish commonwealth, whose tenants, as anointed, were types of the Anointed One.

When it is said that Jesus is the Christ we are to understand that he is *the* anointed, standing above all other anointed. Of him they were only types. He is the threefold anointed — the anointed prophet, the anointed priest, the anointed king. In this he meets the three-fold wants of man — ignorant, guilty, and enslaved. Prophet, to instruct us; high-priest, to cleanse us and intercede for us; king, to emancipate us, rule over us and lead us to victory. There is also something exclusive in his pre-eminence. He supplants all others. We are to listen to no other prophet; we are to apply to no other priest; we are to obey no other king, for Jesus only is *the* Christ. How much then is embraced in this proposition!

But this is not all. It gathers within itself the fulfilment of the brightest chain of Jewish prophecies. The Jews shared with the heathen the hope of the golden age. But in the Jew it was strengthened and defined by their prophets, and centred in the person and ministry of the Messiah. Far back in the dim light of the beginning, it shone like the star of the morning, even in the darkness of the curse. "The seed of the woman shall bruise the serpent's head." The promise grew brighter and clearer as it was repeated to Shem, to Abraham and to the patriarchs. "The sceptre shall not depart from Judah, nor a lawgiver from between his feet until Shiloh come; and unto him shall the gathering of the people be." (Gen. xlix: 10.) And again, "I shall see him, but not now; I shall behold him, but not nigh; there shall come a Star out of Jacob, and a sceptre shall rise out of Israel." (Num. xxiv: 17.) Moses foretold his coming, saying, "A prophet shall the Lord your God raise up unto you of your brethren, like unto me; him shall ye hear in all things whatsoever he shall say unto you." (Acts iii: 22, Deut. xviii: 18.) When we come on down to the Psalms and the prophets the light is fuller and clearer. In the Messianic psalms, and especially in Isaiah, the evangelistic prophet, the character and mission of the Messiah are set forth with a minuteness, a pathos, and a wealth of imagery most wonderful and attractive.

Remember that Messiah and Christ are the same — that one word comes from the Hebrew and the other from the Greek — and you will see that to say that Jesus is the Christ, is to claim that these rays of Jewish prophecy concerning the Messiah, all centre in Jesus of Nazareth. Perhaps it is not enough that I say that Messiah and Christ are synonymous. One passage can make that certain, "Andrew first findeth his own brother, Simon, and saith unto him, We have found the Messiah, which is, being interpreted, the Christ." (John i: 41.) How full of meaning, then, is this proposition? It bears the full import of all the sacred anointings of prophets, priests and kings, and claims a fulfilment of the brightest prophecies of the Jewish people. 'Those golden threads of prophecy which came streaming down through the ages, giving hope to the chosen nation, brightening their days of darkness, and inspiring their sacred songs, all centred on the person of Jesus of Nazareth, who with his own hands wove them into a chaplet of divine glory, and in the presence of the people crowned himself the long-expected Messiah — the anointed of the Most High.

Nor is this all. The proposition in the text is two-fold. Not only is Jesus the Christ, but he is the Son of God. The first part affirms his Messiahship. The second part affirms his divine Sonship. It is not here said that he is *a* son in some restricted sense, but that, in the fullest, highest sense, he is *the* Son of God. But did not the Jews expect the Messiah to be thus divine? And, consequently, does not his Messiahship necessarily include his divine Sonship? Certainly they ought to have so understood their prophecies. his divinity is clearly stated. Isaiah said his name should be "The Mighty God" (ix: 6), and he should be called "Immanuel" (vii: 14), which means, God with us. Again, in the forty-fifth psalm he is addressed thus, "Thy Throne, O God, is forever and ever." Surely from such expressions they ought to have known that the Christ would be divine. But the question is not what they *ought* to have believed, but what they actually *did* believe. His humiliation, and his death upon the cross were as clearly foretold as was his divine nature, and we know that the cross was, to the Jew, a stumbling-block. (I Cor. i: 23.) The literature of the first Christian centuries, when there were frequent discussions between the Christians and the Jews, shows clearly that while a few might have believed that the Christ would be divine, the popular opinion was that he would be simply human. Of this there are clear indications in the gospels themselves. For instance, Luke says, "All men mused in their hearts of John (the Baptist) whether he were the Christ or not.' (Luke iii: 15.) They knew John's parents, and they knew that he was only human. They could not, therefore, have thought that the promised Christ would certainly be divine. Again is this clearly shown when Jesus asked the Pharisees, "What think ye of the Christ? (That is, the Christ of Prophecy.) Whose son is he?" They did not answer: The son of *God*, but said, the son of *David*. And when he asked, "How then doth David in spirit call him Lord, saying, the Lord said unto my Lord, Sit thou on my right hand, till I make thine enemies thy footstool? If David then called him Lord, how is he his son?" (Matt. xxii: 42-45.) No man was able to answer him, for no one there thought that the Christ would be the divine Son. Thus the plainest predictions of their prophets were not understood. The divine Sonship of the Messiah was not received by the people. It was because he claimed to be the Son of God that they rejected him, and finally put him to death. They would have received him, perhaps, had he claimed to be nothing more than the Messiah. But he claimed *both*, and the proposition of the text includes both, in the fullness of their meaning. Simple, sublime, and comprehensive then is the proposition of the text — Jesus is the Christ, the Son of God. It claims for the poor Nazarine that he is the only prophet, the only priest, the only king anointed over the true

Israel of God. He alone is divinely authorized to instruct us in our ignorance, to cleanse us of our sins, to intercede for us, to rule over us and to lead us to victory. He is the only begotten Son of God. He is the first and the last, the Alpha and Omega, the beginning and the end, the mighty God, the Prince of Peace. Coming with such high claims we may, yea we must ask, " What sign showest thou?" What evidence does he present? What proof is offered in support of this proposition?

II. *The proof submitted.* John offers the " signs " which Jesus did. " Many other signs truly did Jesus in the presence of his disciples which are not written in this book, but these are written that ye might believe that Jesus is the Christ, the Son of God." By this he claims that Jesus bore with him his own credentials. I will not attempt to elaborate the proof thus submitted, but will endeavor to show its nature and its application to the proposition.

By signs we are certainly to understand him to mean the miracles which Jesus did. Miracles are often called signs. In many places where our version has the word miracle the original has the word sign. This name presents the religious end and purpose of miracles. They are the indication of God's presence and approval. They are typical also. I believe that the miracles of the New Testament are all, in a sense, typical of the higher work of the Christ — that they were not performed simply for the benefit of the sufferers who were by them relieved of their sufferings, nor yet simply to attract the people, but that they point to Jesus as the physician of the soul. Coming into this world to seek and to save the lost, he should demonstrate his power over all the consequences of sin. Without such demonstrations how could he reasonably ask men to commit their highest interests to him? These signs appear to me to be a complete demonstration.

Let us see. The consequences of sin are both internal and external — both spiritual and physical. The soul within is tempest-tossed by sin. Darkness and chaos are there. What could be a more striking type of this internal wreck than were the demoniacs in the days of Jesus. Reason seemed to have deserted its throne. The poor demented sufferer raved like a hopeless maniac. He fled from home and sought an abode among the tombs. He tore off his raiment. He could not be bound. His eye had a wild, frenzied look. All these were signs of the wreck and ruin wrought within by sin. The demoniac was a type. Can Jesus heal him? Can he cast the evil spirit out? Can he restore him to his right mind? Can he still the raging tempest within? Let us read some of the testimony of the evangelists.

In the first chapter of Mark, I read this: —

"And there was in their synagogue (at Capernaum) a man with an unclean spirit; and he cried out saying: Let us alone; what have we to do with thee, thou Jesus of Nazareth? Art thou come to destroy us? (He knew that Jesus had power.) I know thee who thou art, the Holy One of God. And Jesus rebuked him, saying, Hold thy peace and come out of him. And when the unclean spirit had torn him, and cried with a loud voice, he came out of him. And they were all amazed, insomuch that they questioned among themselves, saying, What thing is this? what new doctrine is this? for with authority he commandeth the unclean spirits, and they do obey him."

Turn to the fifth chapter and read the account of his healing the demoniacs in the country of the Gadarenes.

"And they came over unto the other side of the sea, into the country of the Gadarenes. And when he was come out of the ship, immediately there met him out of the tombs a man with an unclean spirit, who had his dwelling among the tombs; and no man could bind him, no, not with chains; because that he had been bound with fetters and chains, and the chains had been plucked asunder by him, and the fetters broken in pieces; neither could any man tame him. And always, night and day, he was in the mountains, and in the tombs, crying, and cutting himself with stones. But when he saw Jesus afar off, he ran and worshipped him, and cried with a loud voice, and said, What have I to do with thee, Jesus, thou Son of the Most High God? I adjure thee by God, that thou torment me not. (For he said unto him, Come out of the man, thou unclean spirit.) And he asked him, What is thy name? And he answered, saying, my name is Legion; for we are many. And he besought him much that he would not send them away out of the country. Now there was there nigh unto the mountains a great herd of swine feeding. And all the devils besought him, saying, Send us into the swine, that we may enter into them. And forthwith Jesus gave them leave. And the unclean spirits went out and entered into the swine; and the herd ran violently down a steep place into the sea (they were about two thousand), and were choked in the sea. And they that fed the swine fled, and told it in the city, and in the country. And they went out to see what it was that was done. And they come to Jesus, and see him that was possessed with the devil, and had the legion, sitting, and clothed in his right mind; and they were afraid."

Thus he demonstrates his power to remove the internal effects of sin. Is this not a sufficient demonstration? But, what are its *external* effects? All manner of disease and death itself. Has he shown his power? See him heal the nobleman's son (John iv: 46-54); the poor paralytic (Matt. ix: 1-8); the man who was leprous from head to foot (Luke v: 12-16); the impotent man at the pool of Bethesda (John v: 1-16); the man with dropsy (Luke xiv: 1-6); the man with a withered hand (Matt. xii: 9-13); and all those who came to him with their diseases. He demonstrated his power over disease in its many forms. More than this, he demonstrated his power over death itself. See him in the house of Jairus calling his daughter back to life. (Matt. ix: 18-26). See him, when he meets the procession bearing to the grave the remains of the only son of a widow, draw near and touch the bier, saying, "Young man, arise." The dead obeyed him. (Luke vii: 11-16.) And see him, again, when he stood by the grave of the four-days dead and cried with a loud voice, "Lazarus, come forth," and at that quickening call he came forth, still wearing the raiment of the dead. How full, and even overwhelming is the demonstration! In the chamber of Jairus where the death angel still lingered; by the bier of the dead as they carried him to the grave; and by the grave of the four-days dead, he manifests his power over death. His miracles were signs of his higher work and pledges of his power to accomplish it. He has power over the consequences of sin, both internal and external.

But what is the relation between his miracle and his doctrine? I answer that his doctrine rests upon his authority, and his miracles demonstrate his authority. There is danger of our forgetting the important fact that his doctrine rests upon his authority. He did not attempt to prove his doctrine. Neither did he argue from his doctrine to his authority, but from his authority to his doctrine. The doctrine rests upon that. How, then, do his miracles show him to be the Christ, the Son of God, and hence supreme in authority? Miracles in themselves, separate and apart from what he declared himself to be, can prove nothing. We must connect them with what he claimed for himself. I put the matter briefly thus: Miracles show God's presence and approval. What the worker claims in working the miracles is, therefore, approved of God. But Jesus claimed that he was the Christ, the Son of God, and wrought miracles in support of this claim. Hence, this claim was approved of God. Again, he performed the works which demonstrate his power to accomplish the higher purpose of his mission. Thus, as it were, by the signet of the Almighty he stamps with authority his claims to the Jewish Messiahship and Divine Sonship, and by his wonderful works demonstrates before men his ability to save the lost.

But why did John write to establish this proposition? Why did Jesus perform a series of miracles to demonstrate that he was the Christ, the Son of God? What is its importance?

III. *The importance of the proposition thus demonstrated.* Twice during the personal ministry of Jesus did the Father speak audibly in the hearing of the people — at his baptism in the Jordan and at his transfiguration on the summit of the mountain. On each occasion he declared that Jesus was his Son, in whom he was well pleased, and that it was man's duty to hear him. Seldom in the history of the race has God condescended to speak in person to man. We may, therefore, reasonably infer that what he says on such occasions is of no ordinary importance. From the fact that God himself announced it; from the fact that Jesus performed a series of miracles to demonstrate it; and from the fact that the gospels were written that man might believe it, we are forced to conclude that the proposition that Jesus is the Christ, the Son of God, is of the very highest importance. A few considerations will strengthen and justify this conviction.

First. It is the central fact in the Christian system. Every system must have a centre. This is true whether the system is spiritual or physical, moral or political. The planet on which we live is part of a system of planets revolving around one central sun. From that sun they receive light and life. The system of religion established by the false prophet has this for its centre: There is one true and living God; Mahommed is his prophet. Everything depends upon that. Accept that and you accept all. In the Jewish religion the doctrine of the unity of the deity, in opposition to every form of polytheism, is the central doctrine. There is one, true, and living God, and Moses is his lawgiver, is that on which all else depends. Accept that and you must accept everything which belongs to that system. So in the Christian system, the proposition that Jesus is the Christ, the Son of God, is the grand central fact. Everything depends upon that. Accept it and you must accept everything he taught. For this reason the inspired teachers presented it as the problem of the gospel. They brought every argument to its support. Every doctrine, every command, every promise rests upon that as its basis. To support this is to support the divine claims of the entire Bible. For he stands, as it were, between the Old Testament and the New, and extending one hand back over the Old, he indorses that as divine. It is, therefore, divine. Extending the other down over the New he indorses that as divine. It is, therefore, divine. As in geometry, every proposition lies latent in the definition of the figure, so in Christianity everything lies latent in this proposition concerning the Christ. And as one may stand on different planets in our solar system, and each in its revolution points to the same centre, so may we take different standpoints and different views of the divine scheme of human redemption, yet from each point we are directed to the same central fact, the Messiahship and divine Sonship of Jesus of Nazareth. Do you look upon it as a system of doctrine? Every doctrine hinges upon this. Do you look upon it as a system of commandments? Every commandment in the system rests upon the authority of Jesus, and this proposition as a declaration of that authority. Do you view it as a system of blessed promises? All the promises of God are in him. Whatever, then, may be the point from which you view the system you are uniformly pointed to the Messiahship and divine Sonship of Jesus as the centre. It is the sun of the system, and the citadel of revealed truth.

Second. It is the foundation fact in the church of Christ. When Jesus was on his way to Cesarea Philippi he asked his disciples, "Whom do men say that I, the Son of man, am?" And they said, "Some say that thou art John the Baptist, some Elias, and others, Jeremias, or one of the prophets." Then he asked them. "But whom say ye that I am?" And, Simon Peter answered and said, "*Thou art the Christ, the Son of the living God.*" Then Jesus answered and said unto him, "Blessed art thou Simon Bar-jona; for flesh and blood hath not revealed it unto thee, but my Father who is in heaven. And I say unto thee, that thou art Peter, and *upon this rock I will build my Church;* and the gates of hell shall not prevail against it." (Matt. xvi: 16–18.) I know that this passage has been the battle ground of fierce conflicts. What is here meant by the rock? Does it mean Christ, or Peter, or the truth which Peter confessed? The whole matter may be presented thus: "The leading image of these and the following verses is that of two opposing cities, one representing the kingdom of heaven, and the other representing hades. The former is represented as about to be built on a rock. Its builder, its gate-keeper, and its keys are mentioned, and the assurance is given that the gates of the latter city shall not prevail against it. Of the former city Jesus is the builder; Peter is the gate-keeper, for to him the keys are given; and the foundation on which its walls are to be erected, like that of Cesarea Philippi, which was close at hand, and in all probability supplied the imagery, is a solid rock." To suppose that either Jesus or Peter, in person, is to be the foundation would throw the whole imagery into confusion, for Jesus specifically says that he is the chief architect, and he gives the keys to Peter. Interpreting the language according to its imagery, there seems to be no room to doubt that the truth which Peter confessed is the solid rock on which the Church of Christ is built. Destroy this foundation, and the church falls into ruin. Preserve it, and the church may stand against every foe. I care not what may be the pretensions of any organization, if it is not built upon this, it cannot be the Church of Christ, for he has said, "Upon *this* rock I will build *my* church." The true church rests upon nothing else, however true it may be. It rests upon no peculiar view of ordinances; no peculiar view of the operation of the Holy Spirit; no peculiar view of the doctrine of the divine decrees; no peculiar view of the fall of man and the depravity of human nature; no peculiar view of ecclesiastical polity, but it rests, like the city built upon the solid rock, upon the fact that Jesus is the Christ, the Son of the living God. This is the foundation fact.

Third. It is the saving fact in the gospel of our blessed Savior. "Whosoever believeth that Jesus is the Christ, is born of God." (I. John v: 1.) I believe that most commentators agree that "begotten of God," is much nearer the meaning here than "born of God." So, at least, teach Barnes, Macknight, and others whom I have examined. This is not a meaningless distinction, but I cannot notice its importance now. What I wish you to notice now is that the belief of this central and foundation fact is saving faith. By this belief we are begotten of God. Is it necessary for me to say that I am not speaking of a cold, heartless assent to it? A belief of it which has no more effect on the heart than to believe that the sum of the angles of a triangle are equal to two right angles? Remember that it is written, "with *the heart* man believeth unto righteousness." (Rom. x: 10.) I do not teach that a belief which touches not the heart can save the soul. Neither do my brethren teach any such doctrine. I believe in and try to teach the necessity of a heart-faith in Christ. I believe in heart religion. I ask for a faith which works by love, and purifies the heart.

Let us turn more directly to the statement of the text: "These things are written that ye might believe that Jesus is the Christ, the Son of God, and that believing ye might have life through his name." Some important truths lie upon the surface of this statement. First of all, that saving faith rests upon testimony. John wrote that men might believe. He presented testimony to produce faith. In the next place it is necessarily implied that the testimony is sufficient to produce faith. "These things are written that ye might believe." In the third place it is assumed that men have power to believe when the testimony is presented. In the fourth place, the proposition to be believed is that "Jesus is the Christ, the Son of God." And in the last place, *this belief is the faith by which men have life through the name of Jesus.* There are many other things equally true, but they are not the channels by which life comes to men. How simple and yet how comprehensive is this faith. How important, beyond all computation, is the proposition. Who can estimate its value? It is the central fact in the Christian system; the foundation fact in the Church of Christ; the saving fact in the gospel of our blessed Savior.

We need not wonder then that the apostles of Christ and the inspired teachers of the church uniformly presented it as the problem of the gospel. We need not wonder that they brought argument from every possible source to establish it firmly in the minds and hearts of men. When Paul began the work of the ministry in the city of Damascus the burden of his preaching was to prove that Jesus was the very Christ. (Acts ix: 22.) In the synagogue in Thessalonica, "he reasoned with them out of the Scriptures, opening and alleging, that the Christ must needs have suffered, and risen again from the dead; and that this Jesus whom I preach unto you, is Christ." (Acts xvii: 2, 3.) The apostles in Jerusalem "daily in the temple and in every house ceased not to teach and preach Jesus the Christ." (Acts v: 42.) Paul, pressed in spirit, testified to the Jews in Corinth that Jesus was the Christ. (Acts xviii: 5.) When Appollos went into Achaia "he mightily convinced the Jews, and that publicly, that Jesus was the Christ." (Acts xviii: 28) And so, wherever they preached, the force of their arguments was brought to bear in support of this.

Again, we may now more clearly understand why this was made the confession of faith in the early churches. Before one was baptized he was required to confess with his mouth the faith of his heart in Jesus as the Christ, the Son of God. We can see with what propriety it is called The Good Confession. (I. Tim. vi: 13.) It bears with it so many sacred memories. The angels sang in the song of good will to men, "For unto you is born this day in the city of David a

Savior, which is Christ, the Lord." (Luke ii: 11.) God, the Father, announced it at the Jordan when, pointing by the descending Spirit to Jesus, he said, "This is my beloved Son, in whom I am well pleased." (Matt. iii: 18.) And again, on the Mount of Transfiguration he spake from out the brightness of the cloud, saying, "This is my beloved Son, in whom I am well pleased: hear ye him." (Matt. xvii: 5.) Jesus himself before Pontius Pilate witnessed this good confession. (I. Tim. vi: 13.) Moreover, it is the good confession because in making it we publicly declare in in favor of Jesus. And finally, it is the good confession because it is unto salvation. "With the heart man believeth unto righteousness, and with the mouth confession is made unto salvation."

THE GLORIOUS GOSPEL.

But if our gospel be hid, it is hid to them that are lost; in whom the god of this world has blinded the minds of them that believe not, lest the light of the glorious gospel of Christ, who is the image of God should shine unto them. — ii Cor. iv: 3-4.

If you desire to select from this text some clause which presents its salient point, and is so brief that you can easily remember it, I suggest that you take this, "The glorious gospel of Christ."

Have you never observed how we often fancy we understand things simply because we are familiar with them? Familiarity is so easily mistaken for knowledge. I have a little book called "Catechism of Common Things," which has brought this matter to my mind repeatedly. I have been surprised to find how little I really know concerning the most familiar articles about my home. The very fact of my perfect familiarity has prevented my pausing to ask questions. I felt as if I knew all about them. The same is true of words. We become familiar with them — we have a general understanding of their meaning — and do not pause to ask for exact definitions. The word "gospel," I think, belongs to this class. We are familiar with it. We see it so frequently, it is upon our tongues more than almost any other one word, and we take for granted, that we know exactly what its full significance is. Perhaps, we may. But even if we do, it will be no waste of time to linger over its meaning awhile.

I will endeavor, therefore, to answer two questions tonight. First, What is the gospel? and second, Why call it glorious?

I. *What, then, is the gospel?* Quite a prevalent idea seems to be that the word stands for religious truth in general. A sermon is preached. Some one who heard it says, as he leaves the house, "Well, that man preached the gospel, to-night," meaning by the remark no more than that what was preached was true — that it was religious truth.

I need scarcely remind you that the literal meaning of the word is good news or glad tidings. The word used in the inspired volume is composed of two words, one meaning good or glad, and the other meaning news or tidings, so that etymologically it means simply good news or glad tidings. Any message, therefore, which contains good news may be called gospel. The message which the Divine Father has sent to his sinful, wandering children through his Son is called the gospel of Christ, because it is full of love and forgiveness, and is radiant with the brightness of hope. The angelic announcement of his birth was gospel, for it was glad tidings of great joy to all the people because a Savior was born.

But the good news of a Savior born — of a Redeemer sent to redeem us — is not the full gospel. The word is used to designate the place or method by which we are to be saved. The term is a name for the entire system of salvation through Jesus Christ. This system has its different elements.

In the fifteenth chapter of First Corinthians, Paul, after saying he had preached the gospel to them in that city, proceeds to state in a summary way what he had preached, saying, "For I delivered unto you first of all, that which I also received, how that Christ died for our sins according to the Scriptures; and that he was buried, and that he rose again the third day according to the Scriptures." Here are certain great *facts* concerning Christ — his atoning death, his burial, and his resurrection. These are fundamental. Yet these facts, important as they are, do not constitute the full and complete gospel. It was not his purpose to make a statement of the entire gospel in this place. He mentions fundamental facts, but there is more in this gospel than its wonderful facts. For we read of the obedience of the gospel, and facts cannot be obeyed. In order to obedience there must be *commands*. This gospel must, therefore, contain certain commands. But facts and commands are not all, for we read of the hope of the gospel, and hope rests upon promises. If there is no promise there is no ground for hope. The gospel must, therefore, contain *promises*. These, then, are the essential parts of the gospel of Christ,—facts, commands, promises.

The order in which I have named them is their logical, scriptural order. First, facts; second, commands; third, promises. And our relation to each of these is different. Facts are to be believed, commands are to be obeyed, promises are to be enjoyed. The order of the process in us also corresponds to the order of the parts of the gospel. First, faith; then, obedience; then, rejoicing. Much of the confusion which manifestly exists concerning this matter, so simple in itself, is to be attributed either to the fact that this order is not observed, or that a part only is presented for the whole. Were I to undertake to produce Christian joy without first producing faith and obedience — that upon which the joy legitimately rests — I would produce confusion. Or were I to preach the exceeding great and precious promises, without showing how enquirers are to appropriate these, I need not be surprised to find that I have bewildered those whom I should have guided along a plain way. How simple was the gospel as preached at first, and how easily understood! How great the mystery which enshrouds that which in our day is sometimes preached!

II. But why call this gospel, so simple in itself, *the glorious gospel?* It is spoken of in the text as full of light and as shining forth with the radiance of heavenly glory. It is called the glorious gospel.

1. I answer, in the first place, that we may call it glorious because *it is the fullest manifestation of the glory of the divine character ever made to man.* The phrase is, literally, "The gospel of the glory of Christ." But Christ is spoken of in the clause which immediately follows, as the image of God. This glory, therefore, does not belong to the Son alone. It is the glory of the entire godhead. While it is the gospel of Christ, it is, at the same time "the gospel of the grace of God." It is the "gospel of our salvation," and the godhead in its fullness is engaged in the accomplishment of this salvation. The Father so loved the world that he gave his Son, the Son, by his death upon the cross, made atonement for sin, and the Holy Spirit came as his advocate and our comforter. Without attempting to draw accurate distinctions as to the three persons in the Trinity, and without pausing to indicate the part each performs in the work of human redemption, I may say that the entire divine nature is manifested by the gospel. In its revelation of the divine character I find its glory. It is so full of God that it shines with unearthly splendor. He is the light of it.

I will not ignore the fact that God is revealed to us by other means nor seek to magnify the importance of the gospel as though it were the only revelation of his being and character. To me all nature beams with his brightness. Were the sun perfectly hid from my eyes by an intervening cloud, concealing his body without obscuring his beams, I would still know there is a sun, for the cloud that hides him is full of his light. Even so creation is radiant with the light of God. He shines through all his works. Intelligence, will, forethought, power, and providence are clearly seen.

Then, too, the earlier pages of this great volume of revelation glow with the brightness of God. The law, the prophets, and the psalms contain disclosures of his attributes and shine with their revelations of his character and his gracious purposes. His unity, his holiness, his justice, his personal providence, his designs of grace, brighten the pages of the Old Testament Scriptures. What revelations of glory in the purity of the law, in the devotion of the inspired psalms and in the lofty utterances of the prophets when visions of the high and holy One were granted them! The living oracles, even as they were given to the Jews, are full of the divine glory.

But the manifestation of God to man has been progressive. As the sun does not burst upon us with the suddenness of the lightning's flash in the fullness of his glory, but slowly uplifts the curtain of night and gilds with his beams the window of day, and brighter grows and brighter until we are flooded with light, so has God slowly and by degrees revealed himself to man. All that go before are but morning beams — harbingers of the day — but the gospel shines full-orbed. It is the fullest revelation of the divine character yet given to us, and in this is its glory. Mercy, grace, forgivenesss, love, fatherhood — in short — the great heart of God is therein made manifest to men.

2. In the second place, it is glorious *from the character of its message*. Not only is it good news, but it is the very best news which could come to sin-smitten, bewildered, lost humanity. As God's gracious purposes were being unfolded in types and symbolic ritual, we are told that angels looked on with eager gaze. These purposes were enshrouded in mystery. But when the time drew near for types to meet

with their fulfilment, and angel messengers were dispatched to tell to the waiting shepherds the advent of a Savior-king, a multitude of the heavenly host heard the message and broke forth in an ecstasy of song, saying, "Glory to God in the highest, and on earth peace, good will toward men." The Prince of Peace comes with a message of peace. He might have come with the voice of the thunder to pronounce the sentence of death. He did not. The angels saw in his advent a new manifestation of good will toward man. The gospel message is glorious because it is full of grace and good-will.

If you will turn to the fourth chapter of Luke, you will find Jesus interpreting the general character of his message and work. It is in the village of Nazareth, where he had been brought up and where all the people knew him. It is the Sabbath day. His wisdom and purity have already attracted the notice of the people. But the circumstances attending his recent baptism were so remarkable that they were even now widely known, and expectation was kindled to feverish eagerness. His seclusion during the period of his temptation has increased rather than allayed this feeling. And now it is rumored that he is coming back to the home of his childhood. The synagogue is crowded. He enters, and all eyes turn toward him as the minister hands him a roll containing a part of their sacred writings. He opens the book, finds the place where it was written: —

The Spirit of the Lord is upon me, because he hath anointed me to preach the gospel to the poor; he hath sent me to heal the broken hearted, to preach deliverance to the captives, and recovering of sight to the blind; to set at liberty them that are bruised: to preach the acceptable year of the Lord.

He closes the book, and he gives it again to the minister,

and sits down. And the eyes of all were fastened upon him; and he said to them: this day is this scripture fulfilled in your ears. He applied this prediction directly to himself, and so gives us an interpretation of the character of his message and work. Good news to the poor; healing for broken hearts; freedom for captives; sight for the blind; liberty for the oppressed; a jubilee for all! He comes to meet the deep wants of our race.

Time would fail me to speak of the fullness of the blessing of this gospel of Christ. Like the poor man of whom we read in the ninth chapter of John, born blind and vainly seeking a guide, the gospel comes and, with holy anointing, opens our eyes. Bruised and wounded, it is for us a balm full of healing and fragrance. Covered with a pollution more loathsome than leprosy, it cleanses, restores and sanctifies. Bound in sin with the fearful bondage of Satan, our condition is sadder than that of the poor, wild demoniac of Gadara, until the gospel gives us freedom and restores us to our right mind, and clothes us with the beautiful robes of righteousness. We are alienated from God, but the gentle, pleading voice of this gospel wins us back. It is the message of reconciliation. We are condemned. It comes offering pardon, full and free. We are as orphans. This is God's message, in which he declares his willingness to adopt us as his children. Through fear of death we are subject to bondages until Christ brings life and immortality to light in the gospel. The nature of this message — the fullness of its blessing — makes it unspeakably glorious in our eyes. It meets and satisfies the deepest wants of our nature.

3. In the third place, this glory appears full-orbed, when we reflect that *it is both designed for all and adapted to all.* I believe that the purpose of the gospel is as wide as the

race, that it is God's gospel for the whole world. I cannot believe that its gracious provisions are for only a select few. The gospel shines as the sun, everywhere and without partiality. For the sun shines not only upon your meadows, and gardens, and vineyards, but upon those of others as well. Yea, he sends out his beams of light and heat every whither, over forests, and deserts, and fertile fields, and the wide waste of waters — everywhere. You cannot fence in his rays and claim them as your peculiar and exclusive possession. No more can you limit the gospel. You may urge your doctrine of election and decrees, you may teach that this message of grace is for only a select and limited few, and yet it shines on full-orbed, for its Creator made it so.

The angels said, " glad tiding of great joy *for all the people.*" They were not Calvinistic angels. Jesus said, in giving the commission, "Go preach the gospel *to every creature.*" And, as if to give peculiar emphasis to the absolute universality of its purpose and provisions, he taught the apostles to begin their work in Jerusalem. There, where he had been buffeted, where he had been mocked and spit upon, where his betrayers and murderers were, — there, in the city of Jerusalem, begin your work, that all the world may know the riches of my grace. Then go everywhere and tell this story of redeeming love to every creature. Wonderful as the gospel is in the fullness of its blessing, it is intended for every one. Its glory is not eclipsed by the shadow of predestination and fore-ordination of any to everlasting death. God takes no pleasure in the death of any, and so has made provision for all.

Moreover, this that is intended for all, is suited to all. The gospel is glorious in its simplicity. The evangelical prophet, in foretelling the highway of holiness, described it as so plain that the unwise and simpletons need not err therein. The gospel is not a profound science, to be understood only by the gifted who have leisure for study, nor is it an abstract philosophy suited to a certain class of thinkers, but — blessed be God that it is so — it is a simple message of love and salvation suited to the masses. Its facts are few and easy to be understood; its commands are plain and simple; its promises, though exceeding great and precious, lie within the range of easy comprehension. The simplicity of the gospel is demonstrated by the fact that among its first converts there were " not many wise men after the flesh, not many mighty, not many noble." In the history of apostolic preaching we find, in many instances, the people needed to hear only one sermon in order to understand it, believe it, obey it, and rejoice in its blessings and its promises. It is glorious in the wide sweep of its grace; it is glorious in its beautiful simplicity.

4. But, in the fourth place, *it is glorious in its results.* As seed sown brings forth grain after its kind, so the gospel brings forth in men results peculiar to itself. It tamed the fiery spirit of the sons of thunder, and made of the bloody persecutor a gentle and devoted lover of his fellow-man. It purifies the corrupt, lifts up the degraded, comforts the sorrowing and reforms the abandoned. It brings light to those who sit in darkness, and sanctifies and soothes the grief of the bereaved. It is a feast to the hungry, a fountain to the thirsty. It gives us songs in the house of our pilgrimage and in the night of our sorrow. It inspires and nurses all the gentler virtues. It begets charity. It fills human hearts with the sweet melody of love. It purifies home and makes it fragrant. It builds asylums, founds hospitals, and furnishes shelter for the fallen that they may reform. Under its gentle rays all goodness, all moral beauty, all true

nobility, all virtues are developed. As well attempt to tell of all the sun does for us in his shining, as to tell the fullness of the glorious results of the gospel. Every flower that blooms is a child of the sun. So every flower that blooms in a human heart and makes fragrant human life is born of the gospel.

Were we to permit a wider range to our inquiry, we would enrich and enlarge our conception of the blessed fruit of gospel truth. It has directed the course of nations. It has silently undermined despotism and overturned the throne of tyranny. It has fostered the spirit of liberty and given freedom to the slave. If we examine the map of the world to-day, we will find that those nations which enjoy the highest civilization are those which have imbibed most freely the spirit and teaching of the gospel.

But we would err were we to suppose this gospel has already borne its full harvest. The precious results already attained are scarce worthy to be called even the first fruits of the golden harvest yet to be gathered. If we are not grievously mistaken in the utterances of prophets, a brighter day is yet to dawn. The wilderness and the solitary place shall be glad, and the desert shall blossom as the rose. Swords shall be made into ploughshares, and spears into scythes; nation shall not lift up sword against nation, neither shall they learn war any more. The prospect is glorious, but as I speak, the vision widens and brightens, and I look into the future which lies yet beyond. For, as the brightness of the transfiguration itself shall pale before the glories of that day, when the countless hosts of God's children shall rise from the sleep of death to be changed into his glory, so do the triumphs of truth here lose their lustre in the light of that day when the ransomed shall enter their heavenly home. Then shall the angelic choir cease their anthem of praises to listen to the new song of those who have been saved by the glorious gospel of Christ.

In conclusion, I briefly present two points for your consideration.

First, let us not consent to the perversion of this gospel. Paul says, "Though we, or an angel from heaven, preach any other gospel unto you than that which we have preached unto you, let him be accursed." Let us be watchful in guarding the purity and preserving the simplicity of this gospel.

And, lastly, by its glorious revelations, by its fullness of blessing, by its marvellous grace, by its adaptation to human wants, by its victories already achieved let us give ourselves to its propagation with renewed zeal, "Let him that heareth say, come."

SPECIAL INFLUENCE IN CONVERSION.

And a certain woman named Lydia, a seller of purple, of the city of Thyatira, which worshiped God, heard us; whose heart the Lord opened, that she attended to the things spoken by Paul.—Acts xvi: 14.

We are naturally fond of the mysterious — especially of mystery in religion. That which shrouds itself in mist and stands half concealed and half revealed impresses the imagination and inspires sacred awe.

To very many, religion is the most incomprehensible and inexplicable of all mysteries. Especially is there great mystery shrouding the entrance upon the Christian life. Conversion is looked upon as a kind of spiritual miracle. It is held that in order to its accomplishment special divine influence is needed; that the ordinary means of grace are not sufficient; that without special divine help, in each case, it is impossible for man to understand the divine message, to believe it; to obey it, and to become a Christian. I desire, therefore, with all candor, and in the light of sound reason and the teachings of the Holy Scriptures, to consider the question: *Is any special divine influence either needed or promised in order that men may believe the gospel and become Christians?*

You may readily see that this question is not simply a speculative one, but that it is an intensely practical question.

Its legitimate fruits make it such. It exerts a powerful influence over men at the very turning-point of their lives.

1. In the first place, it causes men to stand still, thinking they have no power to act. For, in what way can we sup-

press all effort more effectually than by persuading the people that they are absolutely unable to do anything?

2. Still further, it naturally causes those who think a special influence is promised, to wait for it. Many are postponing the time of their turning for no other reason. Christians have frequently told me they would have turned to the Lord much earlier had it not been they were waiting for some special influence. And are we not forced to fear that many go down to their graves waiting for it?

3. In the third place, the tendency of the theory is to turn the attention of the people away from the gospel. If they have not the ability to understand and believe it without special enlightenment, if it has not power unless specially energized why should they give earnest heed to it? They look elsewhere for what they need. In some moment of quiet waiting, or of agonizing prayer, they hope the Lord will speak directly to them.

4. A fourth result of this theory is that through its mysticism it tends to produce skepticism and infidelity among persons whose reason is well developed and dominant. The theory appears so contrary to sound reason and so manifestly unjust in its conclusions that they reject it. But, they have been taught that the theory is an essential part of scripture teaching. They, therefore, reject the scriptures as a revelation from God, for certainly the Author of reason cannot be the author of a doctrine so unreasonable. While I speak, there comes to my mind a striking illustration of this in the case of one of my intimate friends.

These considerations are sufficient to show that the question is an intensely practical one. If, however, the theory is true, we should know it and act upon it; but if it is false we should reject it and let it go down, carrying with it all its consequences. Let us, therefore, examine some of the reasons which may be presented in support of this theory.

1. In the first place, it may be said in support of it, that not *all* who *hear* the gospel are blessed. Some hearts are opened to it and receive it with joy, while others are in no way affected by it. This is a fact. How can it be explained? The same gospel is preached in each case. All influences which we can see in one case are brought to bear in the other. Yet results are different: If results are different, must there not be a corresponding difference in the causes? But, the causes, so far as we can see and estimate, are exactly the same. Must we not, therefore, suppose that, in addition to the causes which are apparent, there was some hidden cause in the cases where such joyous results followed?

In answer to this I ask attention, first, to the fact that this is not peculiar to religion. The same diversity of results appears in reference to any other book or message. "Uncle Tom's Cabin," for illustration, produced a variety of results. I know some men whose lives, politically, were moulded in harmony with its sentiments and the influence which the reading of that book had over them will follow them to their graves. On the other hand I know men whose hostility was awakened by reading it. Then there are others who were influenced neither one way nor the other. These are facts. They are parallel to those cited in reference to the diversity of results following the preaching of the gospel. How will you explain *these* facts? Do you feel compelled to resort to the supposition that a special influence was put forth in some cases, and that it was withheld in others? Certainly not. Then why resort to this supposition to explain the corresponding diversity in the effects produced by the reading of the scriptures or the hearing of the gospel?

Christ gives us the correct explanation in his parable of the sower. See Matt. xiii: 1–9; 18–23. In this parable he predicts that this very diversity of results will follow the preaching of the gospel. In some cases no impression is made; in others it is transient; in others, more lasting; in others, only a small harvest; in others, larger; in others, very large. Here is presented the greatest variety, graded all the way up from no results whatever to the very largest possible. Now, how does *he* explain this phenomenon? Not by supposing any variety in the seed, or that special energizing influences attended the seed in some cases that were withheld in others, but *by the actual diversity of the soil.* This explanation commends itself as reasonable. It places the matter on the same plane and explains it in the same way in which we would explain the corresponding diversity in secular and political matters.

2. Again, it is urged in support of this theory that sinners are represented as dead and their conversion is spoken of as being quickened, or made alive. Eph. ii: 1. The dead have no power to wake themselves. Not until Christ, the life-giving one, stood by the sepulchre and called with a loud voice did Lazarus come forth. So of sinners. They are dead, and it is therefore claimed they have no power. Special influence must go forth to quicken them before they can rise from this spiritual death. The power that regenerates is special. It must be put forth in each case.

Let us examine into this. That sinners are represented as being dead is true. But, is the language literal or figurative? Unquestionably it is figurative. They are compared to those literally dead. They are not absolutely dead. When, then, they are said to be dead in trespasses and sins, are we to understand they are *so* dead that they can neither think nor do that which is good? Christians are also said to be dead.

They are dead *to* sin. Are *they* so dead they can neither think nor do that which is wrong? Certainly not. If, then, when Christians are said to be dead *to* sin it does not imply they cannot do wrong, neither are we to conclude when sinners are said to be dead *in* sin they cannot do that which is right.

Whatever theories may teach, the fact is that in every person in the world good and evil both are found. There is none so good but that evil is in him, and none so bad but that good is in him. The doctrine of total depravity is not sustained by a careful study of human nature. The work of regeneration is the development of the good and the suppression of the evil, until the good becomes regnant. The gospel recognizes the universality of the moral sense and makes its appeal to that. The tone of its utterances and the nature of its call imply that man is not too dead to hear, to understand, to believe, to turn and enter upon the Christian life.

3. Another reason urged in support of this special influence is found in the fact that the gospel is called the sword of the Spirit, and the sword is powerless and ineffective unless it has some one to wield it. A sword can accomplish nothing by itself. The gospel is only a sword.

Very true. But does it follow from this that it must, in some special manner, be used in each case by the Spirit himself? It is called the sword of the Spirit because the Spirit is the maker of it. It is to be used by Christians. If you will turn to the sixth chapter of Ephesians you will find that this sword is a part of the Christian armor and must be wielded by the Christian soldier. Eph. vi: 17. Paul says it is sharper than any two-edged sword, piercing to the dividing asunder of soul and spirit, of the joints and marrow, and is a discerner of the thoughts and intents of the heart. The sword is all right. All we need is faithful men to wield it.

4. The case of Lydia is supposed to be a demonstration of special influence put forth to prepare the heart to receive the divine message — "Whose heart the Lord opened that she attended to the things spoken by Paul."

That *the Lord* opened her heart there can be no question. But, what is meant here by her heart being opened? You answer that she had a wicked, hardened, unregenerate heart, and that the Lord wrought a special work upon it to change it from all this. What evidence have you of this? The facts mentioned concerning her go to establish the very opposite. First. She was already a devout worshiper of God. Second. She was true to her faith when away from home, even among heathen. Third. She was so faithful that she closed her place of business and observed the Sabbath at the sacrifice of her business interests. Fourth. She spent that day in worship although the place where she was sojourning afforded no synagogue. Fifth. She persisted in observing the day with appropriate devotions, although there was no man to conduct the services. These are some of the facts. In the light of them can you say she had a bad heart? Who here can give such evidence of a devout heart as Lydia? What, then, was wrong with her heart! She was a Jewess, and her heart was contracted by narrow Jewish prejudices. Her heart was opened, that is, it expanded. It enlarged from the narrowness of its former faith to the catholic and philanthropic feelings produced by the gospel.

But, *how* was this accomplished? What means did the Lord employ? If you will but glance back over the history immediately preceding this case you will see the Lord working toward this end. The messengers were divinely guided to that place; the message was divinely given; it was divinely confirmed. That message, as given and confirmed, accomplished the good work. The result was, "she attended to the things spoken by Paul." That is *she did them*. Attend is here used in that sense. It is the evidence that her heart was opened, and is an indication of the extent of that work. Her heart was *so* affected that she did what was commanded. That is the best evidence that you can possibly give that your heart is right.

Having examined the ground upon which the theory rests, I now desire to file a few objections against the theory.

1. First of all it relieves all who have not been favored with this special influence of the sin of unbelief. If they cannot believe without it then they cannot be justly held responsible for their unbelief. Nor is this all. If they are not responsible for their unbelief they cannot be justly held responsible for all other sins which flow from unbelief. A theory which legitimately leads to such sad conclusions must be false.

2. Second, the theory makes God a respecter of persons. Some believe and are saved. Others are not. Why this difference? The theory says, God did for some what he did not for others. We cannot hold to the theory and refuse to accept its legitimate and necessary conclusions. It makes God a respecter of persons. But Peter says, "God is no respecter of persons." We must therefore, abandon the theory.

3. In the third place it makes Jesus guilty of cruel mockery for he commands the gospel to be preached to all, knowing that there are many who cannot accept it, — knowing that none can accept it to the saving of their souls unless this special influence is put forth, and yet he will not put it forth for all. They are helpless. The prize is held before them, but their hands are paralyzed. They cannot grasp it.

Still he holds it before their eyes and exhorts them to receive it. He tells them if they do not believe they will be damned, yet gives them not the power which enables them to believe. What cruel, fiendish mockery is this! Believe it of Jesus if you can. I cannot.

Away with the theory. It has no foundation in Scripture. It is contrary to the moral sense of mankind. It is false in its essense and pernicious in its results. It is an aspersion against the divine throne. It defames God. It belies Christ. It is a deep pit between the sinner and the cross. Into it many have fallen. Remove it. Away with it, away with it!

I take up the Bible. I turn the leaves of the New Testament. In the light of its teachings I state to you briefly the case as it is.

We are sinners standing in imminent danger. We need an atonement for sin. We need a revelation to guide us. God has made provision for us according to his abundant mercy. He sent his Son into the world to seek and to save the lost. Christ gave up his own life on the tree of the cross. His blood has been shed. That blood cleanseth from all sin. The Holy Spirit has been sent to reveal the way. This gospel is his message. It teaches the way. The Father calls you to come back from your wanderings in the ways of sin. The Son beseeches you. The Spirit says come. You can hear. You can come. The responsibility rests with you. Flee now for safety to the foot of the cross.

YOUR OWN SALVATION.

Work out your own salvation with fear and trembling. For it is God which worketh in you both to will and to do of his good pleasure. — Phil. ii: 12, 13.

No man desires to be lost. In many cases the desire to be saved may not be very strong, but I cannot believe that a desire to be lost exists in even the most corrupt human heart. It is possible for every man to be saved. God is no respecter of persons. Christ died for all. When he had accomplished his work on earth, and was ready to ascend to the Father who had sent him, he committed the glad tidings of salvation to chosen men, and bade them go into all the world and preach the gospel to every creature. From that moment their work was to preach, their field was the wide, wide world, and their mission was to every creature in it. But why preach the gospel to every creature if there are some who cannot accept it and be saved? To do it would be not only most unreasonable, but it would be cruel mockery. Blessed be the name of our glorious Redeemer, the way of life stands open to all. It stands open now. It stands open for you.

My present purpose is to show how to be saved both here and hereafter. My chief desire is that the answer which I may present shall be the answer given in the Holy Scriptures. Next to this stands the desire to present the answer in a manner so plain and simple that all may easily understand it. I must content myself with little more than a mere statement. I shall aim to be full, but not prolix; brief, but not obscure. It must be remembered that indepedently of revelation we can know nothing concerning the plan of salvation. Neither from the teachings of nature, nor from the light of human reason can we learn the way of life. For all our knowledge in the case we are shut up to what the Bible says. Hence, in what I am about to say my appeal shall be to that alone. Before proceeding to my main purpose, however, it will be well to note a few simple but important facts.

1. No man has a right to throw away either his life or his soul. If it is a man's duty to save his life when in danger of drowning, it is no less his duty to endeavor to save his soul when in danger of being lost forever. You have as much right to take your own life as you have to lose your own soul. You have no right to do either.

2. No man can reasonably hope to be saved who does not put forth some effort to save himself. He must not only will, but *do*. Every man must act for himself. Our friends cannot save us. Great as may be their solicitude for us, and much as they may do, there is a point where efforts must stop — and that point is always short of salvation, unless we are aroused to earnest action. I say it reverently, and because the Scriptures so clearly teach it — God himself will not save us unless we strive to be saved.

3. Our salvation should be the object of our deepest solicitude. We should be in earnest about this as we are in earnest about nothing else. The soul is of priceless value. "What will it profit a man though he should gain the whole world and lose his soul?" Men are in earnest in toiling for wealth, and in striving for worldly honor, but what are all these worth when compared with the soul. Better live as poor Lazarus, the beggar, and die neglected and unknown, if at last you may be borne by angels to the saints' eternal home, than to feast like Dives here, and then lift up your cry of hopeless anguish in torment hereafter.

You are in danger. Awake and flee for your life! Let nothing stop you.

4. Whatever lessons may lie, partly concealed and partly revealed, in our text, this one lies upon the very surface — that God and man unite in working out human salvation. The command is, "work out your own salvation with fear and trembling;" the encouragement is, "for God worketh in you, both to will and to do his good pleasure." God works and we must work. I have nothing to do with theories which stand opposed to this vital truth. I have not time to discuss them. Against them all I wish to place just a few clear passages from the word of God, and then pass on. In the Sermon on the Mount Jesus said, "Not every one that saith unto me Lord, Lord, shall enter into the kingdom of heaven; but he that *doeth* the will of my Father who is in heaven." (Matt. vii: 21.) Again, "Therefore, whosoever heareth these sayings of mine and *doeth* them, I will liken him unto a wise man, which built his house upon a rock," etc. "And every one that heareth these sayings of mine and doeth them not shall be likened to a foolish man who built his house upon the sand," etc. (Matt. vii: 24-27.) And again, "Marvel not at this, for the hour is coming, in the which all that are in their graves shall hear his voice, and shall come forth; they that have *done good*, to the resurrection of life, and they that have done evil, to the resurrection of condemnation." (John v: 28, 29.) And still again, "And being made perfect he became the author of eternal salvation to all them that *obey* him." (Heb. v: 9.) And more yet, "And to you who are troubled, rest with us, when the Lord Jesus shall be revealed from heaven with his mighty angels, in flaming fire, taking vengeance on them that know not God, and *obey not* the gospel of our Lord Jesus Christ." (II. Thess. i: 7, 8.) Turn to one more passage. "Behold,

I come quickly; and my reward is with me, to give every man according *as his work shall be.*" (Rev. xxii: 12.) I could easily add many more. These are enough. If you wish to enter the kingdom of heaven; if you wish to come forth to the resurrection of life; if you wish to enjoy that eternal salvation of which Jesus is the author; if you wish to rest with the apostles of Christ and the saints of all ages when the troubles of life are over; if you wish to escape the sword of vengeance, when in flaming fire and with mighty angels the Lord shall descend from heaven; and if you wish to receive from him in that day, when both the living and the dead shall stand before him in awful judgment, the reward which no hand but his can bestow, then you must earnestly strive for it in this life. Let us then consider as fully as our limits will allow both the work of God and the work of man in the problem of human redemption.

I. *God's Work.*

Salvation is primarily and necessarily of grace. It was commenced, it is carried on, and it will be finally consummated, not by any scheme or merit of our own, but by the grace of God. " God so loved the world, that he gave his only begotten Son, that whosoever believeth on him should not perish, but have everlasting life." (John iii: 16.) The plan of salvation is the offspring of divine love. *We can offer nothing to atone for sin.* Were thy head waters and thine eyes fountains of tears, thou couldst not wash away the stain of thy guilt. The sword of Justice hangs over thee and thou hast no power to stay the avenging stroke. Thou canst not build with thine own hands a city of refuge, and then dwell securely within its walls. Thou hast trampled upon the law of God, and whither wilt thou flee for safety? God is everywhere. Wilt thou ascend into heaven? He is there. Wilt thou descend into the under-world? Lo! God is there. Wilt thou take the wings of the morning and dwell in the uttermost parts of the sea? He is even there. Dost thou say, "Surely the darkness will cover me?" Even the night shall be light about thee. Yea, the darkness hideth not from God. The darkness and the light are both alike to him. But God has laid help upon one mighty to save. He gave his Son to die for men. "Thanks be unto God for his unspeakable gift." (II Cor. ix: 15.)

Paul, in his letter to the Ephesians, says, "For by grace are ye saved through faith; and that not of yourselves; it is the gift of God." (ii: 8.) In another place in the same epistle, he writes, "Christ also loved the church, and gave himself for it; that he might sanctify and cleanse it with the washing of water by the word, that he might present it to himself a glorious church, not having spot, or wrinkle, or any such thing; but that it should be holy and without blemish." (v: 25-27). In his epistle to Titus he says, "But after that the kindness and love (philanthropy) of God our Savior toward man appeared, not by works of righteousness which we have done, but according to his mercy he saved us, by the washing of regeneration, and the renewing of the Holy Ghost; which he shed on us abundantly through Jesus Christ our Savior; that being justified by his grace, we should be made heirs according to the hope of eternal life." (iii: 4-7). How marvelous is God's grace, and how wonderful his work for the children of men! "O the depth of the riches both of the wisdom and knowledge of God! How unsearchable are his judgments, and his ways past finding out! For who hath known the mind of the Lord? or who hath been his counsellor? or who hath first given to him and it shall be recompensed to him again? For of him, and through him, and to him, are all things; to whom be glory forever. Amen." (Rom. xi: 33-36.)

God's work in our salvation is immeasurably great. But please notice, first of all, that *he does not do our work for us.* The text does not say that he wills and does for us, and it cannot be. Though God influences men, yet it is *man* who "wills and does." There are those who appear to think that God will do their work for them, and that they need put forth no effort. They are just floating along. They expect to float into the church and then in some way float into heaven. Now God promises to help those who help themselves. He never does for us what we can do for ourselves. We can plow, and sow, and cultivate the growing harvest. God does not do these things for us. We cannot turn the seasons round and bring the glad sunshine and the refreshing showers. So God sends them. In our salvation there are many things we are commanded to do, and we are able to do them. These God will not do for us. There are many more which we cannot do. These belong to God, and he is faithful.

In the next place, please notice that whatever may be the manner in which God works in us both to will and to to, *he does not force us to do our part.* The will cannot be forced. God never compels a man to become a Christian. Salvation is not simply a question of power, Do not think, O man, that God can save you if he were only willing. He *is* willing. He is waiting for you to will, and to do. Look to your own will. Bend that to the will of God and obey the gospel of his Son. If you remain unforgiven here and are lost hereafter the blame will be yours. God has given his Son to be a sacrifice for sin. He has opened up the way of approach to himself. By the precious blood of Jesus he has purchased redemption. He has sent his message of mercy to you and asked you to accept it. He urges you by his unspeakable love, by the terrors of the judgment to come, and by all the blessed promises of his word to turn and be saved. You are able to do it. A most fearful responsibility rests upon you. May God help me, by the light of his word, to direct you in the work which you are to perform in accepting and appropriating the salvation which he offers.

II. *Man's Work.*

It will greatly assist us in this investigation to remember that salvation is two-fold — present and future — here and hereafter. The text was addressed to those who were already Christians. They were at that time forgiven, and members of the Church of Christ. There was however a salvation not yet attained, and for which they were to work with fear and trembling. It was to give them most anxious concern. We are frequently taught in the Scriptures that one may be truly converted here, and then not enjoy eternal salvation hereafter. He may deny Christ. He may trample upon his precious blood. He may do despite to the Spirit of grace. He may be adopted into the family of God, and afterward so live as to be disinherited. Our salvation is therefore two-fold. The first part consists of the blotting out of all past sins and admission into the family of God on earth; the second consists of a part in the resurrection of the righteous and admission into the family of God in Heaven. By the first we enter the kingdom of grace; by the second we enter the kingdom of glory. In the first we become heirs; in the second we actually inherit. Any complete answer to the question, what must I do to be saved? must comprehend therefore an answer to each of these parts. First, what must I do to be saved here, and what must I *then* do to be saved hereafter? I might answer these in a general way by saying that to secure the first you must *come to Christ*, and that to secure the second you must *continue to follow him*. But as my desire is to be very specific and plain I propose to enter more into detail. How and in what spirit are we to come to Christ?

1. *We are to come with conscious need.* When the three thousand cried out, on that memorable Pentecost, "Men and brethren, what must we do?" they saw their guilt and were deeply conscious of their need. When Saul, prostrate on the ground, asked, "Lord what will thou have me to do?" there was manifest a spirit of humility and entire submission which told of his conscious need. And when the jailor at Philippi, almost frantic with fright, came trembling and fell down at the feet of Paul and Silas, his very question and manner told the want he so deeply felt. Do not come to Christ in a spirit of self-sufficiency. He will not receive you. He came not to call the righteous, but sinners to repentance. He came to seek and save the lost. In coming to Christ let your prayer be that of the poor publican, "Lord be merciful to me a sinner." You are guilty before God and need — not justice — but mercy. Christ's precious invitation is to all who labor and are heavy laden. "Come unto me and I will give you rest. Take my yoke upon you, and learn of me: for I am meek and lowly in heart; and ye shall find rest unto your souls." He pronounces his blessing upon those who hunger and thirst after righteousness, saying, "they shall be filled." You have sinned. This you know. You cannot lay your hand upon your heart and say, this heart has never condemned me. It has condemned you and that right often. I believe there are times in every man's life when he is called to stand before the bar of his own conscience to hear his condemnation. If our own hearts condemn us, let us remember that God is greater than our hearts and knows all things. Surely then he condemns us. We forget many of our sins, but before him there is a book of remembrance. Not one sin is

forgotten with him until it is washed away by the blood of Christ. He can see sin much better than we. Our moral vision is very dim, but his is perfectly clear. We may sin in secret but he seeth in secret, and in the day of judgment our most secret sins will be made known, and before the Judge of all the earth we must answer for them. Your tears cannot wash away a single stain. You need a Savior. Christ is mighty to save. Come to him in conscious need. This is the very first condition of the gospel call.

2. *You must come, led by faith in him.* He is an all-sufficient Savior and as such you must trust him. To the conscience-stricken jailor, Paul answered, "Believe on the Lord Jesus Christ, and thou shalt be saved." In another place it is written, "Without faith it is impossible to please God." Do you say you cannot believe? Why not? Can you believe your friend who has never, in the very least thing, deceived you? Cannot you accept his word when he makes you a solemn pledge? Why then can you not believe Christ? Has he ever deceived any one? Can you point to a single instance where he has failed to keep his word to the very letter? Why, then, can you not trust him? Has he not shown his power to save? Has he not cleansed and saved the worst? Has he not shown his willingness to save. Has he not evinced even an anxiety to save? Can you then doubt his ability or his willingness to forgive you? I can see no room for doubt. He has removed every obstacle. But are you troubled about the kind of faith you are called upon to exercise? Let me notice some features of the faith which saves. First of all, it rests, like all faith must rest, upon testimony. In concluding his history of the life of Jesus, John said, "And many other signs truly did Jesus, in the presence of his disciples which are not written in this book; but these are written that ye might believe that Jesus

is the Christ, the Son of God: and that believing ye might have life through his name." He wrote that men might believe. He presented testimony in order to produce saving faith. Again, the faith which saves lays hold upon Christ, for its object. It is not faith in a creed, or in a church, much less in your own merit and power, but a faith which takes hold upon Christ. John wrote that you might believe that *Jesus is the Christ the Son of God*. This, then, is what you are to believe. It is personal faith in a personal Savior.

3. *You must renounce sin and all that stands opposed to Christ.* You must repent. "Now God commandeth all men everywhere to repent," said Paul when he stood in the midst of Mars hill and preached to the Athenians. If God has commanded all men everywhere to repent, then are *you* commanded to repent. Remember, too, that this command comes not from men, but from God who "has appointed a day, in the which he will judge the world in righteousness." By the certainty and the solemnity of that coming judgment he calls you to repentance. Will you heed his warning voice? But, you say, "I am told that I must see myself as the chief of sinners, and this I cannot do. I know I am a sinner, but then I know that others are even worse than I am. I cannot feel that I am the very worst of the wicked." Now, I do not wish to palliate sins, nor to make you think you are better than you really are; but, let me ask, who told you that you should see yourself as the very chief of sinners? Has God? I have never seen such a requirement in all his word. Men have no right to require in your salvation what God does not require. God calls upon you to see yourself as you really are — condemned and hastening on to judgment. Another says, "I cannot feel as I think I ought to feel. I know I am a sinner, but then I cannot weep over my sins as I think I ought to weep." My dear sir, have you

never thought of this — that repentance has not so much to do with your emotions as it has to do with the purpose of your heart? You may shed your tears of bitter sorrow until the very fountain whence they flow is dry, and yet not truly repent. *The essential feature of repentance is a change of your will in reference to sin.* This change of will is *produced* by sorrow for sin, and *leads* to a reformation of life. Away with all false and fanciful notions about this important duty.

4. *You should publicly confess your faith in Jesus as the Christ, the Son of the living God.* Christ himself has made the promise that, "Whosoever shall confess me before men, him will I confess also before my Father which is in Heaven," and to this he has added that, "Whosoever shall deny me before men, him will I also deny before my father which is in Heaven." A blessed promise and a solemn warning are here placed side by side. Which do you desire — that the glorious Christ shall confess you before the everlasting Father, or that he shall deny you in his presence? What, then, will you do with Christ? Will you by your conduct deny him, or by lip and life confess him? Hear these words from Paul: "If thou shalt confess with thy mouth the Lord Jesus, and shalt believe in thine heart that God hath raised him from the dead, thou shalt be saved. For with the heart man believeth unto righteousness and with the mouth confession is made unto salvation." In the great controversy about Jesus, we are not allowed to be neutral. The martyrs in flames confessed him, angels have confessed him. The Father himself openly confessed him, and Jesus confessed and denied not at the peril of his life. You should publicly confess him.

5. *You are required to be baptized into the name of the Father, and of the Son, and of the Holy Spirit.* In the

great commission to his apostles, Christ said, " Go, teach all nations, baptizing them into the name of the Father, and of the Son, and of the Holy Spirit." (Matt. xxviii: 19.) "He that believeth and is baptized shall be saved." (Mark xvi: 16.) Peter said to the inquirers of Jerusalem, " Repent and be baptized, every one of you, in the name of Jesus Christ, for the remission of sins." (Acts ii: 38.) Ananias said to penitent Saul, "Arise and be baptized, and wash away thy sins, calling on the name of the Lord." (Acts xxii: 16.) From these passages two things appear. First, that baptism is a duty; and secondly, that it has been divinely appointed as a condition of the forgiveness of sins. These scriptures, however, do not ascribe any mystic or miraculous power to this ordinance. They present it as a *condition*, divinely imposed, and speak of it as an act of faith. But neither in the faith nor the obedience which we may render can there be any *merit*. Christ, by his own blood, *procures* salvation. We, by the conditions specified, personally *appropriate* it.

By the way which I have pointed out, you are to come to Christ and receive remission of sins and adoption into the family of God on earth. In other words, you *become a Christian*. Remember our text was addressed to Christians — " Work out your own salvation with fear and trembling." How must I work out this salvation! I have already said that as the first is secured by *coming to Christ*, so this is to be secured by *continuing to follow Christ*. This is a Scriptural generalization. We have noticed already the specific things contained in the first. Let us now notice how we are to continue to follow Christ. By following him is meant, of course, taking him as our pattern — striving to imitate the exemplary life he lived. We are to drink of his spirit and manifest it in our lives. "He that sayeth that he abideth in him ought himself also to walk even as he walked." (I John ii: 6.) The way of life is brightened and made glorious by the example of Jesus as he walked before men. Even Renan, the infidel, felt compelled to say that, "all ages will proclaim that, among the sons of men, there were none born greater than Jesus." The character of Christ must be studied. We must learn of him, by what he did, as well as by what he said. What, then, are some of the features of this model character?

The will of God was the rule of his life. When about to come to this world he is represented as saying, "Lo, I come to do thy will, O God." (Heb. x: 9.) When only twelve years of age he went to Jerusalem with his parents to worship. They started on their return, leaving him behind, but missing him they went back and found him in the temple conversing with the doctors and lawyers. When they chided him for not returning with them, his reply was, "Wist ye not I must be about my Father's business." (Luke ii: 9.) And when the time of his death drew near — when the guilt of the race rested upon him — his prayer was, "Father, if thou be willing, remove this cup from me: nevertheless, not my will, but thine, be done." (Luke xxii: 42.) The will of God was the supreme rule of his life. It must be ours in following him.

He was unselfish. He came not to be ministered to, but to minister. He was rich yet for our sakes he became poor, that we, through his poverty, might be rich. (II. Cor. viii: 9). "Let this mind be in you which was also in Christ Jesus; who, being in the form of God, thought it not robbery to be equal with God; but made himself of no reputation, and took upon him the form of a servant. and was made in the likeness of men; and being found in fashion as a man he humbled himself, and became obedient unto death, even the death of the cross." (Phil. ii: 5–9). He denied himself rest and food sometimes, saying, "I have meat to eat that ye know not of. My meat is to do the will of him that sent me, and to finish his work." (John iv: 32–34.)

He was a man of prayer. One would most reasonably suppose that if any could live without prayer surely he could. Yet we often find him engaged in prayer. He would withdraw from the crowd to be alone with his Father. Often through the entire night he would be engaged in active communion with God. In this we must follow him. The life of the Christian must be one of devotion.

He was actively engaged in doing good. "He went about," says Peter, "constantly doing good." He lived to labor. He sought the helpless that he might help them. He healed the sick, opened the eyes of the blind, unstopped the ears of the deaf, restored the paralytic, healed the leper, fed the hungry, instructed the ignorant and raised the dead. He spent his life in ceaseless activities. "I must work the works of him that sent me," is a sentence from his own lips. "Let them who have believed in him be careful to practice good works," was one of the faithful sayings in the early churches. By active lives spent in doing good we follow Christ.

He was gracious in forgiving. His life abounds in illustrations of his forgiving nature. He cherished no malice. He prayed for his most bitter foes. Who can forget the prayer which arose from the cross, "Father forgive them, they know not what they do." We must cultivate a forgiving spirit. If we forgive not, how may we hope to be forgiven?

These are some of the features in the character we are to imitate. To live such a life, in this evil world, requires a struggle. It is called the fight of faith. It is a fight. Enemies are around us and within us. We are tempted, and must be, so long as we remain in the flesh. But thanks be to God he promises to help in every time of trouble. We need his grace to strengthen us and he has promised it. The gift of his son is a pledge that he will give us all we may need. Think not of being borne to heaven without effort on your part. He who enters through the gate must strive. The reward beyond is worthy the strife. We cannot now fully comprehend the richness of that salvation for which we struggle. It surpasses the conception of man. We may know by and by. When from every kindred, and people, and nation, and tribe, and tongue under the whole heavens, the redeemed ones are gathered home, when we shall hear the sentence pronounced against those forever lost, when we shall look upon the face of him whose we are and whom we serve, when we see the king in his beauty and glory unearthly, when we hear that song unsung before, the song of salvation in heaven, as it rises from that countless host of grateful hearts, and when God shall with his own hand wipe every tear away, then — oh, then — may we begin to realize the priceless blessing so freely offered in the gospel. I have sought by the light of God's word to show you how to be saved both here and hereafter. Will you begin your journey heavenward now? Will you come to Christ and then follow him whithersoever he may lead you? Do not delay, I beg you. By the coming judgment, by the cross of Christ, by the soul undying, by the warnings and the promises of the word of God, I beg you, turn to Christ and live.

ORDINANCES OF THE LORD.*

And they were both righteous before God, walking in all the commandments and ordinances of the Lord blameless. — Luke i: 6.

This commendation was written of Zacharias and Elizabeth, the parents of John the Baptist. Its value lies chiefly in the fact that it is divine. The approving words of good men, however precious, may hardly be compared with the approbation of God. Every reverent spirit desires to know what the Lord commends, and to do it. In this case He commends their righteousness, as shown in their walking in all His commandments and ordinances blameless.

There are some features of this text which I think it important for us to fix in our minds in the very beginning. One is that the ordinances which Zacharias and Elizabeth observed were ordinances *of the Lord*. Had they been the ordinances of men, having nothing more than human authority, I am sure this commendation would not have been written of them. The Lord condemns, with clear and solemn condemnation, the religious observance of all such ordinances. They may be beautiful and elaborate, and impressive, yet he does not approve their observance as a part of religious duty. "In vain do you worship me, teaching for doctrines the commandments of men." Note this, too, that these aged servants of God did not make a division of the ordinances of the Lord, and observe some while they neglected others, but they walked in *all* the commandments and ordin-

---

* Preached just before administering the ordinance of Christian baptism.

ances of the Lord. They had not adopted the theory of essentials and non-essentials. They observed all. Then, too, the manner and spirit in which this was done is worthy of notice. It is expressed by the word *blameless.*

There are those in our day who would scarcely have praised them for these things. They have such a distaste for ordinances that they would not think of making the observance of even divine ordinances any ground of praise. Although many of them are very good people, yet even to listen with respectful attention to a sermon on these subjects is a heavy tax on their toleration. And this distaste — or prejudice, I would better call it — arises from several causes. Let me mention a few.

The bitter controversies which have been waged over ordinances is one cause. For, it must be confessed, that some of the most bitter and disgraceful controversies which have convulsed the church have been about these matters. Another cause is found, I think, in the extreme and unwarranted value which some have attached to ordinances. One extreme begets another. Some overvalue ordinances, practically making all religion consist in their observance, and, quite naturally, others go to the opposite extreme and practically ignore them. And still another cause is found in the supposed antagonism between the observance of these ordinances and a spiritual religion. They seek to be spiritual; they desire a heart-felt religion; they look upon ordinances as carnal and ceremonial and cold, and so, for this reason, ignore them. And still another cause is found in the misapplication of certain Scriptures which speak of ordinances as having been abolished. (Eph. ii: 15; Col. ii: 14–20.) These are some of the causes which have produced a very positive distaste for ordinances and especially a dislike for even Christian discussion of them.

We should avoid extremes. While we may have a very wholesome distaste for controversy, yet it is unwise to seek the peace we covet by casting aside what God has enjoined. Nor should we allow any extreme position taken by others to force us to the opposite extreme. The best way to correct any extreme is to stand firmly on the golden mean where truth is found. Nor should cold formalism lead us to conclude that every observance of forms in religion must of necessity be empty formality. The proper observance of ordinances cannot exist without spirituality. We should obey from the heart. And when Paul, or other inspired men, write of the abrogation of the ceremonial law of the Jews, let us not be so unwise as to apply what is said of these Jewish ordinances, to the ordinances of the Lord enjoined in the gospel. Let us seek to know the truth in reference to all matters connected with our holy religion, and to enjoy peace and avoid all extremes.

My purpose this morning is to present briefly something of the functions of ordinances, and to estimate as near as we can their real value. I speak only of ordinances of the Lord.

1. *They are divinely appointed teachers.* They are not idle, meaningless ceremonies. They are stereotyped lessons. They are pillars erected by the divine hand on which the finger of God has written inscriptions for the passing generations of men. Take the oldest of all, the Sabbath. It tells of the Creator, of his work, of his rest, and of a rest that remains for his people. Then, too, what records and lessons were written all over the Passover. It was full of meaning. It told of bondage and deliverance; of the slaying of the Egyptian first-born, and of the sparing of the first-born in the homes of Israel; of hasty flight; of the opened sea; of the engulfed army in

pursuit; of all that was thrilling and precious in the events that clustered about the birth of the Jewish nation. The day of atonement furnishes another illustration. It stood as a marble shaft written over with many of the profoundest problems that belong to the redemption of fallen man. It told of sin and helplessness and forgiveness. It cast its rays of promise on the future, and these finally painted the rainbow over the cross. Baptism also is significant. It speaks of the facts on which our religion rests. It is radiant with the divine promise of foregiveness. It tells of death, it is a burial, it points triumphantly to a resurrection. It is a parable in action. So, again, of the Lord's Supper. How sweet and how tender are the lessons of love which make even these emblems of death beautiful. With his own hand, so soon to be nailed to the cross, our Savior inscribes in letters of heavenly light over this table, "Do this in remembrance of me." This ordinance tells of sin and danger, and divine solicitude, and atoning love, and stern justice, and pleading mercy, and divine wrath, and inflexible law, and forgiving grace, and an open heaven and rejoicing ranks of ransomed souls, and all that salvation means and salvation cost. Ordinances are not empty ceremonies. They are significant. They are divinely appointed as teachers and helpers of men.

2. *In the second place they are a part of God's method of righteousness.* I ask attention to a single passage of Scripture and then to an illustration of it. This is the passage: "Brethren, my heart's desire and prayer to God for Israel is, that they might be saved. For I bear them record that they have a zeal of God, but not according to knowledge. For they, being ignorant of God's righteousness, and going about to establish their own righteousness, have not submitted themselves unto the righteousness of God." (Rom. x: 1–3.) What is here meant by the righteousness of God?

Evidently, not the attribute of God which bears that name. For they were not ignorant of God's righteousness in that sense. They knew that he was righteous. Moreover, Paul cannot here be speaking of the attribute, for he says, they had not submitted themselves to it and it is not possible for men to submit themselves to an attribute. Nor can we suppose that when he places their righteousness in antithesis with what he here calls the righteousness of God he meant to say that they were opposing their character to the character of God.

What, then, is his meaning? I answer, that by righteousness he means the plan or method by which they are made righteous. The context points to this. The word which Paul uses cannot be fully represented by any one word in English. By the substitution of a phrase we have his meaning in our own tongue. They were ignorant of God's method of constituting men righteous; they go about to establish their own method of constituting men righteous; and so they did not submit themselves to God's method of constituting men righteous.

The illustration to which I refer is found in the incidents of Christ's baptism. You remember that when he asked to be baptized, John said, "I have need to be baptized of thee, and comest thou to me?" And Jesus' reply was, "Thus it becometh us to fulfil all righteousness." That is, thus it becometh us to observe all God's methods of constituting men righteous. Baptism is *a part* of the divine method or plan of constituting us righteous. Since, then, ordinances are a part of the divine method of constituting men righteous, and if Christ could say that for this reason it was becoming in him to submit to them, certainly it is not becoming in us to contemn or ignore them.

3. Still further, *our treatment of ordinances is esteemed as*

our treatment of their author. This is reasonable. An ordinance is an observance established by authority, and to despise it and trample it under foot is to despise and trample under foot that authority. And so Paul says, in the lesson which I read, in speaking of the Lord's Supper, "whosoever shall eat of this bread and drink of this cup unworthily *shall be guilty of the body and blood of the Lord.*" That is, the way in which they treat this ordinance of the Lord is regarded as the way in which they treat the Lord himself. If we are indifferent when he has said, "Do this in remembrance of me," it is regarded as indifference not simply in reference to an institution of the Lord's house, but as indifference toward the Lord himself. If you profane this ordinance, if you turn it into a drunken revel, if you make of it only a feast to satisfy animal hunger, if you pervert it and prostitute it, the matter does not end there, but is reckoned as an indignity toward Christ. So of baptism. In speaking to the Jews, of John and his baptism, Jesus said: "And all the people that heard him, and the publicans justified God, being baptized with the baptism of John; but the Pharisees and lawyers rejected the counsel of God against themselves, being not baptized of him." (Luke vii: 29, 30.) And, on another occasion when he asked them concerning the baptism of John, whether it was from heaven, we are told that they reasoned with themselves, saying, "If we say from heaven, he will say, why then believed ye him not! and if we say, of men, the people will stone us, for they be persuaded that John was a prophet." (Luke xx: 4-6.) They easily saw that if they admitted its divine origin they would condemn themselves as guilty of rejecting divine authority, and this was so plain and conclusive that they deliberately agreed to return a falsehood for an answer to Christ's question. In fact, all the force and authority of an ordinance is found in its origin. We should stand by every ecclesiastical ordinance with the question, "Is it from heaven or is it of men?" If of men we may reject it, but if from heaven we cannot, without setting at defiance the authority of heaven.

And this leads me to say, in the fourth place that

4. *Obedience to ordinances is a test of loyalty.* All commands *may* be tests of loyalty. Christ says, "Ye are my friends if ye do *whatsoever* I command you." And again, it is written, "If you love me you will keep my commandments." The Scriptures are full of this test of love and loyalty. But some things commanded are more decisive tests of loyalty than others. Among things enjoined upon us by divine authority are some so manifestly right and in such perfect accord with our inclination that we may observe and do them with no regard for the authority which enjoins them. Marital love, parental love, filial love, obedience to civil rulers, truthfulness, fidelity, honesty and many other things commanded of God may be obeyed with no thought of the command or its authority. Some things are commanded because they are right, while others are right only because they are commanded. When the candidate for baptism this morning humbled herself to submit to this ordinance, what reason can she have for this act save the all-sufficient one, the Lord has commanded it? It will be bowing down to take his yoke. It is an open and public acknowledgment of his authority. In this view of the case it seems to me there is a manifestation of wisdom in placing at the very threshhold of the Christian life an ordinance that is inconvenient, distasteful and humbling. It makes it only a more efficient test. So when I hear it reviled and ridiculed it confirms my conviction that it must be of God. He tries us. He tests our loyalty. But if others revile there is a brighter side presents itself when we remember that,

5. *God has seen fit to join special blessings to obedience to this ordinance.* When Jesus came up out of the waters of baptism and paused on the bank of the Jordan to lift his heart to God in prayer, the heavens were opened and the voice of the Father was heard confessing his Son. The Holy Spirit, like a dove in visible form, descended and abode upon him. This event stands at the opening of his ministry. After that ministry had been fulfilled, — after his example had been placed before men, after his words of life had been committed to chosen embassadors, after the agony of the garden, with bloody-sweat, had been endured, after his blood had been shed upon the cross and death had been conquered by his resurrection and he was ready to be received back to the Father, in his own name he commanded his apostles to "go into all the world, and preach the gospel to every creature," adding the promise, "he that *believeth and is baptized shall be saved*, but he that believeth not, shall be damned." And when we come to the time, in the unfoldings of the divine plan, that these commissioned ones are to enter upon the work committed to them we hear them give answer to the agonizing cry, "Men and brethren, what must we do?" They promptly reply in the words of Peter, "Repent and be baptized every one of you in the name of Jesus Christ, for the remission of sins, and ye shall receive the gift of the Holy Spirit." God meets obedience with blessings. The promise of God joined to an ordinance gives to it a significance and value not its own.

Let us here pause a moment while we glance back over what has been said. We have learned that the ordinances of the Lord are divinely appointed teachers; that they belong to God's method of constituting men righteous; that the treatment of an ordinance is esteemed as if we so treated its author; that they are tests of loyalty, and that God has seen fit to join special promises to their proper observance. With these facts before you I leave it with each of you to form your own conclusion as to the way you will bear yourself toward the ordinances of our Lord.

I will detain you to add only one other thought, and that is, that,

6. *Obedience to ordinances should always be from the heart.* There are no empty forms and idle ceremonies in the gospel. It is a spiritual religion. It deals always with the heart. In writing to the church in Rome, Paul thanks God that, though they had been the servants of sin, yet they had *obeyed from the heart* that form of doctrine which had been delivered unto them; being *then* made free from sin they became the servants of righteousness. Their obedience was a voice of the heart. Had it not been, had they obeyed the form of doctrine as a mere form, this blessing would not have been theirs. As we go down into the waters to be buried with our dear Savior, it should be with a heart contrite and penitent, for we have sinned; meek and humble, for we are unworthy; loving and trustful, for the Lord has spoken in mercy, and his promises are sure. It is the sealing of the soul's vows. It is the public declaration of its sacred covenant with God. It is the open, and formal, and solemn renunciation of the sinful past. It is the entrance upon a new life. Over the baptismal grave is the rain-bow of promise, placed there by the pierced hand of Christ. "He that believeth and is baptized shall be saved."

SAFETY IN SHIPWRECK.

Except these abide in the ship, ye cannot be saved. Acts xxvii: 31

Paul is on his way to Rome. He is a prisoner. The hostility of the Jews in Judea had shut out all hope of justice for him there and so he appealed to Cæsar.

Let us join him as the vessel lies at Fair Haven, a harbor on the south of Crete. Julius, a centurion of Augustus' band has him in charge. The ship hails from Alexandria in Egypt and is bound for Italy with a cargo of corn. She is a large craft, and, in addition to her cargo, carries as passengers and crew two hundred and seventy-six souls.

It was about this season of the year and sailing was dangerous. Paul, although a prisoner, ventured to advise against putting to sea, and warned them of dangers and loss. But, as the harbor at Fair Haven was not a commodious one to winter in, it was determined to set sail. One day when the south wind blew softly they weighed anchor, and were soon out upon the blue waters of the Mediterranean.

But, not long after, there arose a tempetuous wind called the Euroclydon. If you will read the twenty-seventh chapter of Acts, from the fourteenth verse to its close, you will find how, for many days, they were driven and tossed by this tempest. Oh, the terror that comes in a storm at sea! No sun, no moon, no stars. The vessel has sprung a leak. Cargo overboard. Pumps at work. Night comes on, but no sleep; day dawns, but it brings no relief. At last all hope has perished and the darkness of despair settles down upon them. They must perish in the sea. But when that cheerless day came Paul gathered the sailors about him on the deck of the laboring vessel, and, raising his voice above the storm said, "Sirs, ye should have hearkened to my counsel, and not have set sail from Crete; thus would ye have been spared this harm and loss. And now I exhort you to be of good cheer; *for there shall be no loss of any man's life among you, but only of the ship.* For there stood by me this night an angel of God, whose I am and whom I serve, saying, 'Fear not, Paul; thou must stand before Cæsar: and lo! God hath given thee all that sail with thee.' Wherefore, sirs, be of good cheer; *for I believe God, that what hath been declared unto me shall come to pass.* Nevertheless, we must be cast upon a certain island."

The storm continues without abatement and the danger seems only to increase. It is now the fourteenth day. About midnight there are indications that they are nearing land and orders are given to heave the lead. Twenty fathoms. They sound again. Fifteen fathoms. They are rapidly approaching land, and danger of being dashed upon the breakers gives fresh alarm. Quickly as possible four anchors are cast out astern and they anxiously await the dawn of day.

While they thus wait, that transpired which called forth the words of the text. For the sailors, under pretext of carrying out some anchors from the bow, lowered the boat over the ship's side. Their real purpose was to save their own lives and leave the others to their fate. Paul detecting this, said to the centurion and to the soldiers. "*Except these abide in the ship, ye cannot be saved.*"

Place this by the side of that confident assurance he expressed a few days before. "No loss of any man's life." He said he believed God. He is a man of faith. Yet when the crisis comes, he is watchful and cautious and active. There are those who find difficulty in reconciling these things. They detect, as they suppose, a wavering of Paul's faith. To me, nothing appears in his conduct, however to awaken such a suspicion. His conduct was perfectly consistent with his expression of confidence. DIVINE PROMISE DOES NOT IGNORE HUMAN INSTRUMENTALITIES. This fact is the basis on which the two phases of his conduct are to be harmonized. Paul recognized this as a principle underlying the promises of God. Yea, more: he shows that according to his view *divine promises find their fulfilment through human instrumentalities, wherever these are available.* He believed in God's power; he believed in God's fidelity; he believed the word of God spoken by the angel, yet he recognized the need of watchfulness and skill and prudent effort on the part of all on board.

The soldiers with their short-swords cut the ropes and let the boat drift to sea. All on board the ship, renew their strength by partaking of food. The ship is lightened by casting the remainder of the cargo into the sea. Then when the day dawns they select a place to run the ship aground. They cut the anchors adrift, loosed the rudder bands, hoisted the mainsail and strand her on the beach. The stern was rapidly broken by the sea. Some swimming and others on spars and broken pieces of the wreck sought the shore until all were safe on the island of Melita. *Thus was the gracious promise of God fulfilled.*

I cannot think upon the conduct of Paul in this interesting event without contrasting it with that of some very good people in our own day.

1. Had he been like them he might have stood upon the deck as the ship rode at anchor that night and said, " I will show *my great faith*, before these heathen. God has prom-

ised that no life shall be lost. I have given this assurance to the passengers and the crew. The ship is foundering; the sea is raging; the storm shrieks through the rigging; in the lull of the storm I can hear the sound of breakers; I know the ship must go down, but God has promised and he is able to fulfil all that he has promised. I will show my faith by manifest unconcern and inactivity."

My friends, have you never heard such expressions? Is it not true that absolute passivity is regarded by many as the manifestation of the highest degree of faith? Justification by faith, in order to be justification *by faith*, must rigorously exclude all human agency. It must be faith alone. And, in the ordinary affairs of life, we are supposed to show great faith only as we refuse to exert ourselves in the use of ordinary means.

A few years ago Mrs. Girling, a religious fanatic in England, proposed to live by faith. Several other women gathered about her. They did nothing for their support, claiming that God would care for them, and give them their daily bread and all needed good. The life of the English philanthropist, Geo. Muller is put before the world as, *par excellence*, the "Life of Trust," because he does not make direct appeal to the benevolence of the people to give him support in his charitable work, but only prays God to supply his wants. Now and then, too, we are told of "faith cures." They are called such because they are accomplished, it is claimed, without the use of means. The patient trusts God to do the work. So, in the matter of salvation, sinners are exhorted to "only believe." All effort on their part is discouraged. They must be saved by faith, and human endeavor is a manifestation of weak faith. Perfect faith holds its arms and waits, trusting God to do the work in his own good time.

Such theories lack the element of common sense. They are pernicious. Worse than all, they are unscriptural and anti-scriptural. I respectfully submit that Paul was a man of quite as great faith as any of these modern teachers, and yet his vigilance and prompt efforts to save himself and others, employing ordinary means to do it, were not inconsistent with his faith. *Divine promise finds its fulfilment through human effort, wherever that is available.* The thought of this proposition underlies his theology and his conduct.

2. Or, had Paul been like others of our day, he would have said, "*Let God have all the glory.* He has granted me a vision and has given me a sure promise. The danger was very great. Hope perished. The danger now is imminent. The sea is wild with rage and the sound of the breakers is as the sound of doom. Yet God is able to save us. Let him get great glory to his name and magnify his power in the presence of these heathen. I will stand with folded arms. No effort will I make. All the glory shall be his." Paul might have so said; but, it is certain, he did not.

Yet we are taught in our day that to put forth effort to save ourselves is to become our own saviors. That if the sinner makes any effort, or does anything looking towards his recovery from sin and its dreadful consequences, his salvation ceases to be a matter of grace, and he takes the glory from God. I flatly deny the correctness of this conclusion. As to the glory, — I hold there is more given to God in the doctrine of man's free agency and responsibility than in the doctrine of his passivity. Do you suppose Paul and the few brethren who were with him, felt any less grateful when they reached the shore in safety, as they did, than they would have felt had they been rescued without effort on their part? And, can you suppose that when the struggling saint stands safe within the vail he will restrain one note of praise because he struggled along the rugged way.

3. The fact is this: *God saves by rendering needed aid.* He does what we cannot do. This all readily recognize in the realms lying beyond the range of matters religious. God gives man his daily bread, and yet "in the sweat of his brow" he gains it. What would you think of the farmer who would enter his closet in the spring and remain there praying God to give him abundant harvests, and yet do no work? Or, here is a young man who desires wisdom and knowledge. He prays for it, but does not study. Or, again, here is a young girl who longs for skill at the piano, but she will not practice. She has faith, and prays and trusts that God will give her skill. What do you think of these? The truth of the matter is that when we take these theories away from religious interests and apply them to the affairs of every-day life, they appear absurd. We exercise more common sense and sound judgment in ordinary matters than in religious.

4. If what I have presented be true, then there are three doctrines, at least, which must go down.

The doctrine that all men will be saved goes down. It cannot be true, if there is human agency in salvation, for not all will make the effort.

The doctrine of arbitrary choice and eternal decrees goes down, for that wholly and distinctly repudiates the agency of man in his salvation.

The doctrine of passivity goes down, for that affirms that man is absolutely unable to do anything.

Well, let them go down. If they sink into utter oblivion the world has lost nothing worth holding. No truth, no light, no comfort, no strength, no help has been lost. Let them go down and let the light of revelation and the dictates of sound common sense come up. Let them go down, for they have been a hinderance to many. O, my brother man, if you have been saying salvation is of God in such a sense that it lies wholly beyond the reach of your efforts; if you have been saying the entire work has been done, so that nothing remained for you to do; if you have been saying you are unable, and are yet waiting for some power to be given you of God, cast away these delusions and hear the spirit calling, "Save yourself;" "flee for refuge!"

THE MANIFESTATION OF FAITH.

What doth it profit, my brethren, though a man say he hath faith, and have not works? Can faith save him? If a brother or sister be naked or destitute of daily food, and one of you should say unto them, Depart in peace; be ye warmed and filled; notwithstanding ye give them not those things which are needful to the body, what doth it profit?. Even so faith, if it hath not works, is dead, being alone. Yea, a man may say, Thou hast faith and I have works; show me thy faith without thy works and I will show you my faith by my works. — James ii: 14-18.

We are required not only to believe, but to manifest our faith to the world. God does not permit any one to hide his faith. It is something too precious to be concealed. Though the exhibition of it should bring upon us the hatred of men, and lead us through bitter persecution, even to a violent death, still we are required to confess and deny not. Moreover, a strong, living faith cannot consent to be silent. It cannot live shut up in one's heart. It must out. It will show itself. When a genuine faith takes hold upon us we are compelled to speak and to act under its directions. It will not suffer us to be idle. It enthrones itself in the heart, and then, by the words of the lips and the works of the hands it proclaims its presence and its power. We cannot be possessed of a living faith without at the same time being characterized by obedient lives. Faith alone is dead. It cannot benefit any one.

The comparison in the text is obvious and striking. The sense of this Scripture is, that, faith in itself, without the acts fitly corresponding to it, and to which it would prompt, is as cold, and heartless, and unmeaning as it would be to say to one who is destitute of the necessaries of life, " depart in peace; be warmed and filled," and not give them the things which are needed. Faith is not, and cannot be shown to be genuine, saving faith, unless it be accompanied with corresponding acts: just as our good wishes for the poor and needy (when we have it in our power to help) cannot be shown to be genuine but by actually ministering to their necessities. He who refuses to give to the needy, when he is able to do it, shows, beyond a doubt, that he has no genuine sympathy for them, although his profession of sympathy may be very great; so he who does not work, shows that he has not genuine saving faith, though he may lay great claim to it.

But what kind of works is to be given and accepted as proof of faith? Clearly, those works which spring from faith and can be produced by nothing else. There are many good works which may exist, and actually do exist, where there is no faith. An infidel may be generous, liberal, kind, affectionate and philanthropic. The natural and noble impulses in men often bring forth good fruit to bless others. Such works, therefore, cannot certainly prove the presence and power of faith within us, since they often are where faith evidently is not. Faith, however, is not in the least opposed to such good works, but by strengthening the good already within, makes us abound more and more in doing good to all men as we have opportunity. We may become so fruitful in self-sacrifices for the good of others as to leave little room to doubt the genuineness or strength of our faith. A man who lives by faith will be more affectionate and forbearing in his family, more sympathetic and charitable toward the poor and needy; more willing and gracious in forgiving, and more ready to expend his energies and his means in every good word and work.

There are works, however, which spring from faith, and

which can be produced by nothing else; and these, after all, must furnish the clearest proofs of the presence of faith. These works may be classified under one general head — *works of obedience.* Faith looks up to God and is guided by him. It resolutely and persistently rejects all other guides. To it, God's will is the highest law possible. But it is not sufficient to say, in this general way, that the works which furnish the best proof of faith are works of obedience. This is sufficiently exact, but is not sufficiently minute and specific. Let us descend into a more detailed description of some of their characteristics, and illustrate our meaning by incidents in the lives of those who have lived by faith. I do not undertake, however, to point out all the marks peculiar to these works, nor do I hold that all the features of them which I may present are to be seen in any one single act of faith.

1. *Where there is no apparent reason for doing the thing commanded, and where we are, therefore, compelled to do it simply and alone because God has commanded it.* Were any other reason apparent, save the fact that God has commanded it, then that other reason might be the motive which prompts us to do it, and hence the doing of it could not certainly prove our faith. For instance, when Abram was commanded to leave his native land, and go forth, he knew not where nor why, he obeyed the divine injunction and thus gave proof of his faith. There was no apparent reason why he should leave his home and become an exile. No doubt he loved his kindred and the land of his birth. He saw no reasonable prospect of improving his circumstances by seeking a new place. Why then should he go? Why did he go? For this reason, and for this alone: God had commanded him to do it. Again, when, many years after this, God said: "Take now thy son, thine only son Isaac, whom

thou lovest, and get the into the land of Moriah; and offer him there for a burnt offering upon one of the mountains which I will tell thee of"—what reason could have induced him to do this? There were many apparent reasons why he should not, but there was only one reason why he should. God had commanded it. Of this there could be no doubt. The command was emphatic and specific. He obeyed simply and alone because God had commanded. What higher reason could any one have? Faith says this is the very highest possible.

2. *Where there is no apparent connection between the thing commanded and the end to be gained.* A certain end is to be accomplished. We are commanded to do certain things in order to reach this. But there is not the most remote connection, so far as we can see, between the end and the means. They are not related to each other as cause to effect. Take, as an illustration of this, the capture of the city of Jericho. That city was taken by faith. We read, that, "by faith the walls of Jericho fell down, after they were compassed about seven days." But how does it appear that the taking of that city was an act of faith? The Israelites took many other cities, and they took them, too, in obedience to God's command, yet these other cases are not mentioned as acts of faith. What is there peculiar to this, which marks it as an evidence of faith? Evidently, this, that there was no apparent connection between the means to be employed and the end to be gained. God said to Joshua, "Ye shall compass the city, all ye men of war, and go round about the city once. Thus shalt thou do six days. And seven priests shall bear before the ark seven trumpets of rams' horns: and the seventh day ye shall compass the city seven times, and the priests shall blow with the trumpets. And it shall come to pass, that when they make a long blast

with the rams' horns, and when ye hear the sound of the trumpet, all the people shall shout with a great shout: and the walls of the city shall fall down flat, and the people shall ascend up every man straight before him." This was the divine plan for the siege. But in all the history of wars, and in all the science of warfare, who had ever adopted such a plan? What apparent connection between the means and the end? The adoption of the plan was a trial and a triumph of their faith. Their own judgment and experience would certainly have suggested some plan more apparently rational. But God intended they should walk by faith, and so while he clearly presents the end to be accomplished, and reveals in detail the means to be employed, he hides from sight and from reason the link which unites the one to the other. We may find, in the conclusion of this discourse, that he sometimes applies to our faith the same severe test.

3. *Where there is no apparent necessity for doing the thing commanded, and where reason and experience pronounce it foolish.* The faith of Noah furnishes a striking illustration of this. He was a man of remarkable faith. "By faith, Noah, being warned of God of things not seen as yet, moved with fear, prepared an ark to the saving of his house; by the which he condemned the world, and became heir of the righteousness which is by faith." What necessity presented itself? What signs of a universal deluge? What reason for expecting one? What, in his own experience, or his research into the experience of those who had lived before him, could suggest even the probability of a coming flood? What prophecy in the movement of the waters above the firmament or what ominous sign in the movement of those beneath? None! For sixteen centuries man had lived upon the earth, and there had been no deluge. The earth had moved steadily on in its appointed course.

The seasons had come and gone in their regular order. There had been sunshine and shower, making fruitful fields. The sowing at seed-time had been followed by the gathering of the golden grain at the time for the harvest. The laws of nature are moving on with their usual exactness and are producing their uniform results. But God said to him, "Behold I, even I, do bring a flood of waters upon the earth, to destroy all flesh, wherein is the breath of life, from under heaven." He commanded him to build an ark. He gave him the dimensions therefor, and told him of what material he should make it. Now, see him prove his faith. He goes to work doing as God had directed him. The ignorant laugh at him. He works on. Away up in the high land he is felling trees. He says he is preparing to build a great vessel. There is no large body of water near, but he says he intends to build it right there. They call him crazy. He works on. He tells them a great flood is coming, by which both lowland and highland will be covered. He exhorts them to repent. They mock him and turn away. Their wise men seek to instruct him. They tell him there never has been a flood. They lecture him upon the uniformity of the operation of the laws of nature. They argue that such a flood is a physical impossibility. But he answers all this by telling them what God has said, and works on. Years come and go. There are yet no signs of the fulfilment of the prophecy. Still he preaches to the people and works on. O, the patience, and the long suffering and the heroism of his faith! Ridicule, and wit, and sarcasm, and logic, and science, and philosophy, and everything, brought against him — nobody is converted, and nobody pays him for his preaching — yet, he preaches on and works on! O, for a faith like that!

4. *Faith endeavors to do everything God commands, and*

to do it exactly as God commands it to be done. This is an important feature of genuine faith. When faith affirms that the will of God is the highest law possible, it teaches, at the same time, by necessary implication at least, that there is no other power or authority in heaven or upon earth which can excuse us from obedience to that will as it is expressed in the very least of all his commandments. If God's will is supreme and universal law, then, that will, so far as revealed to us, must be supreme law to us, in matters both great and small. If he has right to command that anything be done, then, clearly, he has right to tell exactly how it shall be done, and if he condescends to give the details of the manner in which it shall be done, then faith will, with the same diligence and energy, seek to follow out the details and specific directions, that it employs in accomplishing the general end. Let us recur, for a moment, to the faith of Noah. He was commanded not only to build an ark, but God gave him specific directions as to its size, proportions, and the materials of which it should be made. Now, his faith is shown perhaps more in the exactness with which he followed out all the details than in his obedience to the general command to build an ark. Again, when Moses had received instructions to build the tabernacle, God said, "See that thou make all things according to the pattern showed to thee in the mount." It was, therefore, as clearly his duty to make it according to the pattern as it was to make it at all. This point must be clear. So, at least, it appears to me.

Before leaving this point, however, let me indicate one or two applications of it. First, its bearing upon the theory of essentials and non-essentials. This distinction arises, I apprehend, from a failure to draw the line accurately which marks the boundary between the province of faith and the province of reason. Reason may be employed in deciding whether God has commanded me to do a certain thing. But it cannot, without being guilty of usurpation, go further and undertake to decide whether it is essential or not, and thus decide whether it is binding or not. A strong and intelligent faith protests against such usurpation and ignores all such classifications of divine law. A second application of this point is to the popular idea of Christian charity. There is certainly great need of charity, and there is a legitimate field for its exercise. But I submit that those cases, in which God clearly tells us both what to do and how to do it, cannot properly be included in this field. In such cases there is no room left for us to be charitable, or uncharitable; liberal, or illiberal. The only question is whether we will be faithful or faithless. When once it has been decided that a command has been given to us by divine authority, then whether it be great or small, apparently important or unimportant, in harmony with the dictates of reason or above reason, necessary or apparently unnecessary, a genuine and intelligent faith urges us to obey, and to perform the duty with scrupulous exactness.

5. In the last place I notice this test of faith: *Where the thing commanded requires great self-denial, and self-sacrifice.* This may be regarded as a test of the strength of faith. It is equally a test of its genuineness. The greater the difficulties which lie in our way, the brighter shines that faith which enables us to surmount them. The darkness of the night brings out the stars, and so the trials and difficulties of life cause our faith to shine with unusual lustre. How often may we see this? Time would fail me to mention the illustrations of it which appear on the pages of the history of God's people in all ages — of the martyrs and confessors who were tortured, not accepting deliverance, who had trials of cruel mockings and scourgings, yea, moreover, bonds

and imprisonment. They were stoned, they were sawn asunder, were tempted, were slain with the sword. They wandered about in sheepskins and goatskins; being destitute, afflicted, tormented (of whom the world was not worthy). They wandered in deserts, and in mountains, and in dens and caves of the earth.

Faith led Saul of Tarsus to turn from his friends and admirers, and the bright prospect of earthly honor opening before him and to condemn himself to perpetual exile. He was a despised and homeless wanderer on the earth. He was troubled on every side, yet not distressed; he was perplexed, but not in despair; persecuted, but not forsaken; cast down, but not destroyed. The faith which led him through the furnace of fiery trial sustained him. God never forsakes those who are faithful to him. When the three Hebrew children were cast into the white blazing fire of the furnace God did not take them out, but he did that which was much better. He came down and walked with them through its flames. So he will do with us, my brethren, if only we walk by faith. We can endure anything if Christ be with us.

Faith led Moses to forsake royal honors, the pleasures of the palace, the treasures of Egypt, and the high social standing of the house of the Pharaohs, and to identify himself with the poor enslaved people of God. He endured as seeing him who is invisible. It caused faithful old Abram to offer his son, his beloved Isaac, in obedience to God's command. O, how much stood in his way! With a father's warmest affection he loved that boy. Must he now offer him as a burnt offering? It was morally wrong to kill. Must he slay his own son? Moreover, God had promised that through Isaac his seed should become as the sands upon the sea shore, and as the stars in the heavens — innumerable — must all this fail? Can faith surmount all these difficulties? It did. I do not know how theologians classify his faith — whether it was evangelical, or historical, or faith in the mere words — I don't know, and less do I care — but give me just such a faith.

Having described and illustrated some of the features of those works which furnish the highest proof of the presence and power of faith within, let me hasten to a conclusion, by making a brief application of these principles to present duties. Not only in living the Christian life, but also in coming to Christ for the pardon of our sins and adoption into the family of God, we must walk by faith. The first question to be answered is always this, What does God say? What are the commandments of Christ? What is the divinely appointed way of coming to the Savior? What are the conditions of admission into the Church of Christ? After a careful study of the teaching of Christ and the practice of his apostles, I present this answer: First, you are required to believe, with all your heart, on the Lord Jesus Christ. Second, you are required to repent of all your sins. Third, you are required to confess with your mouth the faith of your heart; and in the fourth place, you are required to be baptized into the name of the Father, and of the Son, and of the Holy Spirit. These are the divine requirements, and this the divine order. All these are for, or in order to the remission of sins.

For proof and illustration of this I refer you to Christ's conversation with Nicodemus (John iii: 5), to the great commission given to the apostles (Matt. xxviii: 19; Mark xvi: 15, 16; Luke xxiv: 46, 47); to the conversion of the three thousand on the day of Pentecost (Acts ii: 37, 38); to the conversion of the Samaritans under the preaching of Philip (Acts viii:12); to the conversion of the Ethiopian (Acts viii: 35-39); to the conversion of Saul (Acts ix:1-18; xxii:16); to the conversion of Cornelius (Acts x: 44-48); to the conversion of Lydia (Acts xvi:14, 15); to the conversion of the Philippian jailer (Acts xvi: 25-34); to the conversion of the Corinthians (Acts xviii: 8); to what Paul wrote to his brethren in Rome about the faith of the heart and the confession with the mouth (Rom. x:10); and finally, to what he wrote to these same persons about having been made free from sin through obedience (Rom. vi:17-18). I submit these Scriptures without argument. How, now, may we show our faith?

1. By striving to do all that God requires. If there are four steps required we will not take three and then stop. The Israelites were required to march around the walls of Jericho once every day for six consecutive days, and then on the seventh to march around them seven times, and then when they heard the sound of the trumpet they were to raise a loud shout. When all this was done they could rest assured that God would fulfil his promise. But would it have done for them to march around the city only once on the seventh day, and then having raised the shout expect God to fulfil his promise? Could they have claimed it? Would they have shown their faith while thus manifestly disregarding divine directions? Why march around the city for seven days? Why march around it seven times on the seventh day? Yea, why march around it at all? There can be only this answer: *God said do it*. But would he not have delivered the city into their hands if they had encompassed it only once on the seventh day? I do not know. I know that in such an event they would have had no right to claim the ful-

filment of the promise. I know still farther that faith would not lead them to try such an experiment.

2. By striving to do it just as God has ordained it should be done. Faith seeks neither substitutions nor modifications of ordinances. It asks for the divine mode, and having found it; it clings to it. Now, Christ has ordained Christian baptism. Sinners are commanded to be baptized before they are received into the kingdom of Christ. The command is not generic, but specific. *One certain, definite thing* is commanded. Faith seeks to find what that one, definite act is, and having found it resolutely rejects all proposed substitutions. What, therefore, is baptism? It will not do to trifle with this question. What do we *know* about the primitive practice? We know that those who went out to hear the preaching of John the Baptist, were "baptized of him in the river Jordan." (Mark 1: 5.) We know that after this John baptized in Enon, near to Salim, "because there was much water there." (John iii: 23.) We know that after Jesus was baptized he "went up straightway out of the water." (Matt. iii:16.) We know that when Philip went to baptize the Ethiopian nobleman, "they went down both into the water, both Philip and the eunuch," and after the baptism they came up out of the water. (Acts viii: 38, 39.) We know that Paul, writing of this ordinance says, "we are buried with him by baptism." (Rom. vi: 4.) We know that in another place he says, "buried with him in baptism, wherein ye are risen with him." (Col. ii:12.) These are some of the things which all may *know* if they will read. Now, put them together and what do we have? We have going to a river, or place where there is much water, a going down into the water, a burial, a resurrection, and a coming up straightway out of the water. This is the divine way. We must

show our faith by accepting the divine way, and persistently rejecting all proposed substitutions.

3. We may show our faith by obeying when there is no apparent connection between the things commanded and the result to be secured; between the means to be employed and the end to be gained. Now in the case before us the result to be secured is the forgiveness of past sins. The things commanded are faith, repentance, confession and baptism. Not one of these alone, but all of these together are for remission of sins. But is there any apparent connection between the end and the means? Is there between faith and forgiveness? between repentance and forgiveness? between confession of Christ and forgiveness? Were I to answer these in the affirmative perhaps few, if any, would object to the answer. I now ask, is there any *apparent* connection between Christian baptism and the forgiveness of sins? I answer most emphatically, No! But is there any connection? Have they been joined together by the divine will? Has baptism been commanded for salvation or in order to the remission of sins? The word of God only can answer this. In Mark xvi:16, Christ says, "he that believeth *and is baptized* shall be saved;" and in his conversation with Nicodemus he said, "Except a man be born of water and the Spirit he cannot enter into the kingdom of God." When those on the day of Pentecost cried out, "Men and brethern, what must we do?" Peter, answering said: "Repent, *and be baptized*, every one of you, in the name of Christ *for the remission of sins.*" I might add passage after passage to the same effect. These are enough. The baptism of a proper subject is for the remission of sins. This makes baptism a test of faith. It must be an act of faith. The connection between faith, re-

pentance, confession, *and* baptism, and the forgiveness of sins, is no more apparent than was the connection between marching around the city of Jericho and the falling of its walls.

4. Show your faith by following Christ in his appointed ways, great as may be the self-denial and sacrifice required. We are not threatened with persecution now as were those who followed Christ during the infancy of the Church. I thank God that we are not. But there is self-denial and sacrifice even now in being a true disciple.

O for that faith which says:—

> "In *all* my Lord's *appointed ways*,
> My journey I'll pursue,
> Hinder me not, you much loved saints,
> For I must go with you.
> *Through floods and flames, if Jesus lead,
> I'll follow where he goes.*"

Begin to follow Christ now. Begin the work of faith to-night. Our glorious Lord and King is coming. It is written, "Behold, I come quickly, and my reward is with me to give to every man according as his work shall be." "The Lord is not slack concerning his promises, as some men count slackness; but is long-suffering to us-ward, not willing that any should perish, but that all should come to repentance. But the day of the Lord will come as a thief in the night; in the which the heavens shall pass away with a great noise, and the elements shall melt with fervent heat; the earth also and the works that are therein shall be burned up." You may not believe this, but it is true. It is God's truth. Men would not believe Noah. When he warned them, they laughed and mocked him. They said: "Has such a thing ever been? What sign is there in the heavens above, or the earth beneath?" That did not change God's truth. At last the time came. It was the day of doom. The Ark was closed. Then were the windows of heaven opened and the fountains of the great deep were broken up, and the earth became one mighty, boundless, shoreless sea. The same God who foretold the deluge of waters and told Noah to preach, now foretells the deluge of fire and bids me call you to the Ark of Safety. That Ark is Christ. The way to him stands open to-night. Who will come? Who will enter in and be saved!

THE EXTERIOR AND THE INTERIOR OF OUR DEEDS.

Though I give all my goods to feed the poor * * * and have not charity it profiteth me nothing.—I. Cor. xiii: 3.

Whosoever shall give you a cup of water to drink in my name, because you belong to Christ, verily I say unto you he shall not lose his reward.—Mark ix· 41.

The New Testament deals with the most profound and delicate ethical questions with the quiet air of perfect confidence. It develops a system of ethics peculiar to itself, both in its doctrines and in its methods of statement. For it is not elaborated into the philosophic formula of the schools, nor arranged according to scientific methods, but its doctrines are embodied in examples and illustrations scattered here and there through the volume of the book.

The texts just read are expressions of the divine judgment concerning human conduct. The first comes to us from Paul; the second is from Christ.

They form a striking antithesis. In the first we see a man of wealth scattering his goods among the poor until he is himself a pauper; in the second, only an ordinary act of hospitality — the simplest and easiest — that of giving a cup of water to the thirsty. But, great as is the antithesis of of the acts themselves, it is surpassed by the startling antithesis between the sentences of divine estimate pronounced upon them. Of the first it is said, "It profiteth me nothing," while of the second Christ says, "Verily, I say unto you he shall not lose his reward." How striking the contrast!

We instinctively ask, What reason can justify these sentences? If any reward be given why not make it proportionate to the amount done? Both acts are good, apparently. They belong to the same class — that of giving to the needy. The one gives a fortune to the hungry; the other a cup of water to the thirsty. Yet the giving of the cup is lifted above the giving of the fortune. If we look upon the acts only, ignoring what lies behind them, every one must feel this is not equitable.

It is not, until we remember there are two sides to every deed, that we are prepared to solve this difficulty. There is that which we see, and there is that which lies concealed from human sight. There is the thing done, and the motive which prompts it; the form of the deed, and its incentive; its body and its spirit; its exterior and its interior. Every just moral judgment must recognize both. When this principle is applied to the cases we are considering we may understand why God lifts the giving of a cup of water above the giving of a fortune. Considered as to their exterior only both deeds are good and worthy of praise. It is not until we pass below the surface of the things done and weigh the motives out of which they sprang that we can see that the divine judgment in these cases is equitable. "Though I give all my goods to feed the poor, *and have not charity*, it profiteth me nothing." See how the motive is uncovered and how sentence is pronounced in view of that. Pride may have prompted the gift, or a desire for praise, or an unworthy wish to perpetuate his name, or it may have been only an effort to rescue a sinking reputation — I know not what the real motive was, but I know that the right one was wanting. "And have not charity." Although the deed attracted the attention of men, and was thought notable and praiseworthy, God, who fully knows the secret springs of actions, saw rottenness in its heart. On the other hand, while the giving of water to the thirsty received no recognition from others, and was probably soon forgotten by the recipient, Christ marks in the book of rememberance, and says the giver shall not lose his reward. And notice how in this case also he lays his finger upon the motive saying it is done "*in my name, because you belong to Christ.*" This is the motive, and this it is that brings the blessing upon the giver. As said the aged Samuel when he stood in the house of Jesse, "The Lord seeth not as man seeth, for man looked on the outward appearance, but the Lord looketh on the heart." So is it now, and so will it be in the day of judgment.

I think we may understand this matter better, also, if we will call to mind the end which God has in view in all he enjoins upon us. For he looks not so much to the things done, considered in themselves, as to that which is manifested and developed by the doing of them. This distinction is real, and it is of vital importance. A man, for instance, does not look upon his family as he looks upon his factory. The end in view in each case is different. He is at the head of an immense factory, and he is at the same time the head of a family. He looks upon his factory and all connected with it, with a business eye. He estimates its worth by the merchandise it enables him to place upon the market. What can it turn out in tangible results? He has no special concern about the thoughts flying through the minds of the workmen, the purposes which rise and swell in their hearts as the work goes on. Machinery will do as well, if only it gives the same results. Flying bands and whirling wheels and buzzing spindles will do as well. But, when he goes to his home after the day's work is done, and looks upon the family group, it is with a different eye. He has another end in view. If he be a wise father and good, he looks not so much to results outward as to results inward. Those things which tell of love and loyalty stand highest with him there. What has been done by the children may have no value in the markets, and be worthless in the eye of business, but if the things done tell of a loving heart and an obedient spirit and a noble purpose, they are good in his fatherly eyes. Here he wishes to see love grow, fidelity grow, truthfulness, purity, nobility — all that makes exalted manhood and pure and beautiful womanhood — develop and grow strong. So of God. This world is not his factory, but his great family. He looks upon it with the eye of a good father. The tasks which he gives us are for our development. In the doing of them the heart must be rightly exercised. They become the voices of affection. All obedience to ordinances, all cross-bearing, all self-denial, all forms of all good works are the voices by which the heart speaks out its love. All goodness grows by doing good out of worthy motives. The giving of the cup of water was a voice of the heart, telling of love for Jesus and those who are his. This very act made that love stronger. It helped the giver, and so, in the eyes of the Father, it was good.

The study of these cases this morning has evolved a principle of vital importance. By the analysis of deeds we find that to each deed there are two sides; that God looks upon both, and that his estimate in each case is formed in view of the motive from which the deed springs. Mark well this principle. It is not that good motives may justify bad deeds. We are not dealing with that question. It is not involved in the texts. Both deeds mentioned in the texts were good when considered only as to their exterior. The principle is this — *good deeds may become void of merit through the absence of right motives.* Or to put it in another way, *the motive is an essential part of every moral act.* An act should be right not only in its exterior but in its interior. This principle is fundamental in its character and it is far-reaching in its application.

Every student of church history, every observer of ecclesiastical matters in our own times, must have noticed the tendency to give undue and almost exclusive attention to the exterior of religious observances. Like the Pharisees, we are careful to make clean the outside of the platter. What is the character of the questions which have been prominent and still are prominent about ordinances, about church government, about worship, and about everything connected with religion? Have not these been questions which deal with the outside of such matters? The *form* has received attention; the *spirit* has been ignored as if a thing of little worth.

Take Christian baptism, as an illustration. The one great and overshadowing question is, What is it, as to its outward form? Such fierce battles have been waged over this that other questions — vital questions — concerning it have been forgotten. Learning on this side; learning on that side; zeal on this side; zeal on that side. Often bitterness on both sides. Now, I am not here to say that to have the ordinance right in its form is a matter of no importance. Not at all. But I stand here to say, with all possible emphasis, that it may be right in form and yet not be acceptable before God. Let us insist on the interior of this solemn act being right. In what spirit? From what motive? With what purpose of heart? With what devotion to Christ Jesus? These questions need to be brought to the front. Though you may be buried beneath the waves of the Jordan itself, yet if thy heart is not right it profiteth thee nothing.

Or, take the Lord's Supper as an illustration: What are

the *ritualistic* qualifications? That's the great question. Men, rotten in heart, depraved in conduct, leprous in character may sit down at that table. The emblems may be partaken of with manifest unconcern. Even levity may be overlooked. But, let some devout soul, who may be wanting in some formal or ritualistic preparation, reverently and lovingly partake, or let one eat beyond the boundaries of the same faith and order, and whole communions will be mightily moved. We all very well know that in the discussions of the question, "Who may partake?" almost exclusive attention is given to outward preparation. We discuss matters of form. We give attention to externalities. What kind of bread, leavened or unleavened? What kind of wine, fermented or unfermented? What time? Can it, under any circumstances, be observed on any day except Sunday? What kind of a cloth should be used to cover the table? The question of "altar cloths" claimed earnest attention a few months ago among some very good people in this State. It is the old question of phylacteries, of borders to garments of mint and annise and cummin. I stand by this table on which are the emblems of the body and blood of Christ, and say, "though you may be ritualistically right, and though you may have just such bread and such wine as was used by our Savior on the night on which he was betrayed, and though all forms may be faultless unless with loving, reverent hearts you eat and drink in memory of Christ, it profiteth you nothing."

What questions concerning worship have received most attention? Are they not those which deal with forms? I was with young men during their ministerial studies, who held that the *posture* in prayer is an important matter. Not a matter of taste, or convenience, or helpfulness. Oh, no. It was a vital matter. Only a Pharisee could *stand* and pray. It was an essential matter. Some, if I mistake not, have gone so far as to make it practically a test of fellowship. So with the question of music in worship. We are to sing. We are to praise God, making melody in our hearts to him. These are the matters which should receive attention. But, we practically omit the questions which tend to produce greater spirituality in worship, which help the heart to devout devotion and are deeply concerned over the place where the choir should should sit; books with music, books without music, or no books; tuning-fork or no tuning-fork; organ or no organ. These are the questions which often receive more attention than those which deal with the heart. We delight to engage in properly adjusting the machinery. I once saw a chart designed to show how to worship. It was a curious and striking illustration of this point. The doing of certain things according to certain forms was worship. It seems to me there are many who need to learn that, though we may have hymns from the angelic choir, and melodies such as are heard in the upper sanctuary, and though we may have forms of worship absolutely faultless, and have not love, it profiteth us nothing.

I might go on adding illustration to illustration without number, for this principle is fundamental and applies to all we do. We need to apply this principle to the questions of church government, church organization, and church work. They have been bones of contention. I beg you leave such bones for those who love dry bones more than spiritual meat. Even dogs do not contend when there is an abundance of meat. Only over bones do they fight. So with Christians. Let us seek to bring into greater prominence inward states and the devotion of the heart. Is thy heart right? *Is thy heart right?*

This principle needs to be applied also to giving. Though

you give all, and have not love, it profiteth you nothing. others may be profited, but you will not. While on the other hand a cup of water rightly given secures a sure reward. Much of our giving, even to good works, does not bring down upon us the divine blessing. We have fairs and feasts and we resort to all manner of devices to induce people to give. They may be led thus to give and to appear liberal, but it profiteth them nothing. *Give first thy heart, and let thy heart go with all thy gifts.* Let giving be worship. Like Mary's ointment let it be fragrant with the fragrance of the heart. Then wilt thou be doubly blest — blessed *in* the giving and blessed *for* the giving.

I close with a word of caution. I fear one thing may result from this sermon which may prove injurious to some. I fear there may be some one who, while I insist upon giving due attention to the interior of our deeds, will swing to the extreme of totally ignoring their exterior. This I would guard against. The thing done — the form — is important. If your heart is right you will be anxious to do the right thing in the right way. Get the heart right. Give that. Let all you do be the expressions of the heart. Love more. Do more good. Live in fellowship with God, and verily I say unto thee thou shalt not lose thy reward.

THE UNIFYING POWER OF THE CROSS.

And I, if I be lifted up from the earth, will draw all men unto me. This he said, signifying what death he should die. — John xii: 32-33.

The "if" in this text is not to be taken as expressive of doubt. Christ knew from the beginning of his ministry that he would be crucified. In his conversation with Nicodemus, which occurred in the early part of his ministry, you remember he said, "As Moses lifted up the serpent in the wilderness, even so must the Son of man be lifted up." In the latter part of his ministry he spoke plainly and repeatedly to his disciples of his death by violence, saying, "The Son of man shall be betrayed unto the chief priests and unto the scribes, and they shall condemn him to death, and shall deliver him to the Gentiles to mock, and to scourge, and to crucify him." And not only did he foreknow the nature of his death, but he understood beforehand its profound significance as a fact in the government of God, and its essential worth in the solution of the problem of man's redemption. To Nicodemus he explained that he should be lifted up so "that whosoever believed on him should not perish, but have eternal life."

When he uttered the language of the text he was near the time of his crucifixion, and the shadow of the cross which had rested upon his heart all the while, now casts a deeper gloom. It was Tuesday; on Friday he must die. The context reveals in some degree the sorrow which even then he felt flooding his heart, — "Now is my soul troubled; and what shall I say? Father, save me from this hour? but for this cause came I unto this hour." He had already entered upon his great baptism of suffering. To me there is a sacredness in any great sorrow, and especially in the great sorrow of our Savior and this sacredness attaches itself to this text. With tender touch and loving hearts let us seek to unfold its meaning — for I feel it is full of meaning and redolent of love.

1. Jesus herein declares his purpose to *unite* men of every race and rank into one harmonious and fraternal bond, by drawing them to one common centre. "I will draw *all* men," not in the sense that each one of the entire race will actually be drawn to him, but that from all classes, and conditions, and nations I will draw.

It was the request of the Greeks to see him that called forth the response of the text. For "there were certain Greeks among them that came up to worship at the feast; the same came therefore to Philip, saying, 'Sir, we would see Jesus.'" As Philip was the only one among the twelve who had a pure Greek name, it is supposed that he was of that blood, and that this was probably the reason they approached him with their request to see the new teacher, now attracting so much attention. This request was presented to the Master by Philip and Andrew, and it awoke within him thoughts of his atoning death upon the cross and the world-wide provisions of his grace. I will be lifted up, but not for the Jew alone. That uplifting will be the widening of my work and mission. It will possess an attraction over the wide world — to civilized and savage, learned and illiterate, Greek and Jew alike. It will break down opposition, and form out of the most heterogeneous and discordant materials a kingdom of surpassing glory.

This purpose marks the opening of a new era in the

religious history of the world. Not only was the purpose unparalleled, but the thought was new. No religious teacher prior to this had even suggested such a thing. All other religions were ethical. Each nation had its gods and its system of religion, as it had its laws and its system of government. Even the divinely-given religion of the Jew was never intended for any other than the chosen nation. It was limited in its provisions, its application and its territory. But the religion to be established by Jesus was designed for the whole world. Its Author proposed it as the religion for the race. It is catholic in spirit, its provisions are universal, its field is the world. Nor was this an ambition kindled within it after its splendid victories made universal dominion appear possible, but in the hour of comparative obscurity did its founder entertain and declare this great purpose!

It was so new, so unlike anything the world had ever known or heard before, that his immediate disciples and their early converts were slow to apprehend and understand it. They seemed to regard it as a revision and enlargement of Judaism. The story of Peter's vision on the housetop in Joppa, and of the commotion and controversy occasioned by his visit to the house of Cornelius, and the history of the Jerusalem council, reveal to us how slowly the light dawned upon their minds. The development of his catholic purpose met with very strong opposition from his own followers then; and, sad to say, in different ways it has experienced the same opposition from his professed followers since. And even now we are slow to understand the riches of his grace, the wideness of his mercy, and the catholicity of his purpose. The narrowness and bigotry of man is like the little land-locked sea of Galilee, which is shut in from all the world, and its waves wash the shores of no land but its own; while divine mercy is like the Great Sea, bearing upon its bosom the commerce of the world, and with its blue waves it washes the shores of all the nations.

> There's a wideness in God's mercy,
>   Like the wideness of the sea;
> There's a kindness in his justice,
>   Which is more than Liberty.
> For the love of God is broader
>   Than the measures of man's mind;
> And the heart of the Eternal
>   Is most wonderfully kind.

In the broad philanthrophy of Christ is an argument for his divinity. Whence came this gracious, catholic purpose, set forth in the text? We know that the age, the country, the education, the society of early years exert a wonderful moulding influence over every one. The seeds of that definite form and character which we eventually assume will be found to lie within our early history. But Jesus was born and reared in the midst of a nation and at a time proverbial for religious bigotry. By natural birth a Jew, trained from infancy by a Jewess, a regular attendant of their synagogues and their temple service, how came he to be the founder of a religion so broad in its philanthrophy, so catholic in its spirit? His gracious purposes strongly suggest, if they do not fully demonstrate, that he came forth from the bosom of the universal Father. The Father of our race, must be the Father of Christ, its lover and Savior.

The nature of his kingdom is new. He forms it into a perfect union by drawing each one to a common centre. It was formed and is governed by the power of attraction. There had been universal dominions before his day, but they were formed and sustained by the force of arms. That which he proposes to establish is, like our solar system, to be held in unity and harmony by a hidden power which holds each part to a common centre. Nor does he propose to destroy all individual peculiarities. Mercury and Venus and Mars and Jupiter and Saturn retain their features of individuality, and yet they harmoniously combine to form one system. Then, too, some are much nearer their central sun than others. And, yet, each fills its appropriate place. It is a grave mistake to suppose that the union which should characterize the kingdom of Christ among men is a dead, a slavish uniformity. Great variety is consistent with perfect unity.

It is important for us to know, since this is the character of his kingdom, exactly what that centre is toward which all are drawn and around which each revolves along his appointed course. Should we suppose that to be this centre which is not the centre, confusion must appear even though harmony prevails. So it was with the old astronomers. They supposed the earth was the centre of the system to which it belongs. Upon this supposition other parts appeared to be deranged. When, however, they found the sun to be the common centre perfect harmony appeared. So, should we suppose any creed or doctrine or ordinance or theory of church organization, or a special interpretation of any passage of Scripture, to be the centre when, in fact, it is not, all would appear to be in fearful discord. We are not left, however, to grope in a vain search for this centre of gravitation and government in the spiritual kingdom on earth. The text states it — "And I, if I be lifted up, will draw all men to *me*."

2. Jesus Christ is himself the centre, and personal, heartfelt attachment to him is the controlling principle in the life, as it is also the final test of Christian character. The basis of Christianity is not a theory, nor a system of formu-

lated doctrines, but it is a person. In Christianity, Christ is the alpha and the omega, the beginning and the end, the first and the last. Its two great questions are, "What think you of Christ?" and "What, then, shall I do with Jesus?" He who in heart and life gives the true answer to these questions is a Christian. He has been drawn to Christ and is obedient to him as the planets are obedient to the sun.

A study of the historical development of the church as recorded in the New Testament will serve to illustrate and demonstrate this. If we go back to the time of the personal ministry of our Lord, before the existence of the New Testament Scriptures, we see him gathering, chiefly from the fishermen of Galilee, the nucleus of the church. He does not propound to them a system of abstract truth, as the Greek philosophers did, to which he demands their assent; nor does he present for their acceptance a plan or constitution for the organization of societies to be called churches, and call upon them to adopt it and aid him in putting it into practical operation, but his simple request was, Follow me. He makes himself the centre of a group of personal friends, and he is the bond by which they are held together in the fellowship of a fraternal band. They loved him, they followed him. Their confidence in him was the cord by which they were held. They willingly left all for his sake. Persecutions could not drive them away from one so dear to their hearts. This devotion to him was the central principle of character in each, and the vital point around which their lives developed into spiritual strength and moral beauty. They could not, even after three years of discipleship under him, have passed an examination in a modern theological seminary. Yet during all this time he had been preparing them to evangelize the world! He had not been drilling them in dogmatic theology, and the science of church government, so much as he had been binding them with multitudinous cords to himself.

At a later period, when they had fully entered upon this world-wide mission, we find that everywhere they went they preached Jesus. They told the story of his gracious life and his sacrificial death over again and again and again, and sought to win and to bind the hearts of the people in loving devotion to *him*. In him they saw all fullness dwelling. Their converts were not converted to doctrines, to churches or to men. They were converted to Christ. All faith, all obedience, all hope had value only as they centred in his person and work. He was the object of saving faith as he was the substance of their simple confession of faith. He was held before the people as their only teacher and guide, and as the one who alone could give rest to their weary souls. They were to wear no yoke but his. Above all other love should be their love for *him*. He was the living vine into which believers were engrafted, and from him they drew the vital current which sustained their spiritual life. Paul's experience was also the experience of the whole body of believers, — " I am crucified with Christ; nevertheless I live; yet not I, but Christ liveth in me: and the life which I now live in the flesh I live by the faith of the Son of God, who loved me, and gave himself for me." Christ was their life.

It is to be feared that controversy over many other things has perverted this simple faith of the early Christians. These controversies have lifted minor points into undue prominence. Questions concerning divine sovereignty, human agency, Christian ordinances, spiritual influence, church government, and many other matters have grown, through controversy, to occupy controlling positions in many ecclesiastical organizations. The result has been to displace, in a greater or less degree, the simple heart-trust in Christ which made the early Christians what they were. It is to be feared that most of that which now passes for religion is little more than ecclesiastical morality. It is practically Christless. His loving presence, his sympathetic mediation, his kingly authority are obscured by the clouds of this religious conflict.

Then, too, may not *we* be making a mistake in the method of our labors for Christian union? Do we not need to make a more practical use of the fact that the only union worthy the name is union in Christ? Is it strictly true that the Bible is the basis upon which we are to unite? Would it not be much nearer the truth, yea, would it not be the exact truth, were we to say that we are to unite around Christ and in him? Is not true Christian union first of all a union of hearts? And does not the New Testament teach that in this union there may still be harmonious variety? As when from the circumference of a circle we advance along its radii toward its centre, we must come nearer and nearer together, so must we, as Christians, come nearer each other as, from our remote positions, we come nearer and nearer to Christ, the centre of the spiritual kingdom. "I will draw all men to *me*." It was in this way that the most discordant elements in society were harmonized in the first churches. They became one in Christ. The Jews and the Gentiles were as far from each other as pole from pole, and yet Paul could say, in writing to the Ephesians, "But now, in Christ Jesus, ye who sometimes were afar off, are made nigh by the blood of Christ. For he is our peace, who hath made both one." From each extreme they drew near to Christ, until they became one in him. His attraction was so strong that it broke down the middle wall of partition between them. If, therefore, we are to succeed in our labor for union we must rely upon this same attraction. Turn individual hearts, with their deepest devotion, to *Christ*. Let his magnetic power sway our own hearts —

> As still to the star of its worship, though clouded,
> The needle points faithfully o'er the dim sea,
> So, dark as I roam through this wintry world shrouded,
> The hope of my spirit turns trembling to thee.

In his church, Christ himself is the centre, and personal, heart-felt devotion to him is the controlling principle in Christian life, as it is also the final test of Christian character.

3. In his atoning death upon the cross, we find the magic power which draws the hearts of men, which reconciles discordant elements and moulds believers into one fraternal band. "And I, if I be lifted up from the earth, will draw all men to me. This he said, *signifying what death he should die.*" Paul finds this attracting power in the bloody tree, saying, "Ye who were sometime afar off are made nigh by the blood of Christ." The history of preaching demonstrates the fact that the power which wins men to Christ is focalized in the cross. German theology is practically without the cross and so is shorn of its power. Unitarianism is weak from the same cause. Never has there been a preacher, from Paul's day to this, who has done much for the conversion of souls, who has not made much of the cross. To the Jews it was a stumbling-block; to the Greeks it was foolishness, but unto them who are called Christ crucified is the wisdow of God, and the power of God. It is wonderful power. No analysis can fully reveal its hidden potency, and yet it may be a delight and a help if we hold before us for a while this morning a few of its prominent features.

1. In its revelation of divine love I find power. Love draws. Herein is love. God commendeth his love towards us in that while we were yet sinners Christ died for us. In the cross I find the genesis of our love for God. For we love him,

because he first loved us. There are problems which have been solved by the cross too profound for my comprehension. I do not undertake to explain the deep philosophy of the atonement. But one thing I do understand, although its fulness passeth knowledge. I know that the cross is radiant with love. While all that Jesus did was but the unfolding and expression of his love, yet chiefly in the cross of Calvary do I see this love displayed. In the manger at Bethlehem is love incarnate; in the ministry of Jesus is love working; in the scene at the grave of Lazarus is love weeping tears of sympathy; in the garden of Gethsemane is love sweating, as it were, great drops of blood; but on the cross is love enduring the agonies of a fearful death and swelling with a strength and fulness that breaks the heart. Here is love that has height without top, depth without bottom, length without end, breadth without limit. Let us seek with all saints to comprehend its fulness. Let us believe in its genuineness and reality. It is love that draws us with its silken cords and binds us to the cross.

2. In its revelation of danger and of safety I find power. Is there anything in God to fear? I answer yes, and point to the cross. That is a revelation of the danger of sin, and a fearful demonstration of divine wrath against it. He was made sin for us. Every pang he felt was a pang of suffering for sin. He suffers upon the cross as our substitute. That cross stands before the world as God's warning.

At the same time it is a place of security for us. We flee to it for refuge, and are safe. Its blood saves us. As the blood that was sprinkled upon the door posts of the Israelites in Egypt preserved from danger all within, on that dreadful night when the first born of the Egyptians were smitten by the angel of death, so the sprinkling of this blood is our defense and shield. Under the seal of Christ's blood we are safe. I have been told that out upon those vast prairies of our Western frontiers, where the grass grows rank and high, there are often in the autumn great sweeping fires. The leaping flames fly with a swiftness greater than that of the fleetest horse. And it is said that, when the frontiersmen see the approaching hurricane of flame, they quickly set fire to the grass on their leeward side and then take their stand in the place thus burned bare, and await in safety the approaching storm. Though it sweeeps about them they are safe. The place where they stand has already been burned bare. So there is one place already burned bare for us. It is Calvary. Standing by the cross, when this world shall be wrapped in its winding sheet of flame, we shall be safe — perfectly safe. There is safety here; there is safety nowhere else. Many have fled to it because of its revelation of danger and of safety. Will you? It seems to me that when any one comes to understand its revelations of love, of danger, and of safety they must feel so driven and drawn to it that they cannot withstand its power.

> "In the cross of Christ I glory,
>   Towering o'er the wrecks of time;
> All the light of sacred story
>   Gathers round its head sublime.
>
> When the woes of life o'ertake me,
>   Hopes deceive, and fears annoy,
> Never shall the cross forsake me;
>   Lo! it glows with peace and joy.
>
> When the sun of life is beaming
>   Light and love upon my way,
> From the cross a radiance, streaming,
>   Adds more lustre to the day.
>
> Bane and blessing, pain and pleasure,
>   By the cross are sanctified;
> Peace is there beyond all measure
>   Joys that through all time abide."

PAUL'S CHAPTER ON CHARITY.

Though I speak with the tongues of men and of angels, and have not charity, I am become as sounding brass, or a tinkling cymbal. And though I have the gift of prophecy, and understand all mysteries and all knowledge; and though I have all faith, so that I could remove mountains, and have not charity, I am nothing. And though I bestow all my goods to feed the poor, and though I give my body to be burned, and have not charity it profiteth me nothing. Charity suffereth long, and is kind; charity envieth not; charity vaunteth not itself, is not puffed up, doth not behave itself unseemly, seeketh not her own, is not easily provoked, thinketh no evil; rejoiceth not in iniquity, but rejoiceth in the truth; beareth all things, believeth all things, hopeth all things, endureth all things. Charity never faileth, but whether there be prophecies, they shall fail; whether there be tongues, they shall cease; whether there be knowledge it shall vanish away. For we know in part, and we prophecy in part. But when that which is perfect is come, then that which is in part shall be done away. When I was a child, i spake as a child, I understood as a child, I thought as a child; but when I became a man, I put away childish things. For now we see through a glass, darkly; but then face to face: now I know in part, but then shall I know even as also I am known. And now abideth faith, hope, charity—these three; but the greatest of these is charity.— I. Cor. xiii :1-13.

My text this morning is the entire thirteenth chapter of First Corinthians — Paul's popular chapter on charity. And I think it speaks well for the heart of religious people generally that this chapter is so popular. Perhaps no chapter in the entire Bible is more so. And, just as I would say it speaks well for the taste of a people to find that that hall in a gallery of art, where the best paintings are, is the most popular, and to see the largest group standing constantly before the finest painting in the entire collection, so here, as I see men and women passing through the Bible — God's great gallery of spiritual verities — it speaks well for their spiritual taste that this chapter is so universally popular; that before Paul's picture of charity there is found such a group of ardent admirers. This single fact is full of pleasant thoughts for me.

I think it worthy of passing notice also that this chapter was written by *Paul*. Had we selected one, from the sacred writers of the New Testament, to give us an ode to charity, I think we would have united in selecting John. We would do this on the ground that men, as a rule, exalt that most which is chief in themselves. The æsthetic exalts beauty in nature, in letters and in art; the utilitarian exalts utility, and would merge all virtues into that; while the modern epicure, like the ancient, lifts the question of present enjoyment above every other, and makes pleasure the chief end of life. In the character of John, the beloved, love stands high above all else. So in his writings love is made the inspiration and the measure of individual Christian life, "He that loves is of God, for God is love." In the writings of Paul, the educated and inspired logician, we find *knowledge* holds a high place. Having been thoroughly delivered from the rigorous thraldom of Phariseeism, his love of *liberty* in Christ is intense; and yet charity is placed above knowledge and liberty even by him. Even Peter, who had so painfully learned the lesson of *watchfulness* and *sobriety*, also places charity above these. This fact is significant. Not only is it very strong testimony to the pre-eminence of charity, but it contains one of the innumerable evidences of the inspiration of these writers. Their writings come not from the spontaneous outflow of individual temperament, but from one common spirit, which, while it does not destroy the individuality, so bridles and guides it that all speak the same thing. This unity of sentiment in the writings of men so different in tendencies points strongly to one common source of all they wrote.

If we take a sweeping view of the entire letter in which this chapter is found, its very position is remarkable. This is the most severe letter written by Paul. The church at Corinth was so split up into parties, it had so grossly perverted the ordinances, and some of its members had fallen into such shocking sins, that its condition called for apostolic censure. He censures the schismatic, pronounces the sentence of excommunication against the incestuous, reproves brother for going to the civil courts against brother, shames them for sins by which they defile their bodies, rebukes their licentions use of liberty to the injury of others, warns them against idolatry, condemns them sharply for their degradation of the Lord's Supper, and upbraids them for their unseemly jealousy and rivalry over their varied miraculous gifts. He writes as one who had no sympathy in his heart, yea, not even a heart within him. It is a vigorous warfare against sin and moral apostacy. But, near the close of this vigorous attack he pauses, and pours forth this tender and beautiful tribute to the intrinsic value and practical worth of charity. This chapter falls into the midst of the severity of the letter like a May day into midwinter. It is as if the snow lying upon the streets and house-tops to-day should suddenly vanish, the cold, heavy clouds should flee away, the bitter winds sweep back to the ice-caves of the North; and the soft winds of the South, fragrant with the breath of the flowers, and joyous with the twittering of the birds in the green foliage, should tell us that one of the mild days of May was upon us; and then, when it has passed, we swing back into winter. So is this chapter among the chapters of this letter.

In its study I present three points for consideration,

namely — The full and exact meaning of charity in this place; its value as stated here; and the best means by which we may cultivate it in ourselves.

I. *What is here meant by charity?*

I suppose it may pass without the saying that it does not mean alms-giving. I presume also that all know "love" is regarded as the best single word in English by which to render the Greek word here translated "charity." In this day of much-lauded, spurious charity, however, it is needful, I think, to note that,

I. *Paul does not mean that easy-going latitudinarianism which is born of indifference and want of conviction.* Men may be tolerant of religious differences because they feel no concern about the questions out of which these differences arise. They have no convictions of their own. With them there are no clear distinctions between truth and error, right and wrong. There may be among the Chinese to-day great political questions agitating the Celestial Empire, but these give me no concern. They are too far removed from me. I am indifferent. So there are those who can stand even in the midst of religious agitations and convulsions, where truth and right are involved, and maintain a careless indifference. The unauthorized decrees of councils and the traditions of men are as much to them as the clearest utterance of the word of God. The hearty belief of error is as good as a hearty belief of truth. They pride themselves on their toleration and charity.

He who knows anything of Paul needs not to be told how abhorrent to him such indifference would be. He could not praise such charity. With all the intensity of his ardent and honest nature he sought truth, and held it with greater tenacity than he held to life itself. He was too earnest to be indifferent.

2. After a very careful study of what Paul ascribes to charity, I find the most accurate statement I can frame of what he means is this, *good-will toward man, intensified and sanctified.* No one word seems able to convey to the popular mind the thought which was lying in his mind at the moment he wrote. Even the word he used was not enough, by itself, to do this. He felt the need of elaboration and extended description. This is an objection I have to the word love; for, whatever may be found in it when used in its largest and strongest sense, it does not convey to the ordinary mind an accurate representation of what was in Paul's mind. Were I giving word-for-word translation, I would feel bound to use the word love. But as I am seeking to translate thoughts rather than words I am constrained to take such a phrase as will best carry the original thought to you.

An examination of his description, from the fourth to seventh verse, shows that it is something which bears upon the relations between man and man, and that its exercise in us is directed toward our fellows. Moreover, the things which spring from it show, by their nature, they must be born of good-will. I, therefore, say it is good-will toward our fellow-men. But it is not that soft and vague good-will which is content with dreaming of good for others, and is rather good-wishing than good-willing. It acts. It does things hard to do, and suffers things hard to endure. It is regnant in character and over life. It is intensified until it becomes positive. It rises up to such strength and supremacy that all other feelings go down under its power. Envy goes down, jealousy goes down, vanity goes down, the feeling of revenge goes down, party spirit goes down, all the feelings which make men harsh and cruel, narrow and selfish, go down under its beneficent reign. It is good-will *intensified.*

Again. It it not simply the good-will of the humanitarian. It is not the philanthropy of generous impulse. There are some natures so benign that, without the warmth and inspiration that comes of the spirit of religion, they send forth from themselves spontaneously that which makes the lot of others better. They shine like the sun, because it is their nature to shine. But these natures are rare. Paul speaks of that which comes of religion. It is the good-will born of God's good-will and modelled after that. It rises in the heart, conscious of divine mercy manifest toward it, in the gracious forgiveness of greivous sins. It lives and flourishes in the light of God's good-will toward a fallen world. It is *sanctified* good-will. I know this is not the definition of dictionaries, but I think it is better because I think it gives to you Paul's thought more accurately and more fully than any one word can. Charity here means good-will toward our fellow-men, intensified until it becomes regnant and sanctified because it is born of the religion of Christ.

II. *Paul's estimate of its worth.*

The twelfth chapter closes with this verse, " covet earnestly the best gifts, (miraculous gifts); and yet shew I unto you a more excellent way." Then he writes in the thirteenth chapter to show that more excellent way, and especially to point out its excellence. The chapter is engaged chiefly in showing the unequalled worth of charity.

In the first three verses he gives a statement of its value by a contrast which seems an exaggeration, and it is certainly startling. He places it in contrast with four things generally held in high esteem, but especially so in the Corinthian church. They prized the gift of tongues, and he contrasts charity with that. In his rapture, of which he tells us in his second letter, he had heard angelic language which could not be clothed in any language of man, and he places charity in contrast with that, saying, "Though I speak with the tongues of men and of angels and have not charity, I am become as sounding brass, or a tinkling cymbal." Gifted with an eloquence that soars above the tongue of men and speaks with the tongues of angels, my utterances are but the soulless clanging of cymbals, if this heavenly virtue makes not fragrant all I say. Knowledge, to the Greek, was above the price of rubies — that knowledge which is the reward of diligent study. But many prophets in this church were gifted with that *deeper* insight into mysteries which comes of inspiration. Both are placed in contrast with charity when he says, "And though I have the gift of prophecy, and understand all mysteries and all knowledge * * * and have not charity, I am nothing." The sage and the prophet are nothing without charity. Again, the power to work wonders had been bestowed upon many, and it was esteemed valuable in itself, and a mark also of peculiar favor. But he who has this power to its highest degree is declared to be nothing if charity is wanting, — "Though I have all faith, so that I could remove mountains, and have not charity I am nothing." And, finally, he places it in contrast with that form of self-sacrifice and good work which had such a remarkable development in the first churches that it seems exaggerated and abnormal. "Though I bestow all my goods to feed the poor, and though I give my body to be burned and have not charity, I am nothing."

Behold the man pictured in these three verses! We need not pause to question whether it is possible to actually have such a character as this, with charity left out. He but supposes a case. Behold the man! An orator, a sage, a giant, a benefactor, all in one. More eloquent than Demosthenes, wiser than the combined wisdom of the seven sages of Greece, mightier through faith than a Hercules, and more liberal than the disciples in the Jerusalem church. Yet in this character, wrought of such extraordinary elements, charity is wanting, and Paul writes of it, "it is nothing." No profit will come of its faith and its works, and its matchless eloquence supplied by its varied and profound knowledge is as "sounding brass and clanging cymbals!" What a startling statement of the essential worth of Christian charity. For the justice of this verdict he proceeds to assign three reasons: —

1. In the first place, he shows *its effect upon character and conduct*. This he does from the fourth to the seventh verse. He here describes charity, not in the abstract, but in the concrete. Better, perhaps, he is describing a character in which this virtue is the dominant principle. He takes a man in whom good-will is so intensified that it is regnant and so sanctified that it is pure, and shows how he bears himself under the provocations which may come upon him in his intercourse with others. Let me place each item before you, on this wall, and number them that we may the more distinctly note each feature —

1. Suffereth long.
2. Is kind.
3. Envieth not.
4. Vaunteth not itself.
5. Is not puffed up.
6. Doth not behave itself unseemly.
7. Seeketh not her own.
8. Is not easily provoked.
9. Thinketh no evil.
10. Rejoiceth not in iniquity.
11. Rejoiceth in the truth.
12. Beareth all things.
13. Believeth all things.
14. Hopeth all things.
15. Endureth all things.

Here are fifteen characteristic features in the conduct of him who is under the domination of charity. You observe that almost all are negative. The magic reformation is wrought by dissipating evil. When charity comes to the throne of all these out of which tumults and riots and anarchy come flee the realm. Quick temper goes, harshness flees, envy disappears, boasting is heard no more, self-conceit vanishes, selfishness, passion, evil suspicion and ill-will find no longer a home in that realm.

When the night comes wild beasts go forth seeking prey. To their victims it is the reign of terror and of death. But, with the rising sun the shades of the night vanish, and the ravenous beasts disappear. So, it is in us. When the sun of charity goes down these evil things rise up and go forth to their work of terror and darkness and death. But, with the rising of charity, they disappear. And, while it continues to shine, they cannot be found. Travellers tell us that there are in some ancient lands the ruins of cities so preserved that the streets, the temples, the dwellings and every part of them remain as if deserted but a few years. Here life once flowed in full tide, and commerce and pleasure and ambition and civilization held sway. But now you enter these homes or walk these streets and the owls and the bats and foul beasts find their habitation there. Turn back the tide of life and commerce there, and these must disappear. So, when God made man he made that which is more magnificent than ancient cities. He built a temple in which good-will should reign. But good-will was dethroned. Then came evil birds and foul beasts, and the time of desolation. Now, through the power of the religion of Christ good-will comes back and is crowned. This is the power that drives out evil and fills the temple with life. Its reign is benignant, within its dominion is peace, and moral beauty flourishes on every hand.

This is Paul's first and chief reason for his estimate of charity — *its effect upon character and conduct.* The remaining two do not call for extended notice.

2. His second reason is, *the permanence of charity.* "Charity never faileth; but whether there be prophecies, they shall fail; whether there be tongues, they shall cease; whether there be knowledge, it shall vanish away." These miraculous gifts were to answer a certain purpose and then cease. They were the scaffolding around the building. When the building is erected the scaffolding comes down. But when these miraculous gifts went down — when they ceased — faith, hope and charity continued.

Some suppose that he contrasts the permanence of charity with faith and hope also, and that he finds its superiority to them in this. Faith, they say, will give place to knowledge, and faith will be no more. Hope will cease when fruition comes. Hope will be no more. But with this I can hardly agree, for many things now held by faith will then be matters of knowledge; and many things for which we now hope may then be things of possession. I cannot conceive of a time when faith and hope themselves will cease to be. The contrast, as to permanency, which Paul makes, is limited to miraculous endowments, and this contrast had a force then which it cannot have now.

3. His third reason applies now as well as then, — *Charity is a mark of manhood in Christ.* There is growth. "When I was a child, I spake as a child, I understood as a child, I thought as a child; but when I became a man, I put away childish things."

There are well-defined periods in Christian growth. Most of us begin in fear, then live right from conviction and sense of duty, but do not come to fulness of manhood until we come to live from love. Charity marks maturity. Peter teaches the same when naming the Christian graces, he begins with faith and ascends to charity. John but gives us the thought in another form when he says, "Perfect love casteth out fear."

4. There is yet another reason which, while Paul does not mention it, was manifestly in his mind, — *Charity heals church divisions.* The church at Corinth was divided and he knew they needed charity. I rejoice that we do not need it for this purpose. For this church is united from top to bottom. If there is even a personal difficulty within its membership I do not know of it. But we need to learn the value of charity in this direction, as it will help us in effecting Christian union. Our plea has been for the union of all Christians. Are we sure we have presented the New Testament way? How may men be united? In three ways — first, by compulsory authority, reducing all to the same form. This we find in the papacy. Second, by requiring and inducing intellectual agreement, compelling perfect unity in views on all questions. This is attempted in binding men with creeds. Third, by love, which unites hearts, and obscures small distinctions by enriched feeling. I believe that the only true Christian union must begin by binding the hearts of the people together. Ill-will, envy, and party pride will be driven out by nothing else. Let good-will, intensified and sanctified, come in. Let charity preside over all councils held to promote union. Let love dictate all speech, and the good work will go on, until before a united church, the world will be compelled to confess the Christ.

III. I must consider briefly, in concluding, a question which has been rising in importance by everything that has gone before: *How may we cultivate this charity in ourselves?* I pray you turn hungry hearts to this. For, if the most gifted are nothing without it, if it has power to transfigure character, to heal bitter dissensions, to brighten the world and to sweeten life, let us seek it, let us have it, let us cultivate it with the greatest care. I have time to give only two hints: —

1. *Meditate on God's good-will and love.* We cannot command our hearts so that they will obey us, but we may bring them under influences which will melt and mould them. Charity is born of God's good-will. It must feed upon his love. Sit in the light of the cross and think. Think reverently, think deeply, think often, think long. Oh! God's love to man — how far beyond all our thoughts. I pray that you may be able to comprehend with all saints its height, its length, its depth, its breadth, and yet I know it passes human understanding.

2. *Use what you already have.* Let it speak to the troubled to comfort them. Let it give to the hungry to feed them. Let it minister to the children of want. Let it forgive injuries. Let it bear insults. Let it shine in our homes. Let it go and seek lost ones. Let it rescue those ready to perish. It will grow stronger.

As a train swept toward the south a few months ago the engineer saw an object standing on the track. He pulled the whistle-cord but the quick, sharp signal did not cause the object to move. He reversed the engine, — saw it was a human being — a woman — threw himself on the front of his engine and by hazard to himself saved her. She was deaf, and, as her face was turned from the approaching train, she could not see her danger. So, many stand to-day while a greater danger sweeps on toward them. We must rescue them. But, what was the effect upon that engineer? Of the two he was probably the happier. He felt a deep interest in her afterward. Whenever opportunity presents itself he goes to see how that poor old woman does, and carries with him something for her comfort. But more than this, he feels a quicker pulsation in his heart toward others. He would gladly do another deed like that. If you want to be happy, if you wish to forget your own woes, if you wish to have more of good-will in your heart, go out from this place to minister unto others and brighten their hearts and their homes.

THE GROUND OF OUR HOPE.

Be ready always to give an answer to every man that asketh you a reason of the hope that is in you, with meekness and fear. — I. Peter iii:15.

Were some one to ask you, my brethren, the reason of your hope as Christians what would your answer be? It may serve to quicken your interest in the discussion of this matter if you will pause for a moment's thought. Does even the outline of the answer come to your mind? No? And yet, it is self-evident that every hope must have its reason, for hope without reason is like a house without a foundation. Moreover, it is intuitive that every hope should have an adequate reason. To build hope without adequate reason is to build a house upon the sand, — ruin must come, and the more magnificent the house the more fearful the ruin.

No doubt the early converts to Christianity were frequently asked concerning the ground of their new hope. In turning to Christ then the change was more radical and manifest than it is now. They forsook the temples, and altars, and teachings of their fathers for the doctrine of Christ. They abandoned practices in which, before their new faith, they had indulged without restraint. They endured persecutions with patient fortitude and took joyfully the spoiling of their goods. Even death seemed robbed of its terrors by the brightness and strength of their hope. It was quite natural, therefore, for their pagan neighbors to ask their reason for such a hope, and to ask frequently.

In that they are required to give an answer to these inquiries, I find several things implied. It is implied, in the first place, that a reason existed. This hope was not a delusion, a dream, or the fancy of a disordered mind. In the second place, it is implied that this reason appeared adequate. For better not attempt to give the ground of your hope at all, than to give a reason manifestly inadequate. It is implied further that this reason was such that an ordinary Christian could understand it and state it to others. This letter was written not to a few gifted teachers, but to strangers scattered abroad — to ordinary Christian men and women. Still further, it is implied that the reason was such that when stated even the pagan could understand it; for they were the ones to whom the Christians would have to give answers. This reason, therefore, was not some mysterious matter which could be understood by only the regenerate. And, finally, it is implied that every Christian should be familiar with the foundation upon which he rests his hope. "Be ready always to answer to every one that asketh you a reason of the hope that is in you."

I desire to notice two points: —

1. *The nature of our hope,* and
2. *The ground upon which it rests.*

First, then, as to the nature of hope in general. It seems to me that these three things enter into all hope — that they are its essential elements — forecast, expectation and desire. Hope always looks forward, it never averts it gaze from the future. Of the things it beholds in that future there are some it expects. Among these expected things, some are to be dreaded, others to be desired. Only for these last can we say we hope. Though we may look forward and behold the others, and expect them to fall to our lot, yet we cannot be said to hope for them, since we do not desire, but dread them. Forecast, expectation and desire combined make hope.

Had I the gift of an artist I would paint hope. I would represent her as bending with eager gaze toward the future, so absorbed in the things to come that she seems unconscious of things present; her figure full of the energy of perpetual youth. I would picture her bright-eyed and sweet-faced, with the light of the rising sun resting upon it. Were I able, I would catch the expression on the face of Stephen, the martyr, as it was glowing with angelic brightness, and place it upon this canvas as the appropriate expression of the radiance of hope. For she is bright-eyed, sweet-faced, youthful, and radiant, drawing her inspiration from a cloudless, blissful future.

The religion of Christ is the religion of hope. Its patience, its endurance, its brightness of joy, its songs of triumph, its inspiration in good works, its fearlessness of death, are all the children of hope. As an anchor thrown to the bottom of the sea holds the ship fast amid storms and tempests, so the Chrirtian's hope, entering into that within the vail, holds him secure amid the raging tempests and the wrecks on the sea of life. You who have read Bunyan's story of the struggles of Christian, remember how Hopeful helped him on through many dark and difficult hours and gave him perseverance to victory and rest. Hope is the light-house which sheds its rays upon the ocean of life — the rainbow resting upon the cloud of trouble — the star shining in the dark night — the ruddy ray of morning — the blossom upon the tree of promise.

Let there be a holy hush in our hearts while I endeavor to recite in reverent gratitude some of the items of our Christian hope.

1. As Christians we hope to be delivered from the power of death and the dominion of the grave.

2. We hope to stand justified at last before the spotless throne of final judgment.

3. We hope to be transfigured and glorified until our vile bodies shall be like the glorified body of the Son of God.

4. We hope to be freed from present infirmities and limitations, so that we shall sin no more, and shall know even as also we are known.

5. We hope to be admitted to the full enjoyment of Heaven, whose glories surpass all human imagination.

6. We hope to meet and to mingle with the ransomed of our race, — the elect of the whole earth, — a host so numerous that no man can number it.

7. We hope to see our Maker face to face, and our Redeemer as he is.

8. We hope to rise forever by the power of a limitless and eternal promotion.

Briefly, this is the creed of our Christian hope. As I sit in solitude and recite it to myself, or in the wakeful watches of the night, meditate upon it, my heart is moved to ecstasy. Partly in doubt, but more in amazement, and wonder, I ask whether I dream or whether I think upon substantial verities, From the pages of inspiration I strive to catch the outlines and to paint the picture of the things that God has prepared for them that love him. I go beyond the Jordan with Elijah, the prophet of fire, and Elisha, his companion and successor, until a chariot of fire and horses of fire part them both asunder, and with eager gaze I watch his rapid ascent. In this chariot of flame, drawn by steeds of fire, he sweeps upward with the swiftness of the whirlwind. Without the pain of death he enters heaven. So to every waiting, watching Christian may glorious translation come at any moment! Then I witness the ascension of our Lord. He passed through the gateway of death back to his Father and his home. Death had no longer dominion over him. He, in his resurrection and ascension, is the first fruits of the great harvest being gathered to God. He bore our humanity back to the throne. It is glorified humanity. What he is to-day is a type and a pledge of what his followers hereafter shall be. Or I pause and wait with Paul when, rapt in holy vision, he was caught up to paradise, and saw and heard things too glorious to be told in human speech. The revelation was so sublime that a thorn was given him in the flesh, lest he should be exalted above measure. How beautiful beyond our brightest thinking, then, must be the paradise of God! Still further searching, I turn the pages of the Apocalypse and read of the countless blood-washed ones who worship with hallelujahs before the throne; of the new heavens and the new earth; of the holy city, new Jerusalem, coming down from God out of heaven, prepared as a bride for her husband; of its walls and its gates and its beautiful streets; of the pure river of the water of life, clear as crystal, proceeding out of the throne of God, and of the Lamb; of the tree of life, so fruitful, and its leaves for the healing of the nations; of the fulness of light where the Lord giveth light, until with John I reverently fall at the feet of the angel which showeth me these beautiful things prepared for us by grace.

The ground for such a hope, in order to be adequate, must be broad and deep and firm. And yet, when we turn to find the reason we are impressed, first of all, with what appears to be great *un*reasonableness. It seems as contrary to the course of events, to the working of natural law, to the testimony of our own experience, and to our observation, that we are almost overwhelmed by what seems to indicate the utter absence of adequate reason.

Take one or two items. I stated that, as Christians, we hoped to be delivered from the power of death and the dominion of the grave. Yet what appears more unreasonable? The reign of death over our race seems absolute. Countless generations have gone before us to the grave. In the midst of universal defeat does it not seem unreasonable for us to hope for victory? And, again; we hope to stand justified before the spotless throne of final judgment. Conscious of sin, with our own hearts condemning us, with many indications that this consciousness of sin is universal, how very unreasonable it seems for any hope for justification before a spotless throne. How unreasonable appears our hope that our bodies will be glorified; that we shall be freed from present infirmities and limitations; that we shall be received into heaven, and that we shall advance forever in spiritual life and wisdom and glory! When, therefore, we are asked to give a reason of our hope, what shall that answer be?

(1.) We certainly cannot give an adequate reason in the nature of man. Such blessed things as these are not evolved from human nature under the reign of natural law.

(2.) Nor is there within us a prophetic intuition which gives assurance of these things. There is that within which begets dreams of such things, but we feel after the dreaming that they are only dreams.

(3.) Nor can reason, by a series of deductions, build an adequate basis for such a hope. The brightest intellects have given their energy to these questions and their search has ended in doubt. They have stood on the beach and gazed out upon the mist-covered sea, unable to penetrate that mist.

(4.) Nor is there moral worth and merit in us to furnish an adequate reason. It is to be feared that many are deceiving themselves by building upon this sandy foundation. Morality alone is not enough, good works cannot purchase justification and heaven and eternal life.

In my search for an adequate reason I visit the schools of philosophy in vain. My own heart tells me that the claim of personal merit will not do. My dreams are unsatisfactory. I wander from place to place seeking to know something of what lies beyond, and whether, and then why, we may hope. The deepest feelings of my nature urge me on. My questions are too great, too intensely personal to admit of rest and silence. At last I enter an humble chapel. The people are plain, earnest and happy. I tell them I am a seeker for truth and certainty with reference to what lies beyond this brief life. I ask them for light. One of their number, a man of years and venerable in appearance, rises and tells me of their full and joyous hope. I listen enraptured. "But what ground," I ask, "have you for such a hope? What reason can you give? The hope itself is beautiful, and meets the deepest yearnings of my nature, yet in a matter so important I cannot feel satisfied with anything short of certainty." And the aged man replies, "The reason for our blessed hope is short and simple. I can give it in one sentence. *The promise of Almighty God, our Father, through Jesus Christ, our Savior.* This is the reason of our hope; and we have been taught to give it to every one that asketh us." Like the spring time after winter, like the day-dawn after darkness, like the bursting of the sunshine from the shadow of a cloud, comes the brief and simple answer to my darkened, troubled heart.

I feel that this ground is adequate, why should it be thought a thing incredible with me that God should raise the dead? He, too, can justify and glorify. He can fulfil all his promises, and I know that he will. I may not understand just how certain promised things can be, but that does not darken with the shadow of a doubt my faith that they will be, provided, only God, the Almighty Father, has promised them. "For men verily swear by the greater, and an oath for confirmation is to them an end of all strife. Wherein God, willing more abundantly to show unto the heirs of promise the immutability of his counsel, confirmed it by an oath; that by two immutable things, in which it was impossible for God to lie, we might have a strong consolation, who have fled for refuge to lay hold upon the hope set before; which hope we have as an anchor of the soul, both sure and steadfast; and which entereth into that within the vail; whither the forerunner is for us entered, even Jesus."

Here is strong consolation, because here is well-grounded hope. The two immutable things on which it rests are the promise and the oath of God. It is impossible for him to lie. His oath-confirmed promise and his blood-sealed oath are enough. The anchor hold of hope is sure, and so the trusting Christian is steadfast. He has fled for refuge and has found it. The consolation of the Christian is not in his own strength; his hope of heaven is not based upon his merits. His comfort is that God has *promised* eternal life and blessedness to his people, and that he cannot prove false to his word. This is his simple, yet all-sufficient answer to every one that asketh a reason of the hope within him.

Since the Christian hope is so precious, embracing victory over death; justification at the final judgment; an eternal transfiguration; freedom from present infirmities and limitations; an abundant entrance into heaven; a blessed vision of God, our Father and Redeemer; the fellowship of the ransomed forever, and perpetual spiritual growth and exaltation — making it precious above all price, I cannot close without adding a few earnest, brotherly words.

1. Let us strive for the full assurance of hope. The promise of God is sure, but it is conditioned to each individual. Give heed to the exhortation of Paul, saying: "We desire

that every one of you do show the same diligence to the full assurance of hope unto the end; that ye be not slothful, but followers of them who through faith and patience inherit the promises." We need diligence and patience and perseverance. We need to comply with conditions, so that each one may say of the divine promise, it is God's promise to *me*. We need to be diligent and faithful in this, so that we may have the *full* assurance of hope.

2. Let us make more use of our hope in our every-day life. Think not of it as of something to be used only in the dying hour. Hope is not be used as the life-preservers on a boat are to be used. They lie unused and almost unnoticed until there comes a wreck, and then they are hastily put on to buoy up and to preserve from sinking into a watery grave. So are some with reference to hope. Not until there comes a wreck, not until the hour of dying do they seem to think of using their hope. But we really need it every day. We need the strength of its inspiration, the radiance of its light, and the blessedness of its sweet and peaceful joy. We need it to soothe our spirits, to brighten our skies, to solace our hearts. Make more practical and constant use of the hope that God has given you.

And, last of all, let me speak a word of brotherly admonition to those who are "without Christ, and are strangers from the covenants of promise, having no hope." Can you afford to live longer without this blessed hope? The hope that sustained your father and your mother, in life and in death? The hope that transfigures life and conquers death? You need it. Life is empty without it. You may have it as *your* hope. I beg you, flee for refuge to lay hold of this hope set before you. It rests upon the promise of God, and all his promises are in Christ. Only in Christ, therefore, can you find it. Only through loving, trustful obedience does it become yours. He asks you to come to him, to learn of him, to take his yoke, promising you shall find rest to your souls. Oh, the sadness, oh, the bitterness of the thought, should you be lost, that the door of full hope stood open for me, that the voice of mercy called me to enter and yet, day after day, I procrastinated until all my days were numbered and now it is too late! No hope! No ray of hope! Too late, forever too late!

DRIFTING FROM GOD.

Take heed, brethren, lest there be in any of you an evil heart of unbelief in departing from the living God. — Heb. iii:12.

I think it is a well established fact that no one can remain perfectly stationary in this life. The changes which are taking place may be so silent and gradual that they escape ordinary observation, yet they are none the less real. There seems to be, for instance, no change taking place in my body — it appears to be the same it has been for years — and yet science demonstrates that it is continually undergoing modification — that the law of waste and supply is perpetually at work. To cease to grow is to begin to die. Not to go forward is, practically, to go backward.

So is it with our spiritual life. Change is inherent. As the fire-fly shines only when on the wing, so the soul glows only when it is active. When action ceases we darken. Then, too, we are living in a moving, shifting, changing world. The drift of the world, and the undertow of human nature are both from God. He, therefore who comes near to God must make conscious effort to do so. There is no tide in the sea of life to carry him there. He who would abide near God must watch against an evil heart of unbelief. Were I to place a plank, or any substance that would easily float, upon the surface of a large body of water which appears to be perfectly calm, it would seem to lie just where I place it. I might watch it for hours without it seeming to move. But, should I return on the following day, I would find it had slowly drifted from the place where it was. The gentle winds, the tide I could not see, and the motion of the earth combined to displace it by degrees. Thus there is danger lest we drift from God so slowly and gently that we are really unaware of it until we glance back over years. Nor can we, by passing through one tremendous struggle, place ourselves beyond the reach of this danger. As the boatman, rowing up the river, must continue the strokes of his oars to prevent his drifting backward and downward toward the precipice, so by watchfulness, by prayer, by good works, by all appointed means must we continue our ascent. The moment we fold our arms, that moment we begin to drift away.

The history of religion is a history of fluctuations. Israel grieved God by apostasies in the wilderness, so that he is represented as swearing in his wrath that they should not enter into the promised rest. Their goodness was as the morning cloud, and as the early dew that passes away. Only two, of all that went out from Egypt, ever entered into the land of promise. And after the chosen people were settled in Canaan these same weaknesses continued to mar their lives. In fact, their history may be told in two words — *advance* and *retreat*. They drew near to God and were obedient to his will, then drifted away into disobedience, again they drew near and again drifted away, like the ebbing and flowing of the tide. So of individuals. Even Abraham shows marked variations of religious strength and fervor. The same is true of Moses and the prophets, of Solomon and the kings, and of David, the man after God's own heart. The wonderful knowledge which Christ had of human weakness is shown by his repeated exhortations to vigilance and prayerfulness. Watch, watch, watch — what I say unto one I say unto all — *watch*. And Paul had been thinking of the apostasies in the wilderness when he wrote, "Take heed, brethren, lest there be in any of you an evil heart of unbelief in departing from the living God."

I suggest that we limit our meditations to two points: —

1. *The outward symptoms of this apostasy,* and
2. *The remedy for this apostasy.*

(1.) First, then, as to its symptoms. We would err dangerously were we to suppose that only gross sins and sudden, startling falls are the only symptoms. Judas and Julian are not to be typical apostates. Few fall away as they fell. It is with spiritual apostasy as with bodily diseases, — some are shocking in appearance and speedy in their work, while others are more hidden, and do their fatal work silently and by almost imperceptible degrees. Yet these hidden diseases are fatal. Sometimes their covert working makes them only the more dangerous by blinding the eyes of their victim to his real danger. A sudden fall may be followed by a speedy recovery; but a gradual decay, unless promptly arrested, will almost certainly lead to hopeless ruin. It is very important, then, that we earnestly and very diligently search within ourselves for symptoms of spiritual decay. What are some of these symptoms?

(1.) Religious peevishness is one symptom. The man who is habitually petulant, who is of a sour temper and hard to please in religious matters, gives good indications that his spiritual health is bad. Yet, strange to say, some who are thus afflicted mistake it for a sure mark of piety. They seem to suppose that because they can see so many motes in the eyes of others theirs must be remarkably clear. Nothing pleases them. They are as irritable as teething children and confirmed dyspeptics. There is no patience, no charity, no sweetness, no sunshine about them. They find so many things they do not like, and they seem free always to express their dislikes. What they have to say about the church is almost always adverse. Were their hearts right, were they full of the love of God and of love for their fellow-men, were they in good spiritual health, this croaking would cease. Croaking is a good sign that we are drifting from God.

(2.) Another symptom is their loss of relish for spiritual food. They do not earnestly desire the sincere milk of the word that they may grow thereby. Nor can they endure strong meat. To them the Bible has no spiritual attractions. They have no taste for devotion, private prayer and the meeting for public worship are neglected. They find no pleasure in the communion of saints. When they attend the preaching of the word it is not that they may be fed. No, no. They are delighted with oratory, it may be, and they find the public gathering gives them an opportunity to meet with friends. But the simple story of the gospel has lost its charms. They enjoy controversial preaching, for the low state of their spiritual health gives them a relish for controversy. As a rule, those who have the least spiritual life are, of all in the church, most delighted with pugilistic preaching. Other preaching is tame and dry. If the news and the questions of the day are served up in the pulpit in sensational style they are interested. When the preacher is away they are absent. The house of God has lost its attractions because their hearts have lost their love for God and his worship.

(3.) Then there may usually be found another symptom very much like this. It is an increasing relish for trivial, worldly amusements and ungodly associates. Where the carcass is there will the vultures be gathered together. Their taste guides them there. And they plainly tell what their taste is by gathering to feast on a putrid carcass. I suppose there are few ways in which we more clearly indicate our tastes, than by the places we frequent, in seeking our enjoyments, and the persons we choose in forming our associates. When the enjoyment we seek is worldly it is a demonstration that our hearts are worldly, and John, the apostle, says, "If any man love the world, the love of the Father is not in him." Fondness for the circus, the theatre, the ball-room, and for worldly amusements generally, is a sure indication that we have not the love God shed abroad in our hearts. Then, too, if I delight in ungodly associates and find pleasure in their impure and profane conversation there must be within me an evil heart. I am drifting from God.

(4.) Still another symptom is found in the effect which an evil heart of unbelief has on the sight. You know it is of the nature of some diseases to impair the vision. Sometimes it is almost entirely destroyed. This is true of spiritual degeneration. Those who have an evil heart of unbelief, and are greatly reduced in spiritual strength lack spiritual discernment. I suppose every pastor finds those in his flock who are suffering from impaired vision. They cannot see that this is wrong, or that that is dangerous and should be avoided. They say they can't see why the church should object to its members indulging in this or that amusement. Oh, how often we hear them say they can't see! Well, it is to be deplored. But he is a poor spiritual physician who, in such a case, goes to treating the symptom instead of endeavoring to go down to the root of the matter. The primal trouble is in the heart. If you can purify and renew that the vision will be restored speedily. You may set it down, in nine cases out of every ten, that when the moral vision is dim the heart is wrong.

(5.) But, not to detain you longer with the symptoms, I mention only one other, and that is spiritual lassitude. The patient has no inclination to work. He becomes an idler in the Lord's vineyard. Vigorous health delights in employment. It goes to its work with a song. But disease is languid. It has no relish for work. Though there may be much to do, though there may be loud calls for helpers, though the harvest may be wasting, simply because there are not enough reapers, still the weak and sickly cannot summon resolution to enter the field. Many churches are full of idlers because they are full of men and women of weak faith and cold hearts. When the heart pulse is full and strong, when faith is clear and vigorous, when love flows with full tide, there is nothing so delightful as work for the Master. It is sweeter than song, more delightful than dreaming dreams and seeing visions. Labor is an outlet through which the feelings of devotion flow. Have you never observed how the new convert to Christ, in the fulness and freshness of his first love, delights to do some work, whatever it may be, for his Lord and Redeemer? Do you not recall this delight to labor as among the early experiences of your life as a Christian? And am I not right in attributing your lassitude to your loss of love?

Having briefly stated some of the symptoms which usually mark departure in the heart from God, I desire, in all seriousness, to ask you what you think of yourselves. Do you find upon self-examination that you are drifting away from him in whose fellowship we should find our chief delight? Be honest with yourself. If your love has grown cold, if you have ceased to delight in his worship, if you no longer find pleasure in the communion of saints, if you have no mind, no will to work in the vineyard of our Lord, if you find any indications that you have drifted or are drifting from God, do not seek to cloak the fact, fearful as it is, you are apostatizing.

It may be that the cares of this world and the deceitfulness of riches have been the cause, or you may have been borne on the current of the world, or your self-confidence may have given Satan an advantage over you, but whatever the cause of your backsliding may have been, I beseech you, lose no time in healing these backslidings and in returning to your first love. We all need a spiritual revival. We need to renew our vows. We need to lay hold upon all means appointed for our rescue and to use them with great earnestness. I pray that I may be enabled to point out to you the way to recovery.

II. *The remedy for this apostasy.*

1. First of all we must take heed to ourselves. We must look into our own hearts, and make an honest effort to know our real condition. Carelessness has been the cause of apostasy with many of us, and so earnest heed must be the first step in our recovery. It was not until David was caused to see the greatness of his sin that the work of penitence and reformation was begun in earnest. Not until the glance from the eyes of Jesus brought Peter to think upon his great sin did he go out and weep over it with bitterness. And not until the poor prodigal came to himself, not until he realized his wretchedness and how far he was from his father and his home, did he rise to return. Were you gently drifting down the Niagara River, with the mighty cataract below you, the first thing needed for your rescue would be a sense of your perilous condition. And yet, they who are drifting from God are drifting toward a more fearful precipice than that of Niagara. They are drifting toward the pit. When the vessel at sea has, through the carelessness of its captain and pilot, drifted from its course, the first thing needful is that they make their reckonings. There is no hope of its being restored to its proper path until this is done.

2. Call up before your mind, as vividly as possible,

visions of a bright past. Once you were full of zeal, once you enjoyed fellowship with God. That past is bright. It was not until Cowper saw his danger and thought upon this bright past in his life that he began with earnest prayer to struggle back to God and light and joy.

> "Where is the blessedness I knew
> When first I saw the Lord?
> Where is the soul refreshing view
> Of Jesus and his word?"

Thoughts of his father's house and bright visions of the plenty he had once enjoyed there helped the prodigal in his return. Thoughts of these days of blessed experience will give new impulse to our souls. Our sins will appear darker by the contrast. "There is no more effectual means," says Owen, "to stir up backsliders unto endeavors for deliverance than a continual remembrance of former things, and experiences of holy intercourse and communion with God. This will revive, quicken and strengthen the things ready to die, and beget a self-abhorrency. I have known one in the depths of distress and darkness of mind, who, going through temptation to destroy himself, was relieved and delivered in the instant of ruin by the sudden remembrance that at such a time, and in such a place, he had prayed fervently with the engagement of all his affections unto God." When Jacob had come to the place where God had granted him a glorious vision he renewed his vows. So with us. Let us look back to the beginning of our Christian course. Let us recall the earnest preaching, the songs, the whole scene of our conversion. This will help us greatly.

3. Strengthen the things that remain that are ready to die. This was the counsel Christ gave the decaying church in Sardis. This applies to every church, and to each one who finds himself in a languishing state of religious life. Just as

it is important, when the body is prostrate with disease and seems ready to die, that we carefully nourish the strength still remaining, so is it important to strengthen what may yet remain of faith and love and hope in our souls. Every true revival of religion both in individuals and in churches begins this way. There is something good in you yet. This light has not gone entirely out. You may yet fan the dying embers into a glowing flame. Do not be overwhelmed with discouragement. The plant, though dwarfed by the frosts of the winter, may yet be made to blossom and bear fruit when the spring sun shines, and the soft breath of the south wind breathes upon it. You may have thought of giving up your effort to lead a Christian life. You have neglected the meetings of the church because you feel so unworthy. At this critical moment in your life I come to beg you to abandon such a thought. Take courage. Strengthen the things which remain. Many have been as far away from God and as languishing in spiritual life as you, and have yet lived to become shining lights. So it may be with you.

4. Do your first works. The church in Ephesus has left its first love. Christ beseeches it to remember from whence it had fallen, and to repent and do its first works. If we would cease drifting from God and return we must act very much as we did immediately after our conversion. I remember the case of a young man who had so far lost his interest in religion that he determined to abandon even the profession of a religious life. He approached the pastor of the church and requested to have his name erased from the church-roll. The pastor persuaded him to withdraw the request for a while, and asked him, in the meantime, to aid him somewhat in his pastoral work by calling to see a family which had been reported as in very destitute circumstances. He did so. He found the family in deep

need and ministered to them. This was his beginning. He engaged in other good works. Nothing more was heard of his request to have his name erased, until the pastor chancing to meet him inquired if he still desired to withdraw from the church. "Oh no," said he, as he grasped the hand of the pastor, "oh no, and I desire to thank you for your very wise and brotherly treatment of my case. I was miserable beyond all expression that morning, but now I am bright and happy for all my clouds have passed away." He was saved from eternal apostasy by doing good works.

5. Strive for the virtue of genuineness. It is a weakness of human nature to drift into unreal service and heartless formality. At first our songs, our prayers, all our devotions are intensely and vividly real. But we become so used to them that they cease to engage our hearts. We kept up the appearance of religious life for a while; but, by and by, began to feel that such emptiness was base hypocrisy, and that it was better not to appear religious than to do so when it was only an appearance. I am sure this has been the experience of some. What should you do? My advice to you is, strive, perseveringly strive, to make all religious acts vital and genuine. Seize upon your best moments and use them. When you find your heart in a state of prayer, pray. Open the windows, open them toward heaven, and pray. Let it be a season of prayer. Let your best impulses speak out. When you attend church make an honest effort to engage heartily in the devotions of the house of God. Let your effort be to draw nearer to God. If you can do no more, then breathe forth in prayer, "Nearer, my God, to thee — nearer to thee." Better a short, simple prayer, over and over again, striving to engage your heart in its utterance, than the most beautiful and elaborate service

offered without genuine devotion. Strive to be genuine, strive for reality.

I will not detain you longer with these words of brotherly advice, although there are yet a few items I expected to mention. But I suppose they will suggest themselves, and I think it better not to overburden your memory. Carry with you the suggestions I have made, and, I pray you, strive to profit by their counsel. First of all, take earnest heed to yourself; call up bright experiences in your past; strengthen the things that remain; do such works as those in which you delighted in the bright and early days of your Christian experience; strive for the virtue of genuineness in all you do. Do these things, and may God bless you in your efforts to lay your heart upon his altar again.

In conclusion, be assured of God's mercy, that he will receive you. He restored Peter to his apostleship, though he had grievously denied him. He restored unto David the joys of his salvation, although he had polluted himself by gross sin. He will extend his helping hand to you, if you turn with sincere purpose, and with earnest endeavor you seek to come back. Though you may have drifted far from him his eyes rest upon you, and his mercy is ready to forgive and to restore. Think of the father's welcome to the prodigal son on his return, and be encouraged.

JESUS AS A TEACHER.

Rabbi, we know that thou art a teacher come from God; for no man can do the miracles which thou doest except God be with him. — John iii:2.

This is the confession of Nicodemus, a ruler of the Jews. He regarded Jesus as a great teacher. He had probably witnessed some of his miracles, and heard him in his public instruction. It is night. He seeks the great teacher that he may converse with him in private. I can see nothing in the simple fact that he went at night to justify the censure which not only unfrequently is visited against him. His reasons for selecting that time may have been honorable. We know that after this he dared to speak a word for Jesus in the midst of violent prejudice and avowed hostility. When the disciples were paralyzed with fear, and had abandoned hope, Nicodemus joined with Joseph of Arimathea in the burial of Jesus. Does this look like a craven coward?

I desire to speak of Jesus as a teacher. For whatever else he may be to the world we should never forget the fact that he stands out before men as a teacher come from God. The will of God and the way of life must be learned from him. He is divinely anointed to instruct. High above al other teachers he stands pre-eminent. Prophets enlightened by the inspiring Spirit of God, Psalmists whose souls often waited in the Unseen Holy, and Moses with whom the Omniscient had spoken face to face, have delivered their messages. The lessons they taught were only preparatory. The light they shed was only the dim and borrowed light which falls from the stars. The stars fade away before the rising splendors of the king of day. So fade away all teachers when Jesus opens his lips for instruction. In his presence we should reverently bow, and as the favored three on the Mount of Transfiguration, when the cloud had passed, saw Jesus only and heard the voice of the Father saying, "*Hear ye him*," so should it be with us. His right to teach us is an exclusive right. He comes with this claim and his miracles demonstrate that the Father approves it. In our meditation let us notice.

    I. *The record of his teaching*
    II. *Some of the characteristics of his teaching.*
    III. *Some of the subjects of his teaching.*
    I. *Record of his teaching.*

The great Arabian prophet committed to writings dictated by himself those views which he wished should be connected with his name through all time to come. The same is true of the Chinese patriarch, Confucius, and all leading philosophers of ancient times. But it is a fact worthy of notice that Jesus prepared and committed to record no statement of his doctrine. Neither was any one taken under special instruction in order to prepare such a record. He was a great teacher, but he had no organized school to which he invited men for instruction. He went from place to place teaching the multitudes gathered by the fame of his gracious miracles. From the mountain side, and in the temple, from the boat resting at anchor on the margin of the lake and in the quiet of social intercourse, wherever he went, whether at a feast in the house of plenty, or among the famishing children of want, like a bountiful sower he cast abroad the golden seeds of heavenly wisdom. He let them fall. He seemed to feel no concern as to their preservation for future generations.

In a few fragments of public discourses, in parables and in private conversations, scattered, apparently without regard to order, through four brief histories of his life, are to be found the only records of the lessons taught by the most influential teacher the world has ever known. These four sketches were written by as many different men, so that what is related by one is repeated, in many cases, by others. Were we to strike out every repetition, how very short would the remaining record be! And yet it would contain the thoughts which have changed the world's thinking and given the noblest type of manhood and the purest civilization the world has ever seen!

Strange as it may appear to us that Christ left no formulated statement of his doctrine, yet, if we believe in the inspiration of the four evangelists, we must recognize the very form and manner of their records as divine. They were guided by the Spirit of God in selecting and arranging that which was for the instruction of generations then unborn. Men have sought to state in formal propositions these lessons of heavenly wisdom. In volumes of systematic theology, in creeds and confessions of faith they seek to formulate the doctrine of Christ. But, my brethren is not the inspired form the best? It presents these lessons in the simple language of the common people rather than in the technical terms of philosophy. It contains the lessons for practical life rather than problems for speculative thought. It presents them not in the abstract, but in the concrete, illustrated by a life. There is a wonderful reality and simplicity in the faith which comes from these brief but sublime and comprehensive records. "Brethren, let me urge upon you the habitual study of the holy gospels," says Dr. Bernard, "for this revival of the reality and simplicity of faith. Let me urge it more especially upon those who converse in the region of abstract ideas, whether they frequent the ordered paths of systematic divinity, or wander in the free excursions of speculative thought. Dear as the gospel stories are to the simple peasant, they are yet more necessary to the student and the divine; for there are influences in abstract thought and in dogmatic discussion which will drain the soul of life unless fitting antidotes be used; and there is no antidote so effectual, as is found in a continual return to those scenes of historic fact in which the word of God has given us our first lessons in Christ."

In the *form* of the divine record there is a beautiful analogy to the volume of nature. The laws of nature are not formulated after the method of science, nor are its riches classified and systematically arranged. Mountains, and valleys, and fertile fields, and barren deserts, and rivers, and seas, are scattered over the earth without apparent order. Under the rugged mountain are hidden inestimable treasures, and untold wealth lies deep in the caves of the ocean. So the lessons which are to enrich us with eternal life and a heavenly home, which are to set men free from the thraldom of sin and bind up broken hearts, lie half concealed and half revealed under the figure of a parable, or strewn like celestial pearls in private conversations.

II. *Some characteristics of Christ's teaching.*

After reading the brief Memoirs of Christ which have been preserved to us, who can wonder that the multitudes were astonished at his dotrine? Who feels any surprise when those who were sent to arrest him turned with the confession "never man spake like this man." But let us note with some care a few of the characteristic, of his teaching.

1. *It was plain and direct.* The common people could understand him. It abounded in illustrations with which they were familiar. The farmer sowing seeds in a field near

by, and the fishermen dragging their nets to the shore; the frail sparrow flying over their heads, and the delicate lily blooming at their feet; the silent growing of the seed that falls into the ground and the reapers going forth to gather the golden grain are some of the figures by which he conveyed his lessons to men. In this way too he has made some of the ordinary objects and events in life perpetual instructors. These are continually bringing to mind the words of Christ.

2. *It was gentle and affectionate.* With what tenderness must he have said, "Come unto me, all ye that labor and are heavy laden, and I will give you rest. Take my yoke upon you and learn of me; for I am meek and lowly in heart; and ye shall find rest unto your souls. For my yoke is easy and my burden light." How many of earth's weary ones have found in these precious words a cordial for aching hearts! How tender the compassion which breathes forth in this call to rest! And then, again, who can listen to his lamentation over Jerusalem, and mark the flowing tears which steal down his cheek, without being touched with his strong affection. It was only to the corrupt and hypocritical that his words became stern and terrible. In the twenty-third chapter of Matthew he pronounces a seven-fold woe upon his relentless enemies.

3. *His teaching was authoritative.* It was this which impressed the multitude. "They were astonished at his doctrine, for he taught them as one having authority and not as the scribes." The scribes could do no better than to say, "Moses hath said;" but Christ stood before them and with the dignity of authority uttered repeatedly the words, "But *I* say to you." He was divinely anointed to reveal the truth. He did not speculate about things unknown, but testified concerning that which he knew. He could speak

with authority, for in him were hidden all the treasures of wisdom and knowledge. He had the very manner of one confident of perfect knowledge. He never had occasion to correct a single statement that came from his lips. His utterances were infallible.

III. *Subjects of Christ's teaching.*

When we meditate on the sublime and difficult themes which formed the subjects of his instructions, his greatness becomes more apparent. His teaching embraces all that pertains to salvation, duty and destiny. The doctrine of the soul, the doctrine of God, and the doctrine of the reconciliation of the soul to God, give us a general view of the subjects most prominent in his teaching. I wish, however to be more specific.

1. *He taught us more of God's nature and of his special providence over all his creatures.* A knowledge of God must lie at the foundation of every truly religious life. He taught that not a sparrow falls to the ground without God's notice. Not a lily blooms without his care. The fatherhood of God is often and distinctly affirmed. His love is revealed and demonstrated. When Philip said to him, "Show us the Father," Jesus answered, saying, "Have I been so long time with you, and yet hast thou not known me, Philip? — he that hath seen me hath seen the Father." He is the revelation of the character of the Father.

2. *He revealed more clearly the true nature of sin.* It consists not simply in outward action, but in thought and purpose. He is not the murderer only who actually takes life, but he also who in his heart so hates his fellow that he would. In his clear and searching judgment he penetrates the outer vail and looks upon the hidden spring and secret motives which dwell within the heart. With him sin is the refusing of the right as right, knowing at the time it is right,

and choosing the wrong as wrong, knowing at the time it is wrong. He unmasks hypocrisy.

3. *He teaches that the world's great conflict is with sin.* He appears to care but little for outward circumstances. To the poor paralytic he said, "Thy sins be forgiven thee." He saw a deeper affliction than the one which attracted ordinary men. He looked within, and said, thy *sins* be forgiven thee. The Jews were groaning under Roman oppression. They longed to be free. But Jesus saw a more debasing slavery — the slavery of sin. He proclaimed himself a great liberator — not from political bondage — but from the bondage of Satan.

4. *He taught and he demonstrated the reality of the forgiveness of sins.* He presented it as the great boon to be enjoyed as an actual fact in this life. When the Pharisees murmured at his pronouncing absolution in the case just mentioned, he wrought a miracle to demonstrate his ability to forgive. Pardon is no longer something to be vainly sought, but is freely offered to all who will accept it. Your sins and your iniquities I will remember no more forever.

5. *He taught the value of the soul.* This thought underlies all he said and did. But at times it arose into overshadowing prominence, like some mountain peak, in some such expression as this: "What shall it profit a man if he gain the whole world and lose his own soul?" The voice of passion, the voice of worldly care, and the voice of carnal appetite had cried so that the voice of the soul was seldom heard. Its value was forgotten. In fact, its very existence was practically ignored. Jesus gave it a voice and emphasized its value.

6. *He brought life and immortality to light.* He poured a flood of light on the Beyond. The wisest could only guess;

Jesus spoke with the utmost confidence. He spoke of things unseen with as much familiarity as of those things which appear. He taught that this life is to be completed in the life to come. From that he brought thoughts into this which makes it sublime to live. In even a glance at the themes on which he spoke my soul is filled with awe.

How important that we should be his disciples in deed and in truth. The very themes on which he speaks are such as to arrest the attention and awaken a profound interest in every thoughtful mind. He who affects to ignore the gospel records proclaims his own folly.

Again, the nature of his teaching argues his divinity. Where did he gain such wonderful knowledge? He was born a Jew. His mother was a Jewess. He was educated among a narrow and bigoted people. Yet he arose above all the influences of his early years and proclaimed lessons of wisdom for ages to come.

Finally, my brethren, as is the value of his teaching so is our obligation to receive it. "See that ye refuse not him that speaketh. For if they escaped not who refused him that spake on earth, much more shall not we escape, if we turn away from him that speaketh from heaven; whose voice shook the earth; but now he hath promised, saying, Yet once more I shake not the earth only, but also heaven." Let us heed the command of the Father, as, pointing to his Son, he said, *Hear ye Him.*

THE WAY, THE TRUTH, AND THE LIFE.

Jesus saith unto him, I am the way, the truth, and the life; no man cometh unto the Father, but by me.—Jno. xiv: 6.

He who reads the life of Christ with thoughtful attention cannot fail to observe how his whole being seemed to rise as he came near the Cross. His love for his disciples became more personal, more intense, even pathetic; his fellowship with his Father and the upper world seemed more conscious and more precious, and his utterances make manifest the fact that his thoughts were busy with the most profound spiritual relationships. At the supper — the last one he celebrated with his immediate followers — he pours out the deep love and tender sympathy of his heart for them in words which have been a precious heritage to many a believing yet troubled heart since. "It is expedient for you that I go away. Let not your hearts be troubled — I will send you another Comforter." So he sought to quiet them with all the gentleness and tenderness of a devoted mother bending over a sobbing child. His mind moves among the hidden spiritual verities. He speaks of the relationships which can neither be apprehended nor understood by carnal minds. The relation between him and his Father; the coming of the Spirit to be, not only with, but *in* the disciples; the spiritual unity which should exist among them,— these were the high themes on which he spoke during that interview recorded from the thirteenth to the eighteenth chapter of John.

It was while his nature was lifted to this exalted plane that he uttered the words of the text,— "I am the way, the truth, and the life." If we ever come to a full comprehension of what he meant by this, if we ever scale the heights, and fathom the depths, and compass the wide sweep of the meaning of this wonderful saying, it must be in some moment of spiritual exaltation akin to that out of which it was born. Again and again have I turned from this passage with the feeling that it was too high for me and too deep. I have that feeling now. But, if I can bring before you such fragments of its meaning as will make Christ more to us, let his name be praised.

1. *Christ is the way*. Whatever may be meant, beyond and besides, it is certainly meant *he is the way to God and to Heaven.* "No man can come unto the Father, but by me." And, if no man can come unto the Father but by him, then it follows, of necessity, no man can come to Heaven but by him. Not only this, but when he says, "I am *the* way" we are justified, I think, in saying he means there is no other way. The emphasis of the claim makes it exclusive. It means Christ is our *only* way to God and to Heaven.

Sin had closed the way. The flaming sword turning every way to guard the approaches to the tree of life tells how certainly and completely the way was closed. There was no by-path or circuitous route still open. Every approach was closed. And this same fact was taught in significant figure to the Jews. In the tabernacle in the wilderness, and in the temple on Mt. Zion, an apartment was cut off as the symbolic dwelling-place of Jehovah. A thick curtain separated it from the holy place. Through this curtain none dared go save the High Priest only, and he at stated times and with prescribed sacrifices. But, when Christ expired on the Cross, this veil in the temple was rent in twain from top to bottom. The way is open. It is through Christ's flesh. It is called a *new* and *living* way, and is consecrated by his blood.

"I am the way." Christ is the only mediator. If I have thank-offerings for God I must present them through Christ. If I long for divine forgiveness I must find it through Christ. If I desire to approach God in prayer I can do it only through Christ. "There is one God and one mediator between God and man, the man Christ Jesus." I cannot offer prayer but through this mediator. I was once elected chaplain of a Masonic lodge; I would not act because the prayers ignored the mediation of Christ. It is a fundamental — an essential doctrine of the Christian Scriptures.

I can preach salvation by no other way. God's ordained way of dealing with us is through a mediator, and he gives us every reason to believe he will not deal with us in any other way. He is king. He has said whatever you have to present or to ask, let it be through my Son. I will hear you for his sake. You cannot come to me directly. He is the way.

2. *Christ is the truth.* There is a unity in the text which is in danger of being overlooked. Many suppose it mentions three separate and distinct things which Christ claims concerning himself, but which have no relation to each other. They, however, are essentially joined. Neither is complete but in union with the others, and the order in which they stand is the order of nature, because it is the order of man's necessity. First of all is our need of a way to God. But suppose the way opened. How can we find it? In the ignorance which has settled down upon us like thick darkness we would grope in vain to find it, or else by chance discover the provided way. We need the light of truth. Not truth that comes in broken and refracted rays, but full-orbed, sure-shining truth.

The claim is more than that — he speaks truth. There is a difference between truth and veracity. Veracity is the exact harmony between the conception in the mind and the utterance of the tongue. Truth is the exact harmony between the conception in the mind and reality. The conception in the mind may be erroneous, but if the spoken word gives accurate representation of the conception, the man is a man of veracity. But unless there is perfect harmony between the conception lying in the mind and things and events as they actually are, he has not the truth.

When, therefore, Christ says "I am the truth," he claims that in his mind lie the pictures of things and the map of events as they actually are. He claims relation to the absolute. His is no fragmentary knowledge. I am the infallible guide to men because I am the truth. Only the absolute can be infallible. Of men we may say they know truth; but at its best it is only part-knowledge. They cannot come to that fulness which will justify them in saying, we are the truth. Only the divine can do that, because to only divinity belongs absolute knowledge.

The search of the sages has been for truth. The cry of the lost in the great and barren wilderness of sin has been the cry for light, answered only by the mocking echo of their piteous cry. The earnest thinkers of the ages have placed only one question before them — what is truth? They have looked to the stars, they have sounded the depths, they have opened the earth, they have questioned all living things, they have turned their eyes within. Oh, tell us, *what is truth?* We want the sure, the absolute — the infallible. And not until the Teacher, sent from God, had come, was there a voice to say I am the truth.

3. *Christ is the Life.* As we proceed in the study of this high claim of Christ we go into deeper mystery. We easily understood what he meant when he said, I am the way. The claim to be the truth seemed more profound. But, when he says I am the life, he carries us into such deep

mysteries that we cannot hope to fully understand. Life in in its lowest, simplest form is a mystery. We apprehend a few of its phenomena, but what is life itself? The nearest we can come is to say that it is union with a life-fountain according to the law of being in each case. The law of being decides the nature of the life. The union broken is death. In order to life, then, there must be at least two things: First, the life-fountain; second, the union of the creature with the life-fountain. No creature can have life in itself. All creature-life is derived life. Of no creature can you say it *is* life. When, then, Christ says "I am the life," he claimed what belongs only to the Divine. In another place he has said, "As the Father has life in himself, so has he given to the Son to have life in himself." He is a life-fountain. Being a life-fountain he has power to give life. But this life comes to us only by our union with him. Our union with him is begun and is perpetuated by walking in the way and in the light. So we have life. Not only do we have life by union with Christ, but the uniform teaching of the New Testament Scriptures is that in this union alone can we have life eternal. This eternal life is something which begins the moment our union with Christ begins. It is union with Christ. "I am the life." This is the height of his claim. His own resurrection is its demonstration.

I hold Christ before you to-day as the only one who can interpret and meet your deepest wants. There are deep and unutterable yearnings in every soul. There are wants vaguely yet keenly felt. These find their interpretation in Christ. When I study the *supply* in him I learn, by the very supply he brings, just what was the *want* I so vaguely felt.

I am the way. That tells me I am shut out from home, and lost. As a child walks the street and cries out in fright because it has wandered from home and knows not the way back, so with us all. My soul in agony cries for the way.

I am the truth, interprets another part of my want. I am blind. I grope. Vague apprehensions of deeper calamities haunt me. I cry out for light but the echo to my cry is my only answer. I hunger for truth, and my hunger begets dreams and then feeds upon them.

I am the life. Oh, how the fear of death has made me a slave. His shadow rests upon my heart, and he closes with his huge black form the way before me. I cry out in terror. But the tyrant is unmoved by my cry. But blessed be the name of the Most High; there comes one whose very being is life and overthrows the tyrant. What more can we ask? Standing now on the prostrate form of Death, with the barriers of sin broken down and the darkness of ignorance driven back, Christ asks you to accept him because he is the *way*, the *truth*, and the *life*.

> "Thou art the Way — to thee alone
> From sin and death we flee;
> And he who would the Father seek,
> Must seek him, Lord, by thee.
>
> Thou art the Truth — thy word alone
> True wisdom can impart;
> Thou, only, canst inform the mind,
> And purify the heart.
>
> Thou art the Life — the rending tomb
> Proclaims thy conquering arm;
> And those who put their trust in thee,
> Nor death nor hell shall harm.
>
> Thou art the Way, the Truth, the Life;
> Grant us that way to know,
> That truth to keep, that life to win,
> Whose joys eternal flow."

OUR SINS AND OUR SAVIOR.

And she shall bring forth a son, and thou shalt call his name JESUS; for he shall save his people from their sins.—Mat. 1:21.

This name is significant of his entire work for our race. It means savior, and he came into the world to save. Not from the bondage of foreign oppression, as many of that day supposed, nor yet from the temporal ills of life, as many of this day seem to think; but he came to save the people from their sins. His salvation is primarily spiritual and its temporal features are subordinate. Nor did he come to save the people as they are, in their sins; but he came to save them *from their sins*. The leper who had been banished from the camp did not need simply to be admitted to it again; he needed to be healed of his leprosy. So it is not simply admission to Heaven that we need, but we need chiefly to be cleansed of our sins. Sin must be eliminated and the record of it must be erased before we are prepared to enjoy Heaven. Let us give attention, then, to these two points:—

I. *Some of the difficulties involved in this undertaking, and*

II. *The way in which Christ meets them and accomplishes his work.*

I. There are only four of these difficulties which I will mention.

1. First, that which is to be found in the nature of man. Were a planet to forsake its orbit, and rush wildly through space toward wreck it could be restored at once to its place, for its restoration would be only a question of power, and the power that started it on its course could recall it to its

place. Or were the stars to fall from the skies, the power that made them could at once replace them. These matters call for power only. But when man forsook his appointed way and rushed headlong toward ruin; when man fell from his high estate and the work of his restoration is undertaken it is far more difficult. His restoration is not simply a question of power. If saved *as* man he must be saved without violence to his will.

2. A second difficulty is found in the nature of the hold sin has upon us. Were we held simply in its embrace, were it something outside of us, though it were a mighty giant, yet to smite the giant would be to set us free. That, though a great deliverance would still be a simple work. When David kept his father's flocks, he tells us that a lion once came and carried away a lamb, and that he followed after and smote the lion and slew him and so delivered the prey. This was a great yet a very simple rescue. It required only courage and power. To slay the beast was to deliver the prey.

But the hold sin has upon us is very different, for sin is entrenched within us. Like a disease that so permeates the body that every atom is corrupted, and every drop of blood is poisoned, so has sin corrupted and poisoned every part of our nature. He who undertakes to eliminate this poison and to restore health finds his work complicated and difficult. It requires more than power. Or, again, the demoniac is a type of the sinner. Evil spirits have entered in and taken entire possession. The mind, the heart, the will, the entire inner man, is held in bondage. The hold they have upon their victim is of such a nature that no physical force, no simple power, however great, can cast them out. So the nature of the hold which sin has upon us makes the work delicate and difficult. Sin is entrenched within.

3. Then, again, the nature of the connection between sin

and its consequences increases this difficulty. The consequences of sin are natural, as opposed to arbitrary, and are closely linked to sins as opposed to the thought that they are far removed, awaiting our entrance upon another state. But, if we are saved from sins, we must be saved from these consequences. It is not enough, therefore, to eliminate sin, and cause us to cease from sinning. Were this all that was done consequences would abide with us as our bitter portion. The consequences of war do not cease with the cessation of hostilities. Nearly eighteen years have passed since the close of our unhappy civil war, but consequences continue. Suppose I indulge for a number of years in sins which corrupt and enfeeble my body. I may cease sinning in a day, but to my grave I carry the consequences of my sins with me. A house is on fire and you call upon me to save the building. I cannot. No one can. I may quench the flames, but in doing that I do not save the building. The roof, and all the upper story are gone and other parts are damaged. By putting out the fire when I did I prevented the total destruction of the building, but the flames did their work as they went, and I have no power to undo it. The nature of the intimate connection between the fire and its consequences prevented my saving the building entire. So the nature of the connection between sins and their consequences makes the work of saving from sin appear impossible.

4. The last difficulty I shall mention is found in the relation of sin to law and government. Our sins are related to moral law and the divine government. Sin is the transgression of law. Law is the expression of the will and authority of government. Our sins, therefore, involve legal and governmental questions. I state simply the fact. I do not undertake to explain just what these questions are, for I do not know. There are some analogies to the divine

government found among human governments and these help us in apprehending and understanding some of these questions. For the present, however, we have to do with the simple fact that to save us from our sins requires the solution of some problems of law and government.

But I have presented sufficient, I suppose, to indicate some of the difficulties involved in saving us from our sins. We see that it is not simply a question of power or of will. The nature of man as a free agent; the nature of the hold which sin has upon us, binding the inner man and poisoning every part of our nature; the connection between sin and its consequences, and the relation which sin sustains to moral law and the divine government show how difficult and complicated must be the undertaking to save from sin.

II. Let us now consider *the way in which Christ meets these difficulties and accomplishes his work.*

Sin is represented as darkening our understandings, corrupting our hearts, and perverting our wills; as marring our lives and shaping our destiny. It is manifest, therefore, that salvation from sin cannot be complete until it rectifies all these. Our relation to violated law must be corrected, and the demands of justice satisfied. If we read the story of redemption, in the light of these necessities, I think we will find that Christ proceeds with his work along the line here indicated.

1. He, first of all, enlightens the darkened understanding by the light of instruction. His religion deals with the mind first. He informs the mind by the instructions of his heavenly message. He comes before the world, in the beginning of his personal ministry, as a teacher of men. He opened his mouth and taught them; he went about all Galilee teaching the people; he sat daily teaching in the temple, — these and similar expressions used concerning the Christ

indicate the way in which he opened his work. And when he gave commission to his apostles it was that they should go and teach, saying: "Go, teach all nations."

Whatever may be the outcry against that which some choose to call "head religion" I hold that both a sound philosophy and the declarations of Scripture justify me in saying that the religion which does not instruct the mind and enlighten the understanding is not suited to the wants of man. True religion is not first a matter of emotion, or a system of duties, but a matter of knowledge through the light of revelation. The gospel is, for this reason, spoken of as full of light, shining forth. Its messengers are teachers of men, and their power has been greatest wherever they have magnified their office of teaching. I feel sure that our pulpits would have a stronger hold upon the people to-day if they abounded more in instructions on the elementary principles of redemption. To enlighten the understanding with spiritual truth is to begin the work of saving men from their sins.

2. He purifies the heart by the faith of the gospel. Peter said, in the Jerusalem Council, "He hath put no difference between us (the Jews) and them (the Gentiles) purifying their hearts by faith." This is a broad declaration that he purifies the hearts of all by faith. But, Paul says faith comes by hearing the word of God. Purification, therefore, comes through being taught the word of God. Again, John testifies that we love God because he first loved us. This is the genesis of divine love in human hearts. But the love of God for us cannot beget love within us in return until we have first learned the fact of his love. This new love within our hearts has an expulsive power, casting out the love for sin. The process of gospel reformation is

according to the law of substitution. When God would free us from any evil he does so by the substitution of the opposite good. As I would expel the darkness from a room by bringing in light, so he expels moral darkness from our hearts by bringing in moral light. On the Western prairies where rank and worthless grasses grow, beautiful pastures may be made by sowing the seed of the blue grass; so, by sowing in human hearts the good seed of the kingdom of God, may the worthless weeds of wickedness be destroyed. Instruction enlightens the understanding first; but when this instruction is received into the heart by faith it purifies the heart. And this, not because of any inherent purifying virtue in faith itself, but because of the purifying nature of the message believed. Thus our corrupt hearts

> Like the stained web in the sun
> Grow pure by being purely shone upon.

3. The perverted will must be rectified. As the heart is reached by the message of mercy through the understanding, so the will is reached through the heart. The correction of the perverted will is a pivotal point. An analysis of sin shows that its very essence is a wrong will. To will to sin is to sin, whether the purpose of the will finds opportunity to express itself in outward deed or not. There can, therefore, be no salvation from sin until the will is rectified.

In the Scriptures this change is called repentance, for if we make diligent search for the essence of repentance we will find that it is a change of the will with reference to sin. Even godly sorrow is not repentance. Paul says it worketh repentance. It changes the will. This is produced by the motives of the gospel. We find that apostles and other inspired preachers swept the entire range of motives, from the terrors of judgment to the goodness of God, in order to produce repentance. The individual will is right when it recognizes the divine will as its absolute Lord.

4. The outward life must be reformed. This reformation is the legitimate fruit of the rectified will. Genuine repentance leads to a reformation of life. John the Baptist preached repentance, and taught his converts to bring forth fruits mete for repentance. If the course of a ship is wrong it is in vain that the pilot seeks to correct it unless he changes the helm. But let that be properly adjusted and the ship begins at once to turn into its right course. The will is the helm in us. When that is set right a change appears at once in the course of our lives.

This change is manifest not only in our forsaking sins, but in our obedience to God. On the very branches where evil fruit once grew, now grows the fruit of righteousness. The powers once employed in the service of sin now become obedient servants unto God.

All the changes which I have now named bear their legitimate fruit in good works under divine guidance. The understanding enlightened by the gospel changes the heart; the changed and purified heart rectifies the perverted will; the rectified will corrects the evil life; the reformed life adorns the gospel by good works. The man has become a new creature under the illuminating and transforming power of the gospel. But, were the work to cease here it would stop short of the demands of the case. It is true that so far as the man is considered within himself we may say that he has undergone a complete conversion. But more than this moral change is needed.

5. His past sins call for an atonement. Let us suppose for instance, that the changes of which I have spoken, take

place when he is forty years of age. His record lies behind him and that record is darkened by sin. He has no power to correct that record — he cannot obliterate one sin. Every sin must be either pardoned or punished. His own reformation, however thorough it may be, has no merit to atone for these sins of the past. He remains, therefore, enthralled by his past and endangered by the sins it contains. What must be done?

Just here, as I understand the matter, the atoning merit of Christ's death comes in. I can understand how all the changes which resulted in complete reformation could have been produced without the shedding of his blood; but without the shedding of blood there is no remission of sins, and without the remission of sins there cannot be a complete salvation from sin. So it is said "He died for our sins."

The promise of the new covenant is "Your sins and your inquities will I remember no more," and this promise can be fulfilled because "The blood of Jesus Christ cleanseth from all sins." Since he has died God can still be just and yet the justifier of them that believe in Jesus. The record of our sins is erased by his blood, so that Paul could say "There is therefore now no condemnation to them that are in Christ Jesus." How precious is all this. Saved from sinning and saved from the condemnation of sin! Reconciled, reformed, restored forgiven! Yet this is not all. We need more to make our salvation from sin complete.

6. Death is the child of sin, and death has dominion over us. Death itself must die. The child of God goes down to the grave. He is a victim of death, the insatiable monster. He must be rescued from death and the grave, and placed beyond the reach of their power. By the resurrection of Jesus himself we have the assurance that this will be done.

He became subject to death that he might break its sceptre. In his resurrection he became the first fruits of the great harvest to be gathered from the grave.

My hope of life and immortality is not based upon the dim deductions of reason, but upon the demonstration brought by Christ in his own resurrection. By this he has begotten me again to a lively hope. Well may we exclaim with the apostle, "Thanks be unto God who giveth us the victory through Jesus Christ our Savior." He robs the grave of its victims, and death of its terrors and power.

When through him we shall stand upon the prostrate form of death and look into the empty graves where the ransomed have slept, when we shall find that through the merit of his atoning death and high priestly intercessions our sins have been blotted out and no condemnations rests before us, we shall begin to understand the full significance of that name which the angel announced when he said, "His name shall be called *Jesus*, for he shall save his people from their sins." This is the name that is above every name. When he humbled himself and took upon himself the form of a servant and was made in the likeness of man God gave him that name and he has decreed that before that blessed name every knee shall bow and every tongue confess.

In conclusion: This is the salvation and this the Savior you need. You need to be saved from your sins. Perhaps you have been dreamily thinking that what you needed was to be taken to Heaven; that if you were only in better surroundings your needs would be fully met. But Heaven itself could not be Heaven to you covered with the leprosy of sin and alienated from God. Christ knows our wants. He saw that we needed to be saved from our sins, and his mission to man was to accomplish this salvation. The manner in which he proceeds with this great work is eminently rational. He proceeds according to the demands of the case and succeeds at each stage of the undertaking. He is just the Savior you need.

But you cannot reasonably hope to be benefited by his salvation unless you follow his directions. There is something for you to do. Were you sick you would send for a physician, but however great might be his skill, you would not expect to be profited by it unless you followed his instructions. So with Christ, our great physician. He asks you to hear the gospel, to believe it, to repent of your sins, to put him on in baptism, to follow him through evil as well as through good report. Will you do it? Will you now receive his message into your heart? Will you now confess him? Will you obey him and be saved from your sins and all their fearful consequences? He is able to save unto the uttermost all who come unto God by him.

CHRIST'S PURPOSES IN OUR CONVERSION.

I follow after, if that I may apprehend that for which also I am apprehended of Christ Jesus. — Phil. iii:12.

This text may appear obscure. Unless you have given it some attention already the simple reading of it may not convey any clear thought to your mind. For what can Paul mean when he says, "I follow after, if that I may apprehend that for which I am apprehended of Christ Jesus?" It is certain we cannot understand him until we know the meaning of apprehend as used in this connection, or rather, not until we know the meaning of the word which he used and which is here represented by the word apprehend.

The idea in the word he used, is that of seizing hold upon. I think it clear that when he speaks of his having been apprehended by Christ Jesus he refers to his conversion. You remember that, armed with letters of authority from the Jewish Sanhedrim after he had aided in scattering the church in Jerusalem, he proceeded to Damascus to bring believers bound unto Jerusalem for punishment. And that when he was near that ancient city suddenly there appeared about him a light from heaven, brighter than the noonday sun; and that a voice spoke to him out of the brightness of that light saying, "Saul, Saul, why persecutest thou me?" It was the voice of Christ Jesus. I need not repeat the entire story of Paul's conversion. You are familiar with it all. He was seized upon so suddenly and bound so strongly to Christ that it seemed to him as an arrest, and he speaks of it as having been apprehended by Christ.

But what does he mean by saying that he was striving to apprehend that *for* which he was apprehended? The idea seemed to be that he was earnestly endeavoring to seize hold upon that for which Christ had seized hold upon him; that when Christ laid hold upon him and turned him from his course of bloody persecution it was that he might in him, and through him, accomplish certain purposes, and that these purposes of Christ became the controlling purposes of all his after life. The text, therefore, gives us the secret of Paul's wonderful life and ministry. It contains the key to his life-work. It gives us that which made him the strong, brave man that he was. For all that he endured and did, all that he taught and accomplished, from the moment of his conversion until the day of his death, is to be traced to these purposes in his heart.

Every Christian life should be like Paul's in this. In every conversion Christ has ultimate purposes, and these should become the controlling purposes in each individual life. And so, he exhorts his brethren to be like-minded, to walk by the same rule, to mind the same thing, to be followers together with himself, and to mark them that walk according to his example. The text, therefore, gives us not only the controlling principle in Paul's life, but it gives us at the same time, that which should be the controlling principle in each Christian life. *The purposes of Christ in our conversion should become the controlling purposes in all our after-life.*

What, then, are these ultimate purposes in our conversion? becomes a question of vital importance. For it is evident that if we do not understand what these are we cannot understand the nature of the life to which we have been called.

There is a view of this matter too narrow, too hurtful in

its effect to be received by us, and yet too generally accepted. It is that the only end to which conversion looks is final reception into heaven. And yet if this be true there are certain things in the divine economy I cannot understand. Chief among these I place the fact that God leaves his children in this world after their conversion. But why leave them here after their conversion? Why not take them to heaven at once, if that be the only end had in view? After they have been reconciled by the power of the cross, after they have been forgiven through the merit of its blood, after they have been adopted into the family of God according to his marvellous grace, why delay their admission to heaven. The very fact that God leaves them in this world is a demonstration to my mind that there is something he would accomplish in them and by them in *this* world before he takes them to that. What, then, are some of these things?

1. First, that we may be developed into the image of Christ.

I believe in predestination. I believe in the doctrine of predestination because Paul teaches it; and, for the same reason I believe in just that predestination which he teaches. He teaches that we are predestinated to be conformed to the image of God's Son. But conformity to the image of Christ is conformity to his character; and character is the result of growth. Character is not a gift. We may inherit tendencies which largely determine what our character shall be, but we cannot inherit character itself. That must, from its very nature, be the result of growth. Strictly speaking, we cannot say that an infant has any character. It is born with a bias, and this, in conjunction with its environments, will shape its ultimate character. If, then, character is the result of growth, and if we are to be conformed to the character of Christ, we need time in which to grow.

But, you may ask, does not conversion itself, when genuine, accomplish this? I answer, No. Conversion, however radical it may be is but the turning point in one's life; the journey must be, travelled afterward. It contains but the seeds from which the harvest must grow. In conversion a rectified will ascends the throne and the work of its administration is begun.

The nature of the results accomplished by conversion, and the character of the work to be done after that, may be illustrated by the entrance of the Israelites into the land of promise, and the work they were required to do after this country had been formally turned over to them. When the walls of Jericho had been hurled down by unseen hands, and Ai and many other places had been taken, and many kings had been conquered, the land was divided and assigned to the tribes by lot. It was claimed as Jehovah's land. His banner was set up and the whole country formally given to his people. But though thus given to them, was it fully theirs? No; for remnants of original tribes were still there. These were to be subdued. Again and again did they rise up in rebellion and trouble Israel. Many bloody wars had to be fought before the land was wholly theirs. So is it with us. In conversion the victory is so far gained that the government within is formally turned over to Christ. He is enthroned in the heart. But, though this is done, there yet remains much evil within. Again and again does this rise up in rebellion. Battles are to be fought until every thought and imagination of the heart is brought into subjection to Christ. Christ is to be so completely formed in us that every power of mind and body shall become his willing servant.

I believe that this world, where God leaves us, is the best place for the accomplishing of this work. It is his training school — his drill ground. We find here the discipline we need. Our life is not one of ceaseless, cloudless sunshine. It has its disappointments, its trials, its burdens, its griefs; but if we are properly exercised by these they must contribute to our highest good. In the processes of nature winter has its work as well as spring and summer and autumn; and adversity has its place in the processes of grace.

When the precious metal is taken from the mine could it but feel and speak it would doubtless say, "Oh, how glad I am that you have taken me from the mine — from darkness and solitude and silence. I am so glad to be brought up to the beautiful sunlight and the homes of men." But, by and by, it is cast into the hot furnace and passes under heavy hammers. Then it cries out for pain. It had thought the whole work was done when it was brought up out of the mine. But it goes through the furnace and under the hammer, through the furnace and under the hammer, until at last it comes out of these burnings and beatings, shining with new lustre and stamped with a new image. This is the meaning of our furnaces of sorrow and the heavy strokes of affliction which fall upon us.

There is a kind of pear that will not ripen well on the tree. It is plucked from the bough and laid away in a dark place to become sweet and mellow. Could they but speak how would they cry out for pain when plucked, and how would they moan in sadness when laid away. "Oh, why so cruelly tear us away from the branches to which we cling with tenacious hold? Why take us from the kisses of the sunlight and the caresses of the gentle summer winds and hide us away in solitude and darkness?" And so they moan.

But their days of darkness are numbered and they are brought forth ripe and mellow and luscious. So, it seems to me, God sometimes breaks us from the boughs to which we most firmly hold and places us in the silence and darkness of a great sorrow to enrich us. From these we come forth ripe and mellow in heart.

Let us not forget the exhortation that speaks to us as unto children, saying, "My son, despise not thou the chastening of the Lord, nor faint when thou art rebuked of him; for whom the Lord loveth he chasteneth, and scourgeth every son whom he receiveth. If ye endure chastening God dealeth with you as with sons; for what son is he whom the father chasteneth not? * * * Now, no chastening for the present seemeth to be joyous, but grievous; nevertheless afterward it yieldeth the peaceable fruit of righteousness unto those who are exercised thereby. Wherefore lift up the hands which hang down, and the feeble knees; and make straight paths for your feet, lest that which is lame be turned out of the way; but rather let it be healed."

We are turned to Christ to grow like him. Afflictions aid in the accomplishment of this.

2. A second purpose of our conversion is that we may become co-laborers with God in the accomplishment of his gracious purposes concerning others.

This was prominent in Paul's conversion. In the account of it given in his speech before Agrippa he tells how the Lord said to him, "I have appeared unto thee for this purpose; to make thee a minister and a witness of these things which thou hast seen and of those things in which I will appear unto thee; delivering thee from the people and from the Gentiles unto whom now I send thee, to open their eyes, and to turn them from darkness to light, and from the power of Satan unto God, that they may receive the forgiveness of sins, and inheritance among them who are sanctified by faith that is in me." From the moment of his conversion, Paul acknowledged himself a servant of Jesus Christ, both in speech and in deed.

Our conversion means a call to work for our Master. "Ye are not your own; ye have been bought with a price: therefore glorify God in your body, and in your spirit, which are God's." "Ye are the light of the world," says Christ, and then adds, "Let your light so shine before men, that they may see your good works, and glorify your Father which is in heaven." Light does not exist for itself. It exists to shine, and it shines for others. So the Christian does not live for self, — he lives to shine, and he shines for other's good and God's glory.

What is the meaning of Christ's parable of the laborers in the vineyard, found in the twentieth chapter of Matthew? You remember he says the kingdom of heaven is like a householder who went out early in the morning to hire laborers into his vineyard; and that he went out again about the third hour, and again about the sixth hour, and again about the ninth hour, and finally about the eleventh hour, and that each time he found men idle in the market place and sent them into the vineyard. Now, what does all this teach?

"I know what that teaches," says one, "for I've heard it preached on often. It means that God is debtor unto no man. That is what it means." "No," says another, "I think that Christ therein sets forth the various cases of divine mercy to our race, beginning away back in the early morning of time and extending to the eleventh hour of the world's history when the last case was extended through the gospel. The reckoning at evening represents the final judgment in which all must appear. That is what I think the parable means." "Not exactly this," says another, "for I think the day of the parable represents the day of each individual life, and the different hours the Master went to the market place represents the different calls of the gospel, beginning in youth and extending to old age, and that the man who delayed until the eleventh hour and yet received as much as those who bore the heat and burden of the day is designed to teach us that conversion in old age will meet with as rich a reward as conversion in youth."

Well, whether correct in either point or not, I am sure you are mistaken as to the meaning of the eleventh hour man. *He did not delay, but accepted as soon as called.*

But there is one thought which lies upon the surface of this parable, and yet it seems to have been overlooked. It is this: the great desire of this householder to secure laborers. This is shown, in the first place, by the fact that he went out so early in the morning to seek them; in the second place, by the fact that he went out so frequently during the day; and finally, by the fact that he continued to look for laborers until the day was almost gone. He is represented as being *very* earnest in his search for laborers to go into his vineyard. No doubt he represents Christ, so the parable becomes to us a revelation of Christ's great desire for laborers to enter his vineyard.

Then another point: every call was a call to work. From first to last no other invitation was extended. He might have extended others, but it is significant that he did not. He might have said to some, "This market-place is not a pleasant place to spend your leisure. I have a beautiful vineyard near by. Go into that and rest under the shade of the trees." He might have said that—but he did not. Or he might have said to some of these idlers, "You can enjoy yourselves much more in my vineyard than here, I have luscious grapes, and wine old and mellow. Go into my vineyard and enjoy yourselves." He might have said this — but he did not. Or, again, he might have said to others, "I have sent several men into my vineyard to work to-day, I do not ask you to go into my vineyard to work, but I would be glad to have you take oversight of them and see that they do not idle their time away." He might have said this — but he did not. From first to last, from oldest to youngest, the invitation was to go into his vineyard and work.

This is a practical lesson and much needed. Some in the church seem to think they have been invited to rest. They do nothing. All the burdens of the church are borne by others. In most of our churches a very small percentage of the membership does the work. The majority have come in to rest. Well, I think we would be better off without them, and that they have made a mistake in taking membership with us. In New York there is an organization called "The Church of the Heavenly Rest," and their membership should be in that. We desire this church to be "The Church of Heavenly Work."

Others are looking for enjoyment. Religion with them is something to be enjoyed. That's the prominent idea. They are looking for the good wine, and complain if they do not find it. How many complain that they do not enjoy their religion; how few that they cannot find work! Yet, if you are a Christian, the call you have accepted was a call to work. Christ has issued no other. The last commission he has given is as wide as the church. It is a commission to every member — "*Let him that heareth say,* COME." Have you heard? Then, in some way, you must say, *Come.* If you do not aid in extending the invitation you are unfaithful to your Lord.

An examination of the life and writings of Paul would

show that these two thoughts were the prominent ones in his conception of the Christian calling. The building up manhood and womanhood after the divine pattern was the controlling purpose of his ministry. Before this all other questions appear of little worth. The questions of fasts and feasts, of meats and days which his converts propounded to him were speedily answered by the application of some broad fundamental principle, and then he rises to the ruling thought. All things were to serve that. Ah, how the church has suffered from small minds agitating small questions! Let us cultivate some of the largeness which characterized Paul. Let us be forever done with small questions, and let us give heed to character-building.

Paul thought of himself as a servant. His conversion was to him a call to service. The story of his conversion closes with the statement, "And straightway he preached Christ in the synagogues." No time was lost. No persecutions could turn him back, chains and prisons could not cause him to cease from his work. He delighted to call himself a servant of Jesus Christ. To the elders of the church at Ephesus he said, "Behold, I go bound in spirit to Jerusalem, not knowing the things that shall befall me there; save that the Holy Spirit witnesseth in every city, saying that bonds and afflictions wait for me. But none of these things move me, neither count I my life dear unto myself, so that I might finish my course with joy, and the ministry which I have received of the Lord Jesus." Brave, true man, and faithful servant, may we have something of thy spirit!

3. The third among the purposes which lie enwrapped in our conversion is that we may be glorified in heaven. As Paul's life drew to a close he said, "I am now ready to be offered, and the time of my departure is at hand. I have fought a good fight, I have finished my course, I have kept

the faith. Henceforth there is laid up for me a crown of righteousness, which the Lord, the righteous judge will give me at that day." Through the discipline of life he had made meet for the inheritance of the saints in light. He had been faithful as a servant all during the day of life; and now, in its close he is cheered and comforted by the thought of the inheritance and the promised rest. The full meaning of conversion will then have been realized. Its purposes, in each case, are at least three — *growth, labor, rest.*

I desire to urge you, in conclusion, to take more practical views of the Christian calling. When Christ lays hold upon us by the power of the gospel and turns us to himself the matter does not end there; nor are we to suppose he intends us to dream the day away, looking and longing for the glory and the rest that remain for the people of God. He calls us to growth and to labor for the good of others. The Christian life is full of activity. Let it be so with us. It means growth into Christliness. Let that be our aim. And then when the discipline has been endured and the labor assigned us has been faithfully performed, there will come to us the call of the Master to eternal rest and fadeless glory

CHRISTLESS REFORMATION.

When a strong man armed keepeth his palace, his goods are in peace; but when a stronger than he shall come upon him, and overcome him, he taketh from him all his armor wherein he trusted, and divideth his spoils. * * * When the unclean spirit is gone out of a man, he walketh through dry places, seeking rest; and finding none, he saith, I will return unto my house whence I came out. And when he cometh, he findeth it swept and garnished. Then goeth he and taketh to him seven other spirits more wicked than himself; and they enter in and dwell there; and the last state of that man is worse than the first. — Luke xi.: 21-26

This brings us face to face with a curious question — the question of demoniacal possession. Many other incidents in the gospel narratives bring up the same question, for Christ was frequently met by those under the domination of evil spirits and many of his miracles consisted of their exorcism. Nor is the mention of this possession by evil spirits confined to these records of the evangelists. We find mention of the same thing in cotemporaneous secular history.

The Jews accounted for it in different ways. Some, for instance, regarded it as an affliction sent because of a neglect of the temple services; others regarded it as a result of and a punishment for eating swine's flesh; while others supposed that it come of building houses among tombs or over graves; and yet others, of a more philosophic turn of mind, attributed it to climatic influences, and pointed to the fact that it was more common in the regions about the sea of Galilee than elsewhere.

But, did Christ regard demoniacal possessions as a fact, or did he simply accommodate himself to the popular view and make it do service in his work and teaching? He certainly everywhere speaks of demoniacs, not as persons of merely disordered intellects, nor yet as of persons deeply depraved, but as subjects and thralls of an alien spiritual weight. Was this, however, a case of accommodation? I think not; for he addresses the evil spirit as distinct from the man: "Hold thy peace, and come out of him." And even in his private conversations with his disciples, he uses similar language, saying to them, "This kind goeth not out but by prayer and fasting." If the popular idea was erroneous it was an error too grave to have been adopted by Christ. It is also radically opposed to his character as a teacher of truth to suppose that he could adopt it and act upon it. I must conclude, both from the language which he employed and from the manner in which he treated these cases, that he regarded the possession as real.

Enough, however, of these curious questions. Yet I could not enter upon the practical use I propose making of the text until I had given them some attention.

· I. These demoniacs may be considered as in some sense typical of the morally depraved; and their healing may serve to illustrate Christ's work in saving men.

In the demoniac there seemed to be at least two personalities in one body, — the evil spirit and the man's own spirit. The evil spirit held the reins: it sat upon the throne. It would speak with his tongue, and controlled every member of his body. It chained his will and hurried him on toward the precipice. Now and then the man appeared to be in his right mind — he would come to himself. But it was for only a short time. The evil spirit would again trample his own spirit into subjugation and play havoc. As between his own and the evil spirit we find first one in the ascendency and then the other. When the evil spirit ruled he was ruined; when his own ruled he was right — he was his true self.

So of wicked men. In all men there are, as it were, two natures — good and evil. What any individual man may be morally depends upon which rules. For in what do men differ, as to morals, but in this? Good and evil are in each. There is none so good but that evil is in him, and none so bad but that good is in him. In what, then, does the wicked differ from the good? Not that one has a single faculty or gift or organ wanting in the other. Only in this do they differ — in the wicked the evil is regnant; in the other, the good. In every man there are the basilar passions and instincts. These belong at the bottom. If they come to the top and sit on the throne he must be a bad man. If the good is on the throne — if he lives out of his best moments and from his holiest promptings — he must be a good man.

What, then, is needed to make the wicked become righteous? You answer, they need conversion. Yes, but that word has been used so long, and often so roughly in theological warfare, that it has lost its freshness and much of its meaning. Its vitality has been crushed out of it. Not *con*-version, but *in*-version, is what is needed. Place the spiritual on the throne and the carnal on the footstool. Every faculty, every power remains, but their government has been changed.

This Christ does for us by his gospel. He is the stronger man who enters in and strips the usurper of his armor. He casts down the evil and brings into captivity every thought and imagination of the heart to the good. He works a moral revolution. Every faculty and power remains, but their uses are changed. It is for this reason that we so often find the actively, positively wicked make the most useful Christians. See Paul. He was full of energy in his wickedness, he was strong in the service of evil. When the change occurred within him he became the most useful of all the servants of Christ. His was a change of masters within. His best nature, through the aid of Christ, rose to the throne, and this turned his life into a new path.

II. But this is not all. Each part of the text is the counterpart of the other, and by taking the two parts together we have an illustration of the fact that *only the reformation which takes in Christ can hope to be enduring.* For it matters not how thorough the change for good, called conversion, may be, we will be subject to subsequent attacks of evil. Luke tells us that when the evil spirit came back he found the house swept and garnished, and Matthew gives us the additional word, full of significance, it was *empty.* This very emptiness invited a return.

For some reason the evil had disappeared for awhile. It may have been fear of consequences or the rebellious uprising of good — we know not just how it was produced. But however produced we know there was no strong man within to prevent return. The house was empty, though swept and garnished.

Thus some men reform. They say, "The life I'm leading is too bad. I must reform. My vices must be given up." So he begins to sweep. Here goes drinking. Here goes profanity. Here go revellings. Here goes churlishness at home. Here goes a great cobweb filled with dead flies of sensuality. How he sweeps! Then he garnishes the walls. He covers them with bright promises, and adorns them with good resolutions. "What an improvement," says the world. Yes, but the house is empty. No strong man, with his armor, dwelling within to keep it. This emptiness invites a tenant. The evil spirit, with seven others even worse than he, returns and enters. What a picture of negative goodness — of Christless reformation! The evil driven out, but no strong positive good to fill the place made vacant.

Were we to desire to remove the dead leaves from the

branches of the old conservative oak, it would be a tedious undertaking to climb among these branches and clip off these leaves, one at a time. That is not nature's way of removing them. Every spring these dead leaves are removed — but how? When the days grow longer, as the sun moves up along a higher pathway, and the soft breath of the south wind breathes through the branches, a current of new life begins to flow. It moves out through the branches causing the tender buds of a new life to swell and the old dead leaves to fall away. This is God's way.

So was it with you when the love of Christ within your heart began to control your life. You had tried reformation before, but it was a negative, a Christless reformation. You had selected this fault or that vice, and said, "I will cut it off. I will cease from this evil way. I will cast it out and will sweep and garnish and purify myself." But your success was only partial and temporary. The evil returned and found you empty and hungering for it. It came in with increased power. Often you had been brought to the very point of accepting Christ. Yet you did not consent to admit him to your heart. Finally, under a powerful appeal, you surrendered. You came before the people, a penitent believer, and confessed the faith of your heart in Christ Jesus as God's Son and your Savior. You were baptized. From the baptismal grave you arose to walk in newness of life. Happy in your new love you go on your way rejoicing. After a few days you miss this fault, and this, and this. What has become of them? You formed no specific resolution with reference to each; you did not consciously cut it off. Christ formed in you did the work. There was an expulsive power in your new affection. You shed your vices as the tree shed its leaves. A new inspiration gave you a new life.

There is a profound philosophy in the text when considered thus. I wish to further apply it.

1. First, to preaching. We denounce specific sins. We disclaim against the unworthiness and evanescence of earthly indulgences as objects of affection, and then wonder that our efforts to reform men from worldliness and wickedness is not more successful. We seek to cast out evil without implanting and strengthening its opposite good. We undertake to sweep and garnish and yet leave the heart empty. A study of the wants of human nature, and of the history of its renovation, will show that this process is defective. If we would successfully and permanently transform men it must be done by renewing their minds. If we would expel unworthy affections and lusts it must be by implanting affections nobler and stronger. We need to quicken a new love until it becomes so full and strong and dominant that it will by its very strength expel the old.

Dr. Chalmers has truly said, "The ascendant power of a second affection will do what no exposition, however forcible of the folly and worthlessness of the first, ever could effectuate." And it is the same in the great world. We shall never be able to arrest any of the leading pursuits by a naked demonstration of their vanity. It is quite in vain to think of stopping one of these pursuits in any way else, but by stimulating to another. In attempting to bring a worldly man, intent and busied with the prosecution of his objects, to a dead stand we have not merely to encounter the charm which he annexes to these objects — we have to encounter the pleasure which he feels in the very prosecution of them. We must address to the eye of his mind another object, with a charm powerful enough to dispossess the first of its influences, and to engage him in some other prosecution as full of interest and hope and congenial activity as the former. It is this which stamps an impotency on all moral and pathetic declamation about the insignificance of the world. If to be without desire and without exertion altogether is a state of violence and discomfort, then the present desire, with its correspondent train of exertion, is not to be got rid of simply by destroying it. It must be by substituting another desire, and another line or habit of exertion in its place." In short, the process of gospel reformation is according to the law of substitution. One affection is displaced by the substitution of its opposite and stronger affection.

We need to put Christ into the heart as the strong man, well-armed, and able to keep it. He will cast out every evil and unclean thing. As he drove the cattle and the money-changers from the temple and purified it, so will he drive out evil thought, unholy purposes, unworthy affections from our hearts. Christ formed in the heart makes reformation natural, thorough and permanent.

2. This principle finds an important field for its application in the matter of church government and development.

Some are saying we need a stronger, more compact and authoritative organization of our churches. This is the remedy they have to suggest for almost every trouble. They hold that although the New Testament churches may have had the simple congregational form, and although that may have met the demands of the situation then, such a form is not sufficient now. We need something stronger. Well, this may all be true; but I don't believe it. Yet I am no great stickler for the details of any particular *form* of church government. I believe the Scriptures leave some room for the exercise of sanctified common sense in such matters. I cannot, however, agree with those who think that a modification of church organization and government is our great need in church life. Certainly, something is needed, however.

Others say we need more thorough discipline, and by more thorough discipline they usually mean excommunication. They would improve our churches by a kind of ecclesiastical police regulation, and garnish it with exact observances. They would keep the church pure by the outward enforcement of rules, and the prompt exclusion of every offender. Well, it cannot be denied that the church should be purer than it is, and that wisely administered discipline would contribute toward this end. But let us not suppose that the church is for the perfect only. It is a hospital, rather — a place for healing and for help. Do not be in too great haste to cast weak men and women out. What would you think if one should exclude from a hospital all but those of sound health and able bodies? In my judgment it is not by any modification of church government, nor by a more rigid enforcement of outward restraints that the vital wants in our churches are to be met. *We need more religion. We need more of the mind of Christ in us. We need to have him formed within us, so that he shall sway our hearts and direct our lives.* A friend of mine once said, "If the New Testament has made any mistake in the matter of church government it is in taking it for granted that churches of Christ would be easily governed — that they would really need but little outward and formal government." This remark may appear simple, but it is wise — for the New Testament does not undertake to govern by outward restraints, but by inward inspirations, by broad principles implanted in hearts, by lofty motives, by the supremacy of love. Let these be in our hearts and a thousand problems of church government are solved, and a thousand difficulties vanish as the mist.

This principle finds numerous applications, but I have not

time to point them out this evening. Follow up in your own thinking, the line suggested. Wherever men are to be reclaimed from overmastering sins, wherever the power of dominant evil is to be broken, wherever iniquity is to be uprooted, wherever a work of moral reformation is needed, wherever society needs purifying, wherever temples need cleansing, *bring in Christ.* His presence is purifying, and he is the strong man able to resist successfully the attacks of returning evil. Without him the work must be difficult and uncertain.

III. One other item remains to be presented, and though a dark, sad one, it adds force to what has been already said, " The last state of that man " — the man whose reformation was only negative, and which left him empty — " the last state of that man was worse than the first." His reformation was followed by apostasy. The relapse was worse than the first sickness. Evil returned with greater power. So have I seen it in many cases, and the reasons are not far to seek.

(1.) A weakening process is going on in himself by these relapses. His will loses its strength. Overcome again and again it becomes enfeebled. He loses confidence in himself and the inspiration which comes from the hope of success.

(2.) There is a growing process of evil. Some plants when cut off spring up with a more vigorous growth. So when evils spring up again after they have been cut down they appear more vigorous. A Christless, abortive reformation gives vice an advantage.

(3.) The influences from without which led him to cleanse his ways are losing their power. His sensibilities become deadened. That to which he once responded does not touch him now. One can become past feeling, and have to be given over to hardness of heart.

How was Christ speaking to the facts in the case when he said, "The last state of that man is worse than the first!"

To you who are fighting against evil, and besetting sins, struggling in vain to be free, I come with a message of sympathy and help. Do not undertake to overcome Satan single-handed. Do not strive to cast out evil, leaving your heart empty. Christ stands at the door, knocking for admission. Let him in, and as rays of light drive out darkness so will the brightness of his pure presence cleanse your heart and reform your life. Open wide your heart and say, "Dear Savior, come in and deliver me from the bondage of sin; come in and nurture all good, come in and drive out as thou didst drive out the polluting things from the temple of old. I am weak. I need thee to make me strong. Come in, O thou mighty Savior, come in." So welcome Christ to your hearts and you shall be strong and victorious.

THE FRUIT OF THE SPIRIT.

But the fruit of the Spirit is love, joy, peace, long-suffering, gentleness, goodness, faith, meekness, temperance: against such there is no law. — Gal. v: 22-23.

Fruit signifies the fullness of growth; it marks the limit of development. First the blade, then the stalk, then the ear, after that the full corn in the ear, and after that — nothing. You may pluck the seed again and it will spring up, pass through the same stages of growth and reach the same end. This is the process both in nature and in grace.

When, therefore, Paul speaks of the *fruit* of the Spirit I understand that he means the fullness of growth under the multiform working of the Holy Spirit. It is not my purpose this morning to deal with the ways in which the Spirit does this work. We know that the Scriptures teach that he is engaged in our recovery from sin, — that he teaches, comforts, strengthens, sanctifies, — and this simple fact is enough for us to know and recognize just now. Paul is describing the full outcome of all he does, in whatever way he may accomplish it, when he speaks in the text of the *fruit* of the Spirit. Just as we would speak of the fruit of a man's labors, meaning by that the fullest, highest results of all he has done, so Paul speaks of the fruit of the Spirit, meaning the largeness of growth and development under the ministry of the Holy Spirit.

Has it never arrested your attention that Paul used the singular instead of the plural in this connection? He does not say, as he is usually quoted as saying, the fruits, but the fruit. When, in the verses just before, he gives us a long dark catalogue of vice, he uses the plural, saying, the works of the flesh. Why not use the plural here and say the fruits of the spirit? This appears only the more remarkable when we notice he mentions nine different things immediately afterward. The fruit of the Spirit is love, joy, peace, long-suffering, etc. There is a remarkable unity in his view of these matters. In his conception of them there was a striking oneness. How do you account for this?

It seems to me the most rational and simple explanation is that he looked upon well developed Christian characters as the fruit, and these things, named in the text, as its characteristic qualites. Should I point to a tree and say the fruit of this tree is rich and red and sweet and mellow you, would not understand that the tree bore four different fruits, but would readily understand that fruit was one and these were the characteristic qualities of that fruit. So I understand Paul here. The fruit of the Spirit is fully developed Christtian character, while love, joy, peace, long-suffering, etc., are its characteristic qualities. Or, to put the thought in another form, he does for full-grown Christian manhood what phrenologists undertake to do — he reads its character and then indicates it, as it were, on a chart. Here is a man long under the guidance and power of the Spirit. His whole character has been moulded and fashioned by the Holy Spirit. Paul examines him and says, "Love is strong, joy is deep and full, peace, long-suffering, gentleness and all the other qualities are well developed. This character is the fruit of the Spirit." This view of the passage, suggests some things concerning the nature of Christian life which I desire to present, and which I trust may be helpful to you.

It presents a model after which to pattern our lives and a

standard by which to measure our Christian growth. The very fact that it presents full-grown manhood in Christ Jesus gives it these important functions.

It is to be feared that exhortations to grow in grace often fail to accomplish any definite good simply because of the vague conception conveyed by them. To many it means religious ecstasy. To grow in grace is to have the emotions strongly moved. If they can work themselves up to a frenzy of religious enthusiasm, if they can be borne above the plane of ordinary feeling until their brows seem fanned by the breezes of Paradise and they hear the strains of heavenly anthems, they vainly imagine they are growing in grace. I do not speak against deep feelings. I do not object to emotion, strong and full. I would that our religious emotions were more deeply moved. Growth may be helped by such experiences; but they are not growth. Often they are like balloon ascensions, elevating, exhilerating and transporting, yet frequently followed by collapse and disaster. Growth in grace is something more gradual, more practical, more lasting than emotion. It is the development of character along certain lines, according to a given model, and under the inspiration of the gospel motives. Christian growth is more than religious ecstasy, although that ecstasy may partake of some permanency. It is an increase in the qualities of character named in the text until they become the strongly marked features of our character.

Few things can help us so much in right living or contribute so effectually to our Christian growth as to have a clear conception of what God would have us become in Christ. If you have never seriously asked yourself the question what, above all things, would he have me be in character, I suggest it to you as worthy of your earnest thought. What is the ultimate aim of all training, what the purpose of all instruction, of all examples, of all promises? Peter plainly gives the practical use of all divine promises when he says, "Whereby are given unto us exceeding great and precious promises that by these we might be made partakers of the divine nature." The features of character presented in the text are the ones which should appear in our lives. They mark full growth. The more we have of these elements harmoniously combined within us the more of divine manhood do we have. It is a character in which love is the central principle, joy is bright with heavenly radiance, peace flows as a river, long-suffering is without murmuring, and gentleness, goodness, faith, meekness and temperance are manifest to all. A perfect man is Christ Jesus.

The text furnishes a standard by which to measure our attainments in the Christian life. We need a true and worthy standard. There are unworthy ones, and we are in danger of deceiving ourselves by them. To some it is soundness of doctrine. They measure themselves by church standards. If they clearly conceive and fully believe what their church accepts and teaches as true they are satisfied. The standard they recognize is the standard of orthodoxy. Not what they are, but what they believe is the substance of their religion. They vainly imagine they are right, because they profess to believe that which is declared to be true. I hold it to be one of the darkest blots resting upon the history of the church that it has in so many cases exalted subscription to doctrine above uprightness and purity of character. The questions which have divided the church and have led to excommunication and persecution have often been concerning matters which should have been treated as matters of indifference. And it is a sad fact that in our own day the faithful adherent to the creed hides a multitude of sins by this fidelity, while the so-called heretic, though devoted to Christ and the highest good of his fellow-man is excommunicated and anathematized. I hold that the brightest fruit of Christianity is character rather than creed, and that this fact should receive the practical recognition which it legitimately demands. Soundness of heart, the orthodoxy of purpose, the rectitute of life, the nobility of character, have not received the consideration which they justly merit. I would not underestimate the importance of right thinking, but I would exalt the worth of right living. Religion is life. Its product is character.

There is another delusion which I fear will prove the ruin of some. It is the idea that church connection, church membership, is the decisive point. The first question with them is, "Of what church are you a member?" The answer to that decides the whole case. They seem to think that the Lord estimates according to this, and that according to it he will judge us in the last day. With them it comes practically to this — if you are a member of the right religious body you are all right, but if you are not a member of that body you are not a Christian. Their chief concern is to establish the claims of their ecclesiastical organization. They aim above all things to demonstrate that it is evangelical and orthodox and apostolic, etc. Well, it may be all that — it may be all you claim for it — and you may be enrolled as a member of it, but that should not be enough to satisfy you. Do you not remember that in one of the parables of our Lord we read of a certain man who was in the midst of a multitude where all were accepted but himself? He had not on the wedding garment. The inspection there was personal. So will it be when our Master comes to reckon. I pray you place high above intellectual orthodoxy, above church connection, even above Christian doing, the thought of right character. Three verbs can express all of personal religion —

to believe, to do, to be. Their natural sequence, as well as their grade of worth, is found in the order in which I have named them. From believing we rise to doing, and from these develop into being. That is character.

Suppose I am a Christian. I should grow. But in what directions? What must be developed in order to make me a better Christian than I am? I place myself by this fully developed christian character which Paul delineates in the text to learn what is wanting in my character. Look upon that The first thing which arrests your attention is love. It was not by chance that Paul mentioned it first. Am I deficient in love — in breadth, in depth, in richness, in strength, in sweetness? How is it with my love as a Christian? It will not satisfy the full demands made upon my heart to say that I love only those who belong to the circle of my personal friends, or to limit my love to the membership of my own church. Christian love in its fulness must be Christ-like love. It must extend to all classes, reaching up to the highest and descending to the lowest. It must overleap denominational boundaries. It must sweep out in its catholic spirit until it reaches all ranks. It must become a strong, genuine philanthrophy. I must enlarge my affections until I love man as man, without regard to nation, creed or condition. My heart must be knit to every one who loves the Lord Jesus in sincerity, although, in my judgment, many of them may be in error. Even the unbelivers, and even my own personal enemies, should I have any, must be the objects of my love. My Master has taught me to love my enemies, and to pray for them who despitefully use me and persecute me, and he has enforced this teaching by his own example when upon the cross he prayed for his murderers.

I am not afraid of loving my fellows with a love too great. I do not feel there is danger of enlarging my heart too much.

Of all sins for which men will stand condemned in the last day — and the catalogue of these sins is a long one — I am sure there will not be found one to rest under the crushing weight of the divine sentence because he loved his fellow-man too much. God has manifested his love toward the vilest. He so loved the world that he gave his only-begotten Son that whosoever believeth in him might not perish, but might have eternal life. That is the pattern for us; for if God so loved us we ought to love one another. When measured by the divine standard who is there who can honestly say he comes up to the full measure of its requirements? We need more love everywhere — in society, in our homes, in our churches — everywhere. Down with hate. Down with party spirit. Down with religious bigotry. Religion has been blighted by it; the world has been cursed by it. Let sweet, bright love shine out and heal the bitterness of our race. Let us commend the religion of Christ, by showing to the world the spirit of Christ. Let us grow in love, for the fruit of the Spirit is love.

When we turn and look again upon that picture of character sketched in the text, what next do we find? Surprising! The next is joy. It is surprising because it is supposed that one mark of sainthood is sadness. Did you ever notice that all the pictures of saints are sad-faced pictures? And, in your childhood, do you not remember that those whom you were taught to regard as saintly were sad? And their hymns were lamentations. "This world's a howling wilderness," was popular with these sad souls, and they contributed toward making this world a howling wilderness by their howlings in it. I remember one of this type. He was an elder in one of our churches. He would speak in the Wednesday evening prayer-meeting whenever opportunity offered and it seemed to me these opportunities were frequent.

His exhortations were not reviving. They were fearfully depressing. He poured forth words of lamentation. The people seemed too bright. Frequently did he remind us that the Scriptures say of our Savior that he wept, but that they nowhere say that he ever smiled. Leaving us to infer that the proper thing for us to do was to weep, and that the wrong thing would be to smile!

Now, while it is said with touching brevity and pathos that when our Savior stood by the grave of his friend Lazarus, with the two sisters sorrowing by his side that " Jesus wept;" and again when he paused upon the western slope of the hill that overlooks Jerusalem, and saw with prophetic vision the Roman army gathering around it, its walls battered down, its temple destroyed and its people scattered, that he lifted up his voice and wept, and while these manifestations of his sympathy are precious to me beyond all price, yet I know there was something bright about my Master. Had I no other indication of this the simple fact that the children were fond of him would be enough. They are not fond of the sadly sanctified. They dread them with an inborn shrinking. For this reason they have a proverbial fear of preachers. Their sanctimonious mein affrights them. Yet they were fond of my Savior. There was a brightness in his face because there was joy in his heart. Although he is called a man of sorrows and was acquainted with grief, yet it was for the joy that was set before him that he endured the pain of the cross.

The joy of the Christian is not the evanescent joy of the world. The flash and the sparkle of earthly joy is for only a moment. The dazzling glare of fire-works may for a moment seem to put the modest stars to the blush. They seem pale for awhile in its light. But its light goes out and the stars shine on. All earth-born joys soon perish, but the heaven-born abide. If any, in the all this world, have reason to abound in joy it is the Christian. Reconciled, forgiven, adopted, environed with precious promises and helped by divine grace, well may he rejoice. His Father reigns and makes all things work together for his good.

We need more joy. Let our songs be peans. Let our light shine. And there is no light which can shine so far as the light of joy. In the night of sorrow, in prison and chains, when the wintry winds of adversity sweep about us and we are tossed by the tempest, let notes of joy be heard above the voice of the storm. Rejoice in the Lord always; and again I say, rejoice.

And next among the features well-marked in the face of Paul's saint is peace. Not simply that the Christian seeks peace and pursues it, but a blessed peace reigns within, so deep, so sweet that it has transfigured that face. The Christian dwells in the chamber of peace. He avoids contention. He shall not strive, neither shall his voice be heard in the street. Though storms may disturb the quiet of the surface there is an undisturbed peace in his soul. I have seen the ocean in a storm. White-crested waves ran high. Great ships were tossed as a feather. The brave hearts of sailors grew faint. And yet, beneath the tempest-lashed surface were depths untouched, unmoved by the raging storm. So is it with the Christian. His heart rests in God and he is at peace. His troubles pass as a shadow that falls from a passing cloud. Worry is unworthy his profession. He knows in whom he has believed, and is persuaded that he is able to keep that which he has committed to him. Need I say we all need more of the spirit of peace?

But I cannot linger. Take long-suffering and gentleness and goodness and faith and meekness and temperance — take each one by itself, and see if you are not wanting in each.

Then strive to grow in each until, fully developed, they shall be harmoniously combined and be manifest as the well-marked features of your character. Let your character be the rich and ripe and mellow fruit of the Spirit of God.

The next thought I present is this: The means or instrumentalities by which fruit is produced are not to be esteemed on their own account, but are to be valued as fruit producers. All fruit is produced by means. Even that which seems to spring spontaneous from the earth is no exception. The growing twig, the tree, the branches, the blossoms, in short, all that goes before the fruit are the means by which the fruit itself is produced. They are not to be esteemed on their own account. Their value lies in the fact that they produce fruit. What would you think of the wisdom of one who would plant an orchard or a vineyard and carefully tend it year after year with no fruit to reward him for all this? His orchard is for the fruit; his vineyard is for the vintage. If they produce nothing, they are worth nothing.

So the fruit of the Spirit is produced by the use of means, and their value is to be found in the fruit they produce. They are usually called means of grace. They have been ordained to help us. Yet, the mistake is made of regarding them as of intrinsic value. This was the mistake of the Pharisees. They were careful in observing all requirements. They were slaves to them. They did not look beyond these means to the end they were designed to accomplish. When they charged our Savior with violating he Sabbath, his answer contains a principle broader in its application than to the specific question named, — "The Sabbath was made for man and not man for the Sabbath." The Sabbath is the servant of man and not man the servant of the Sabbath. It was ordained, and it exists for his good. So of all ordinances, of all commandments, of all institutions. They exist for man's higher good. In the purposes of the divine Father thoughts of his children have shaped all revelations he has given. Apostles and prophets and evangelists and pastors and the church itself have been given for the perfecting of the saints. It is a sad mistake when we reverse the divine plan. Were we to judge from the history of the church we might conclude that these things were given that they might furnish subject for controversy. Instead of using them as helps we dispute and contend about them until they sometimes seem almost hindrances.

Suppose I had been born a genius, and my talent lay in the direction of the fine arts. Suppose, also, I inherit a vast fortune. I avail myself of every opportunity to improve my talent. After spending much time in the galleries of the old world I return with a rare and beautiful collection of art. In order to develop the taste of the people, I rent a large hall on the second floor, place my collection there, and give notice that the exhibition is perfectly free. A few days after this I visit the place to see how well my entertainment is patronized. I find the stairway leading up to the hall densely crowded. But the crowd does not seem to be moving up, and its standing there hinders others who would. When I come nearer I find they are engaged in controversy, bitter controversy, concerning the stairway. Each expresses his opinion, which is met by an antagonistic view. What folly, what shame, what manifest lack of appreciation of the rare treat provided. Contending about the stairway! For what was it made but to be used so that the people might go up higher and higher, until they reached the place prepared for them? Yet, shamefully great as is this folly, it does not equal that of those who, instead of using the means of grace provided to lift us to a higher plane, turn them into subject of bitter controversy, Take these appointed means and use them. Go higher. By them climb nearer God. Make them your servants. They were designed for that. They are only helps — wisely chosen, divinely appointed — yet they are only helps. Use them as such, and so become richer in experience and larger in all the elements of a Christly character. Let them be but the instrumentalities by which the fruit of the Spirit is produced in you.

I pray that this fruit may abound; that branches may be wide-spread and heavy-laden. I have seen some trees so large and beautiful that their branches reached over the outer wall and bended under the weight of the mellow fruit. The dusty wayside traveller could pluck of the fruit and eat, resting in the shade, and then go on his way refreshed. So may this church be. May it be a source of comfort and help even to the stranger who pauses for a moment in its midst and then pursues his journey. I have seen men and women so rich in grace and in all goodness that their presence was like a benediction, the memory of them like the memory of a sweet song. As the shadow of Peter had healing in it, so there goes forth from these an influence as gentle as that falling shadow and as full of healing. May we become so full of grace that we shall be full of healing.

CHRIST'S LESSONS FROM THE VINEYARD.

I am the true vine, and my Father is the husbandman. Every branch in me that beareth not fruit he taketh away; and every branch that beareth fruit, he purgeth it, that it may bring forth more fruit. Now ye are clean through the word I have spoken unto you. Abide in me, and I in you. As the branch cannot bear fruit of itself, except it abide in the vine; no more can ye, except ye abide in me. I am the vine, ye are the branches. He that abideth in me, and I in him, the same bringeth forth much fruit; for without me ye can do nothing. If a man abide not in me, he is cast forth as a branch and is withered; and men gather them, and cast them into the fire and they are burned. John xv: 1-6.

The emblem of the Jewish theocracy was the vine. David sang of the chosen nation, "Thou hast brought a vine out of Egypt; thou hast cast out the heathen and planted it." And Jeremiah, speaking in the name of the Lord, said, "I had planted a noble vine, wholly a right seed; how art thou turned to the degenerate plant of a strange vine unto me." Josephus tells us that when Herod enlarged and adorned the temple in Jerusalem, he placed a golden vine, hung thick with clusters of grapes over the entrance gate. Some suppose that Christ beholding this in the moonlight said, "I am the *true* vine."

As the words of the text were spoken immediately after he had partaken of the last supper with his disciples, others have supposed that the juice of the fruit of the vine suggested this beautiful imagery to the mind of Christ. The disciples had united in partaking of it, thus confessing their need of his blood and their mutual dependence upon him. As the vital current which flows through the vine gives life to its branches and makes them fruitful, so Christ taught, "I am the vine, ye are the branches; he that abideth in me, and I in him, the same bringeth forth much fruit; for without me ye can do nothing."

Still a third supposition is this: That the symbol was suggested by what they saw as they went from the room where the Lord's Supper was instituted, across the Kedron, to the garden of his agony. The hillsides were covered with vineyards. The branches which had been cut off were dry, and men were gathering and burning them. These fires attracted his attention. Christ seizes upon this scene to teach them the solemn lesson of the vineyard. "If a man abide not in me, he is cast forth as a branch and is withered. They are gathered, cast into the fire and are burned."

This last supposition, upon the whole, appears to me to be the most reasonable.

The principal features of this figure are simple and easily understood. They are these: the vine, the branches, and the husbandman. Christ has so clearly interpreted them that there can be no doubt as to their meaning.

I am the vine, in that, as all the nourishment of each branch and tendril passes through the main stalk, so I am the source of all real strength and grace to my disciples. I am their leader and teacher, and I impart to them all they need for life and holiness and fruitfulness. I am the *true* vine, in the sense of real and genuine. I really and truly give what is emblematically represented by the vine. The earthly is a type of the heavenly. That which the earthly vine is figuratively as a symbol, that which the people of Israel was as a type, Christ is in radical essentiality. He is the trunk-root of spiritual life and fruit.

When he says, "Ye are the branches," he refers to the individual Christians. He does not here speak of "branches of the church," for the very good and sufficient reason that he did not intend his church to be divided as it is in our day. In no place in the word of God do we find such an expression as "the branches of the church." The language is not in the Scriptures, because in the apostolic day the church was united. How sadly in this do we differ from the divine ideal of the church. Believers are the branches, and they are so called, because of their close connection with Christ and their dependence upon him.

My Father is the husbandman. That is, he is the proprietor. The entire vineyard with all its fruitage belongs to him. He has the care of the vine with all its branches. By planting, by watering, by pruning, he gives the increase.

How strikingly the text, therefore, places before us, Christ, his people and God; under the figure of the vine, its branches, and the husbandman! But not simply for the beauty of the figure did he employ it. His purpose was practical. There are lessons enwrapped in this of vital importance, and it is my purpose to point out, briefly and simply, some of these for our profit.

1. We are taught, in the first place, the nature of the Christian life. It springs from union with Christ. It is not moral development and refinement independent of Christ. Man may be morally good, to a degree, but I care not how good he may think himself, or how good he may really be, if he be not engrafted into Christ, he is not a Christian. Not only to build character, but to build it according to a given model, and by the inspiration of certain moral forces, is the purpose of Christ. He unites each branch to himself, not in appearance only, but by the inward current of hidden life.

Paul expresses this truth without a figure in speaking of his own life. "I am crucified with Christ: nevertheless I live;

yet not I, but Christ liveth in me; and the life which I now live in the flesh I live by the faith of the Son of God."

The Christian life is a hidden life. The difference between a Christian and an upright, honest man of the world is not so much an outward difference as an inward. You see them, simply as business men see each other, and you notice no difference. It is not until you go down to the fountain of life, not until you penetrate the heart and learn the hidden springs of action, that you find the essential difference between them. The one is honest from policy, from worldly motives; the other is honest from higher motives. The inspiration to his life is faith in Jesus Christ. He has been engrafted into the living vine and that union is his life.

This union is not simply a formal one, such as many seem to suppose. For they appear to regard this engrafting of a man into Christ as a process quite as formal and materialistic as engrafting a literal branch into a literal vine. Certain specified things are to be accepted as true, and certain appointments are to be observed and the work is done. Instead of this, however, the union is formed through a living faith. You may subscribe to every truth in the Bible and obey every ordinance, but if you have not vital faith in Jesus Christ you are not by all these made a living, fruit-bearing Christian. Nor is this union simply a covenant relation. It is this in part; but this is not the whole of it. The entire body of the Jewish people stood in covenant relationship with God, but we know that many among these were not really and vitally joined unto God. If the force and meaning of marriage is understood to be simply a civil compact or covenant it is unworthy the holy name of marriage. Between the true husband and wife, love and mutual confidence make them one, in a sense in which no civil covenant can. Men united by a business contract, a written agreement, which forms them into a partnership, and they are one in the eyes of the law, so far as their business is concerned, but they are not, as to their lives, vitally joined. A covenant cannot of itself join two persons in vital union. Only mutual personal attachment can do that.

Then, too, let us remember that this engrafting into Christ is a purely spiritual matter. Faith is that which so joins the believer to Christ that the life-current flows from Christ into him, and life flows from the vine into each of the branches. There may be mystery in this, but mystery is not necessarily mysticism. All life is mysterious. Yet every true Christian knows that faith in the Lord Jesus lies at the basis of all his spiritual life and enjoyment. He knows that it forms the bond of union between him and the fountain of his Christian life. This is that which distinguishes Christian life from the simply moral life.

2. We are reminded, in the next place, that all the fruit produced by the immense expenditure of heaven is to be found in individual Christian lives. The fruit grows on the branches and not on the main stem. So the fruit is to be seen in the believer and not in Christ. If the world is to be fed and made glad it must be by Christ's working through Christians. We are the avenues through which blessings flow to the world.

It is a fact, which every careful reader of the New Testament Scriptures must recognize, that Christ deals with the world through his people. The gospel is to be made known, with the fulness of its blessing, through them. The light must be reflected from them. By them he feeds the hungry, clothes the destitute, furnishes shelter for the homeless, cares for the widow and orphan, nurses the sick, comforts the sorrowing, and bestows multiform benefactions. The life current from him must bear fruit. It generates within each believer that which manifests itself normally in fruitage.

If we reflect upon the immense expenditures of heaven we can begin to understand the obligation resting upon us to be fruitful. The liberal gifts bestowed from the beginning of time, when placed together, form the weight of that obligation. We are not our own; we have been bought with a price; we should *therefore* glorify God in our body and spirit which are his. You remember that once, as he went into the city, he saw a fig tree full of life and with the appearance of fruit, and that when he drew near seeking fruit he found nothing but leaves. The tree withered under his sentence of condemnation. Appearance will not do. There must be fruit.

3. The fruit must partake of the nature of the vine. This is the third lesson. Christ himself has said, "Ye shall know them by their fruits. Do men gather grapes of thorns, or figs of thistles?" When James and John would have called down fire upon the Samaritan village his rebuke was, "Ye know not what manner of spirit ye are of. For the Son of man has not come to destroy men's lives, but to save them." It is implied in this that that they should have had the spirit of Christ, and should, out of it, do Christly works.

If, therefore, we desire to know with what works we should adorn our profession, we have but to look to the life our Savior lived. His was a life of sympathetic helpfulness. He found want and ignorance and sorrow about him and he ministered to it all. He did good. His miracles are manifestations of goodness quite as much as they are of power. He gave sight to blind eyes, and health to diseased bodies, and food to hungry men and women. His godlike works were witnesses to his claims of a divine mission. When the two disciples of John came from their master to Jesus asking whether he was the one who was to come, or they should look for another, you remember he referred to his works for answer. So must we sustain our claim to be his disciples. If our religion does not lead us to fruitfulness in Christly works it is not genuine. Profession by itself is worse than nothing. It is hypocrisy. Psalm-singing is not sufficient evidence that you are a Christian. Attendance at church is not enough. Fruit, Christly fruit, is the evidence of our union with Christ.

4. We are taught also an important lesson here concerning the ministry of suffering. "Every branch that beareth fruit he purgeth it that may bear more fruit." The purgings or prunings here mentioned are to be referred to the providences of the Father. Without these prunings the branches will not be fruitful.

A man owned a vineyard which produced no fruit. At last he employed one, skilled in the culture of the grape, to care for this vineyard. A few days afterward he called to see what this vine-dresser was doing, and was grieved to see his vineyard ruined, as he supposed; for it had been so thoroughly pruned it seemed to be destroyed. But when the time for grapes came they appeared in great abundance. He learned the value of pruning.

The problem of human suffering is one of the oldest problems in human thinking. It is natural to suppose it means divine displeasure. When Job was afflicted his friends insisted that his afflictions were sent upon him as a punishment for his sins. Some came to Christ one day, telling him of those Gallileans whose blood Pilate had mingled with their sacrifices. They regarded this as a signal judgment for sins. So the heathen thought when the viper came out of the fire and fastened itself to Paul's hand. And we are often disposed to think of our afflictions in the same way. But

Christ explains that it is not a mark of divine displeasure, it is not as punishment for sin, but it is that we may be more fruitful as Christians.

5. Another lesson is concerning the fate of those who bear no fruit. "Every branch in me that beareth not fruit he taketh away." And again, "If a man abide not in me he is cast forth as a branch and is withered; and men gather them and cast them into the fire, and they are burned." Here there seem to be well marked stages of judgment; the accomplishment of which begins in time and is fulfilled in eternity. They are cast forth even while some appearance of life continues; they wither, losing even the appearances of life; they are gathered at last for judgment; they are cast into the fire, the place where withered branches were being cast, as Christ was looking upon the scene which suggested this figure; and, as fulfilling the sentence of judgment; they are burned. Their fate turned on their fruitlessness. Fearful fate! Too fearful to contemplate, and yet we need the very warning it contains. *No fruit.* There may have been an abundance of leaves, there may have been the appearance of vigorous life, yet there was no fruit. Let us learn that the husbandman looks for fruit and will accept of nothing in its stead.

6. The last point I shall notice is that God is glorified through fruit-bearing Christians. "Herein is my Father glorified that ye bear much fruit." This honors God before the world, because it is a practical manifestation of the excellency of the law which requires it. We are his epistles before men. They read us, and judge of the character of the law by which we profess to govern our lives. When, therefore, they see all manner of goodness and helpfulness and charity in us, they attribute these to the Giver of the law which requires them. Such fruitful lives show the power

of the gospel and the transforming virtue of that grace which can overcome the evil propensities of the heart and bring forth manifold good. The best evidence as to the divine origin of the Scriptures, after all, is found in the divine works with which they induce men to adorn their lives. By their fruit they testify they are inspired of God. And again, such fruitful lives glorify God because the Christian is professedly restored to the divine image, and such a life of practical goodness shows to the world how excellent must be the character after which it was formed.

How wonderful that it is within our power to glorify the infinitely glorious! And by those things in which we glorify him we bring fadeless glory upon ourselves. We shall be remembered, when we are gone, by what we have done. When we rest from our labors our works will follow us. And, in the general resurrection, those that have done good shall come forth to the resurrection of life; and, according to Christ's description of the final judgments, deeds of benevolence will be recited as the welcome is extended to those on the right hand of the throne, while the neglect of these will be mentioned as the sentence of banishment is pronounced against those on the left.

I conclude by offering two suggestions designed to make us more fruitful: —

First. That we seek to make all suffering tend to this. The chastisements of the Lord, are not joyous, but grievous at the time, nevertheless, they afterwards yield the peaceable fruits of righteousness in them that are exercised thereby. Sanctified sorrows are spiritual promotions. They are prunings intended to make us more fruitful. May that be their result in our lives.

Secondly. Let us strive to make the bond between us and Christ more intimate. Let our faith lay hold upon him with firmer grasp. Let the fellowship be closer. He is our life-fountain. The fuller the life current from him the richer will be our lives. Let us not aim simply to *appear* fruitful, but let us strive really to be so. Children may tie fruit to the branches of their Christmas tree until it appears loaded with fruit. But the tree is still lifeless and fruitless. So we may seek to make our lives appear fruitful by a similar method. Only with vigorous life within can we become really so. The barrenness of many lives is to be attributed to the weakness of the life bond and the feeble flow of the life current.

HINDERANCES.

Ye did run well; who did hinder you (or did drive you back) that ye should not obey the truth?—Gal. v:7.

A good start is a good thing, but it is not everything. A good beginning does not insure final success. There may be a fine bloom in the spring, and but little fruit in the autumn. A clear morning may be followed by a cloudy day. A bright child often makes a dull man; and the first-honor man at college, is frequently a failure in the world. The steed may make a good dash from the stand and then come in behind on the homestretch. A new convert may be enthusiastic, and run well for awhile, and then become indifferent through meeting with many hindrances. "Ye did run well; who did hinder you?"

It is a sad fact that with many their greatest Christian activity is immediately after their conversion. They are larger and stronger at the time of their birth than they are at any time after. They have more faith, more joy, more love, more hope, more zeal, more enterprise, yea, more everything that is Christian then than afterwards. They can run swifter, fight more courageously, toil more faithfully, endure more patiently, and sing more joyously. This is wrong; it is unnatural.

Why is it?

I am not to deal with the causes which existed in Paul's day. I do not undertake to point out the hindrances which impeded the progress of the Christians in Galatia. I desire to deal with the present. Nor do I come to you with censure, but I desire to come to you with help. What are a few of the hindrances with us, and how may they be removed?

1. A failure to receive expected encouragement has hindered many.

It is a remarkable fact, that as a rule, we receive most encouragement when we least of all feel the need of it. Success always brings words of cheer. Prosperity calls out professions of friendship. The moneyless man receives few favors, the hungry man few invitations to dine.

As you entered the Christian race you were congratulated and encouraged. We were glad. But you did not so much feel the need of encouragement just then as you did later. Your love was all aglow, and your enthusiasm was full. These encouraging words, with which you were welcomed, ceased at the time your zeal began to abate, and you began to grow weary in well doing. The very fact that they ceased was an added discouragement.

Of this I desire to say three things: —

First, the church *is* at fault. It is not enough that we enlist men as soldiers of Christ; we should train them for duty, and encourage them in the conflict. They often need words of cheer which they never receive. We should stand by them and help them. As I look upon it, the church was organized partly for this very purpose. When all the trees in a forest are removed, save one left standing alone, the tempest may easily overthrow that. But while others stood near about it the storm could not uproot it. Its comrades broke the force of the attack and added of their strength. So it should be in the church.

Then, too, the convert is often at fault in expecting too much from others. They should not expect perpetual congratulations. We congratulate the newly married, but are they to expect these congratulations from us so long as they live? We take a little child by the hand to help it as it is learning to walk, but the child would be unreasonable should it expect us to help it always. Yet there are just such babies in the church. They have been members for many years, and are yet expecting others to help them as they were helped at first. Let me say to you, it is time you were men and women. It is time for you to put away childish things. You are wrong in expecting so much help.

And still further, you are at fault in not extending help to others. As a rule, those who expect the most, extend the least. A pastor once went to a church. He had been there only a short time when a lady came to his study and asked for a church letter. He asked if she expected to leave the city. She answered she did not. He then inquired if she expected to unite with one of their churches nearer her residence. Again she said she did not, and added, "I have been a member of this church more than five years and it is the most unsociable church I ever knew. The members don't visit." "Have none of them called to see you?" he asked. "Yes" she replied, "but that's been a long time ago." "You returned their calls, did you?" "Well, I'm so busy I have no time for visiting," she answered, by way of apology. "But, you think new converts should receive special attention, don't you?" he asked, "And I suppose some have come into the church since you. Have you looked after them and visited them?" "No — well — no I haven't; but that's not my business, or I'd never thought of it just that way, any how. I see what you mean. I'll try to profit by the suggestion. Perhaps, after all, the fault of which I complain, rests largely with me." I present this case as a specimen. There are many expecting too much, and giving too little.

We all need encouragement, more of it than we get. Censure has its place, but we will be sure to indulge enough in censure. Some try to beat the bad out, others drive it out by encouraging the good. We all know we can do better with appreciation and encouragement. Every child will be a better child, every wife a better, happier wife, and the husband a kinder, truer husband, every preacher will be a better preacher, and, in brief, everybody will be better when helped on with words of encouragement.

2. Others fail because they live from impulse, rather than from settled conviction.

The rains fall, the brook is full and its waters turn the mill. The winds blow, the sails are spread and the schooner scuds. Impulse prompts, and men act. By impulse they run well for awhile. But impulse subsides and they stop. It is wise to utilize good impulses. Let them speak; let them act. But there must be something to abide when impulse fails. We must not live simply from feeling. He who has nothing but this must be unstable, and must sooner or later fail. Our trials are too real, too frequent, too protracted. We need deep convictions and pluck.

The life to which we have been called is a warfare. The Christian is called upon to endure hardness as a good soldier of Jesus Christ. I suppose many have enlisted from the impulse of the moment — the martial music, the stirring, patriotic appeal, the excitement of the moment have moved them. They have not really thought of warfare with all that it implies. They have thought of the camp and the drill. The time of trial and of danger comes. They desert.

"But for these vile guns
He would himself have been a soldier."

We need conviction — deep, strong, abiding conviction. When many turned back from following Jesus he said unto the twelve, "Will ye also go away?" Then Peter answered him, "Lord, to whom shall we go? Thou hast the words of eternal life. And we believe and are sure thou art the Christ, the Son of the living God," *We believe and are sure.* That it was which made them steadfast in the midst of general apostasy. They were *anchored* by a deep, strong conviction. Let the multitude go. Let the current sweep like a mighty flood, we remain secure by the strength of well-grounded faith. It was this which kept Paul unmoved in the midst of violent persecution. Speaking of these persecutions as brought upon him by the work of his ministry he says, "For the which cause I also suffer these things; nevertheless I am not ashamed; for I know whom I have believed, and am persuaded that he is able to keep that which I have committed unto him against that day." He had something stronger and more enduring than impulse to carry him through. So must we have.

I believe that one cause of weakness in all our churches is to be traced legitimately to the fact that religion is made principally a matter of emotion. It is wanting in intelligent conviction. It is deficient in instruction. I do not object to impulse. Emotion has its place. Deep feeling is needed for grand achievements. But these must rest upon truth clearly understood and firmly grasped. Teaching must lie at the foundation of strong Christian character. We stand exposed to dangerous assaults from infidelity simply because we are not well-rooted and grounded in the truth. The foundation is not secure because it does not rest upon the rock of eternal verities. Truth clearly apprehended is its own defence.

There is a practical lesson in this for our pulpits as well as our for pews. If we would make men and women strong, if we would establish them so that no raging storm and no dashing billow can move them, we must make them strong in conviction. Let the roots of their lives strike deep into the soil of truth, and be widespread. Light, *light*, LIGHT, is what is needed. When they can say "we believe and are sure," they must stand. When they can say, "I know whom I have believed" no floods can sweep them away.

3. Others fail through the discouragements of sin. I am persuaded that very many are hindered by the consciousness of their shortcomings. Before their conversion they criticised others and said, "If I professed to be a Christian I would not be such a sorry Christian as they. They do things I would not do." They enter upon the Christian life strong in the confidence of their own strength. They run well for awhile. By and by, they stumble. They try again. They fall. This is repeated again and again. Their confidence is vanishing. Their enthusiasm has gone. Their courage fails.

Ah, Satan has entrapped you, my brothers. When you now think of trying again he reminds you of your repeated failures. Memory of sin, like a vampire, sucks away your life-blood. Your are discouraged. Your confidence has given away to a feeling of unworthiness.

You have not been attending church regularly of late. Why? Oh, how many excuses you find! You work so hard during the week that you need Sunday for rest, you say. Or some members of your family have not been very well and you thought you would remain at home with them. Or, you live so far from church. Or, you say, you have not suitable raiment. Or, worst of all — hypocritical and unworthy excuse — you say there are some in the church not living as they ought! How easily you find excuses! Yet, in most cases the real reason is to be found in your own sins. Your failure to attend church is to be attributed to a guilty conscience. Your neglect of the Lord's Supper is to be traced to the same cause. Your fault-finding springs from faults within you. You seek to justify yourself, in a measure, by pointing to the failures of others.

You have drifted away from God, and what should be done? Awake to your true condition. Rest not until the account of sin is settled. Turn back. Give your heart anew to him. Pray earnestly to God to heal your backslidings. There is forgiveness for you. God will pardon and forget. Start afresh, relying not so much upon your own strength as upon divine grace to help you.

We have an advocate with the Father, Christ the righteous; and he is faithful and just to forgive. This is one of the most precious of all the promises of the gospel. Do not think too much or too morbidly upon the past. You may be crushed and kept back by such memories. Be taught humility by your failures, and strengthen the cords that binds you to Christ by your new forgiveness. We should remember our failures only to make us more faithful. Peter was a better apostle, I think, from his having denied his Lord, and afterward being restored to his favor. From that time he had not so much confidence in himself.

You have been hindered, you have made mistakes, you may have fallen away. But I beg you, do not be overwhelmed by a sense of your failures. Do not give over, and cease to make an effort. By the interests of your deathless spirit, by the wooing of infinite love, by the fearful fate of the confirmed apostate, by the glories of heaven, by the blood of the Cross, I beg you to repent and turn and do your first works. Oh, of all sad things this seems the saddest, — to have started for home and then be shipwrecked mid-ocean — to have entered the race and then have fallen by the way. Remember the virgins that slept, the unfaithful servant that during the absence of his lord began to eat and to drink with the drunken. Remember these and be warned. "Ye did run well: what did hinder?" It matters not what may have hindered. Let the past be forgotten, when you renew your vows. God's grace will be sufficient. This moment may decide your eternal destiny. Awake and turn.

OBEDIENCE TO HEAVENLY VISIONS.

Whereupon, O King Agrippa, I was not disobedient unto the heavenly vision.—Acts xxvi: 19.

Paul's defence before King Agrippa rests upon the story of his wonderful conversion. He could explain his conduct in no other way, and he seemed to feel that this furnished not only an adequate explanation, but a complete justification of it. This narrative was his argument. And, on another occasion, when a mob in Jerusalem was wildly thirsting for his blood, he recounts this same story as his defence and justification. He tells of his zeal in persecuting the disciples of Jesus, of his commission to go to Damascus, of the wonderful vision by the way, and his subsequent conduct.

His grand life-work began in this vision. The text I have read contains the gist of his defence — "I was not disobedient to the heavenly vision." It is as if he had said, "No one can understand my recent conduct, which seems so inconsistent with my early life and education, so opposed to the customs of my own people, so full of zeal in the defence of that which I once so zealously opposed, unless they understand the vision out of which the great change came, and in obedience to which my whole life is being shaped. This vision furnishes the key to my conduct, and fully justifies the course I am pursuing."

We cannot fully understand the meaning of this vision, however, if we suppose it consisted only of ocular manifestations. To the vigorous mind of Paul, as he meditated upon it, there was more in it, and that of more practical worth, than was all that he saw with his eyes. These lessons taught him we must gather up and place together as containing its important and influential features. What were some of them?

1. First of all, he was made to feel the nearness of the spirit world, and the reality of the Divine presence as he had never felt them before. Theoretically, he held and advocated these before. He was a Pharisee, and the points of difference between the Pharisees and the Sadducees involved these very questions. The Sadducees denied the existence of angels and spirits, while the Pharisees believed in both. As a Pharisee, therefore, he believed in the doctrine of spirit-existence.

But one may hold to a theory, especially to the theory of the sect with which he is identified, and may zealously defend it without ever fully grasping it as a personal faith, and *feeling* that the doctrine stands for reality. So it is with us. We inherit a faith — we subscribe to a doctrine, without the faith's being our personal faith or the doctrine's being to us the representation of reality. But when the Lord appeared suddenly to Paul, as he was journeying along the highway, and there fell about him the light of heavenly glory, he knew what before he had held only as a doctrine. He was made to feel with a deep certainty what he had heretofore only dimly apprehended through teaching. Ever after he recognized the divine presence and the nearness of the spirit world as well-known certainties.

2. Then, again, he was made to feel his direct and personal responsibility to divine authority, as never before. True, as a Pharisee, he placed peculiar stress on the authority of the Jewish Scriptures, and made great professions of being governed by them, But it was probably with him as with many of us, we look to the Book simply *as* a book, and

are often practically forgetful of the personality of its author, and of our direct, personal responsibility to him. When Paul left Jerusalem the letters he bore from the chief priests were quite sufficient as authority, but when this vision was granted him, and he spoke face to face with the Lord, these letters were forgotten. The question then was, "Lord what wilt *thou* have me to do?" The authority of the Jewish sanhedrim was nothing; it wholly disappeared as there was developed within him a sense of his direct, personal responsibility to God. No councils, no ecclesiastical enactments, no authority, no decrees of men could after that come between him and his divine Lord. Not simply at the time of his conversion, but ever after, the question with him was, "Lord what wilt *thou* have me to do?" To him the Lord was no longer afar off, or vaguely apprehended, nor was his authority forgotten.

3. In this vision he learned also of the possibilities of humanity. When the light fell about him, and the heavenly glory was manifest, the voice that spoke to him out of the midst of that glory was the voice of one wearing a human name. "I am *Jesus*"—the name given at his incarnation, the name which marked him as a man. He had known of of Jesus—had known him after the flesh. When, therefore, the answer came back in response to his inquiry, "I am *Jesus*," he saw humanity glorified.

This thought finds frequent expression in his subsequent writings. It is Paul who speaks of the raised and glorified Jesus as the "first fruits," the type, the promise and the pledge of all the after harvest. It was in remembrance of this vision that he so confidently claims that Christ "shall change our vile body, that it may be fashioned like unto his glorious body." And the promised supremacy of man, as given in the eight psalm, he feels sure will yet meet with complete fulfilment; for he says, "Though now we see not, yet all things put under him, yet we see Jesus, who was made a little lower than the angels, crowned with glory and honor." Jesus exalted and crowned meant the exaltation and crowning of humanity.

4. Last among all things which I shall mention, as having been made manifest to him in this vision, is divine fellowship with human sufferings. "I am Jesus *whom thou persecutest.*" He had given his aid and countenance to the stoning of Stephen, he had persecuted many in Jerusalem and elsewhere, but not until now did he find that in all this he was persecuting Jesus. As a blow upon any member of the body sends pain quivering along the nerves to other parts, so every blow against the least of all the members of Christ's body is felt by him. Christ has said, "Inasmuch as ye have done it unto one of the least of these, my brethren, ye have done it unto me. The union is so intimate that I must feel what every member bears." This union and fellowship was deeply impressed upon Paul's mind, as is clearly shown in his writings. "Christ in us" is a terse expression for a thought which finds frequent and manifest expression in the Pauline epistles.

These, then, are some of the things he saw in that vision: The nearness of the spirit world and the reality of the divine presence; his direct and personal responsibility to divine authority; the ultimate possibilities of humanity; divine fellowship in human sufferings. Few things can so fit any man for the work of the ministry as these. They exerted a controlling influence over Paul. He was not disobedient to the heavenly vision.

The aim of his life, and his conception of duty were changed. He entered upon a new course. Christ's will became supreme in him. Nothing could turn him from the path of duty. Immediately he conferred, not with flesh and blood, but in Demascus began to preach Jesus, and to defend the cause he had sought to destroy. Persecution could not stop him. The incident in the house of Philip, the evangelist, is typical in his devotion. When Agabus, a prophet, took Paul's girdle and bound his own hands and feet, and said, "Thus saith the Holy Spirit, so shall the Jews at Jerusalem bind the man that owneth this girdle, and shall deliver him into the hands of the Gentiles." Those who journeyed with him, and those of that place united in beseeching him not to go up to Jerusalem. Then Paul answered, "What mean ye, to weep and to break mine heart? for I am ready not to be bound only, but also to die at Jerusalem for the name of the Lord Jesus." His devotion to his master was stronger than death.

From the time of his vision of Christ, he sought to build up manhood and womanhood according to the Divine pattern. This was the aim of his endeavors both for himself and for others. "But what things were gain to me," he says, "these I counted loss for Christ. Yea, doubtless, and I count all things, but loss for the excellency of the knowledge of Christ Jesus my Lord; for whom I have suffered the loss of all things, and do count them, but refuse, that I may win Christ, and be found in him, not having mine own righteousness, which is of the law, but that which is through the faith of Christ." His ideal, and the inspiration of his life was Christ. He exhorted his brethren to become followers of him, even as he was of Christ; and, casting aside every weight, and the sin which doth so easily beset, to look unto Jesus as their model and helper. He thought of himself as a character builder, and he used all means furnished in the gospel for this end. In his vision, he had seen sublimest manhood, and he sought to *realize* it. To make the divine *ideal* to become *real* in human character was the aim of all his ministry. All this is implied when he said, "I was not disobedient unto the heavenly vision."

What has now been said of Paul has its lessons for us.

We need visions. The possibility of all growth in men lies in their power to see visions. I know we are wont to turn away from men who think of things that are not as though they were, and to call them dreamers. But after all, these are the men who open the avenues along which we ascend to a nobler life. They are the vanguard in civilization. They are the discoverers, the inventors, the benefactors of our race. They look away from the things that are to the better things which might be.

When the vigorous pioneer went to the wild West to hew from the forests a home for himself, he erected a rude log hut, and was content for awhile to dwell in it. But his industry brought its reward, and he began to think of a better house. It arose in his mind as a vision before it arose as a habitation for himself and his. By and by fortune greatly increases his resources, and he has visions of a home with more comforts and more ample accommodations, and he builds it. So has he gone from the hut to the palace.

The visions we have, the dreams that we dream decide what we shall be. The man who honestly looks to the elements of higher character, and longs for them must go higher. "Blessed are they that hunger and thirst after righteousness, for they shall be filled." But the man who thinks upon things that are base, must himself become base. We need *heavenly* visions. We need to look up. There is a profound philosophy in the exhortation, "If ye then be risen with Christ, seek those things which are above, where Christ sitteth on the right hand of God. Set your affections on things above, and not on things on the earth." The direction of our affections must decide the direction of our growth. We need visions of the glorified Christ. We need to stand nearer to the unseen.

If you understand me to be speaking of that sensuous conception of the spiritual, shown in the wonderful "experiences" so common in some sections and among the ignorant, I have sadly failed to make myself understood. I repudiate these as unworthy and unscriptural. I do not think that these sights and sounds and mysterious voices are any part of conversion. I am glad the masses are coming to a more rational and more scriptural conception of the nature of religion.

Faith is designed to supply us with needed visions. In speaking of Moses' faith, it is said that "he endured as seeing him who is invisible." Paul says that faith is the evidence of things not seen — that is, faith is that by which or through which we see the unseen. This is the etymological meaning of evidence. Again he says, "We walk by faith, not by sight." The contrast implied in this statement is between our walk here, and our walk hereafter, when we shall see as we are seen and shall know as we are known. Now, we cannot literally see, but faith answers for sight — it gives us visions.

There is a vast difference between faith embodied in a creed and faith implanted in the heart. There was a time when I might have written out what I would have regarded as a full and satisfactory statement of my faith, but I could not now. Faith is to me more than any formulated statements could possibly set forth. No more than I can fully set forth in writing all that I see, all that I feel, all the beautiful pictures that rise before my imagination, and the swellings of love in my heart, can I set forth in writing all that my faith is to me now. It is soul-sight. It is an artist, for by it are pictured heavenly visions. It is inspiration. It is the life of the Christian. Through it come the foretastes of heavenly joys. I believe a proposition in geometry, but my belief as a Christian is practically far different from that. The Bible representation of faith is that of a transforming, transfiguring, elevating, all-conquering power. "This is the victory that overcometh the world, even our faith." By faith Enoch was translated; by faith Noah was saved and became heir of righteousness; by faith Abraham became a wanderer in a strange land; by faith Moses was led to choose affliction with the people of God; by faith the walls of Jericho fell down; by faith kingdoms were subdued, weakness was made strong and armies were vanquished.

An evangelist once asked a lady, who was a church-member, concerning her faith. She arose, went to the centre table, took up a book and handing it to him said, "That's my faith." "O, my dear madam," said he, "I cannot possibly read all this during my visit. Can't you epitomize, and state in a few words the principal features of your faith?" Then she went to the window, and throwing the shutters back, pointed down the street to a house on the opposite side, and said, "Do you see that small brown house? Our pastor lives there. Call on him and he can tell you what my faith is." Her faith was in a book. It was a faith which some one else understood better than she. Or, there is reason to suspect, she had nothing worthy the name of faith.

When Elisha was at Dothan, the king of Syria sent thither horses, and chariots and a great host, and they came by night and compassed the city about. They had come to take him and to deal with him as an enemy. And when the servant of the man of God was risen early, and gone forth, behold, a host compassed the city both with horses and chariots. And his servant said unto him, "Alas, my master! how shall we do?" And he answered, "Fear not; for they that be with us are more than they that be with them." And Elisha prayed, and said, "Lord, I pray thee, open his eyes, that he may see." And the Lord opened the eyes of the young man; and, behold, the mountain was full of horses and chariots of fire round about Elisha. Before this miracle he knew not that an invisible army was encamped about them. The miracle did not bring the army, it only enabled the servant to see the angels of God encamped about them for their defence.

The work of faith is similar to this. It enables us to endure as seeing the invisible. It gives us visions of the spiritual world, so near and yet unseen, save by the eye of faith.

It gives us visions of the all-merciful Father, of our glorified Savior, of the work of the helpful Spirit, of ministering angels, of ransomed spirits of just men made perfect, of the many mansions in our Father's house, of the beautiful world above and the glories yet to come. Oh, the beautiful visions of a genuine Christian faith! But I cannot follow this thought further now.

Unto what are you obedient? Is it to the changing circumstances of your lot? Has your life no aim, no inspiration, no plan? Do you float on the tide of events? Are you as a ship on the high seas, without rudder, or chart or pilot? the sport of winds and waves?

Or, are you obedient to carnal appetites? Is the question with you, "What shall I eat, what shall I drink, and wherewith shall I be clothed?" Is there no lofty aspiration in your heart? Is there nothing in you higher than in the beasts seeking prey, or the fowls seeking food? Are you like the rich fool of whom Christ spoke? O, brother man, this is unworthy of you.

Is it to earthly ambition born of visions of worldly glory you are obedient? What is all this worth, if this be all? It fades. The record of it perishes. There sleeps, in our beautiful Hollywood, one of the Presidents of this great land in an unmarked grave. When Paul and Barnabas went to Lystra, the people in a wild burst of enthusiasm said, "The gods are come down to us in the likeness of men." Barnabas they called Jupiter, and Paul they called Mercury. The priests of Jupiter, who were before the city, brought oxen and garlands unto the gates, and would have done sacrifice with the people. A few days pass, and this same people with mob violence drag Paul from the city and stone him until they suppose he is dead. So is it often. The hero and idol of to-day may be the martyr of to-morrow. Few things change so suddenly as popular applause. Let not this be the aim of your life.

Be obedient to heavenly visions. See your personal relation to a better world; the lasting glory to which humanity can attain. Live from your better self. Let the noblest impulses of your heart be the controlling impulses of your life. "Finally, brethren, whatsoever things are true, whatsoever things are honest, whatsoever things are just, whatsoever things are pure, whatsoever things are lovely, whatsoever things are of good report; if there be any virtue, and if there be any praise, think on these things." If you have never given yourself to Christ renounce all else and prostrate cry, "Lord, what wilt *thou* have me to do." Listen to his voice, and be taught; take his yoke, and be obedient. Seek for visions of him as inspirations of your life, and models after which you mould your characters into divine beauty.

THE DIVINE ESTIMATE OF MAN.

When I consider thy heavens, the work of thy fingers, the moon and the stars, which thou hast ordained; what is man, that thou art mindful of him? and the son of man, that thou visitest him? Psalm viii: 3-4.

Our religion receives its love and complexion, in great measure, from our estimate of man. Next to correct views of the divine nature I place correct views of human nature. It cannot be denied that much of what we find in formulated creeds and books of systematic divinity falls little short of systematic slander of humanity. For in many of these books, presented as guides to our faith, we find that affirmed concerning the entire race which we would not very readily affirm concerning the individuals who compose it. They teach that man — that all men — unless they have been subjects of special grace and have passed through a prescribed process, and so have become Christians, are totally depraved. That they cannot think a good thought or perform a good deed — that they are wholly averse to good, and wholly prone to evil.

Now all this, strange as it may appear, is supposed to bring greater glory to God in loving him and seeking to save him. In opposition to such views, which seem to me to be erroneous and hurtful, I desire to present the divine estimate of man. I desire to speak a word for man; not for any class, or grade, or profession, but for man simply as man. He has been trampled down under dogma, under creed, under priest-craft, under ceremony, under iron-hoofed ecclesiasticism. I desire to tell you something of what God thinks of him — simply as man.

In the first place, he is the crown of God's terrestrial creation. Not simply that he stands at the close of that grand drama, but that he stands above all things then made. He is the ultimate reason, in the divine mind, for all other things belonging to this lower creation. The first in design is often last in execution.

We are familiar with the argument for a personal, intelligent creator drawn from the evidences of design manifest in all things about us. The argument is as old as the age of Socrates, and was used with great skill and force by Paley. Nor do I think it can be supplanted by a stronger, because it is of the nature and force of a demonstration. Every new fact brought to light through the researches of science but confirms it. Yet it seems to me the argument has not been carried forward to its legitimate end. It has been made to look backward and upward toward God only. Marks of design demonstrate there must have been an intelligent designer. But let us carry the argument forward, by inquiring the ultimate design of this intelligent designer. It is not enough to know that part is adjusted to part, and that one wheel works with beautiful exactness in another. Beyond all this adjustment and harmonious working there must be some ultimate end to be served. If not, then, though there may be marks of intelligence, there are none of design. A puzzle may show intelligence, but it looks to no ultimate end to be served.

If we inquire as to the ultimate design of terrestrial creation we find it in man. "Thou has made him to have dominion over the works of thy hands; thou hast put all things under thy feet." They were made subject to him to serve him. He is more in the sight of the creator than all they. Before he made the earth and adorned it he thought of man, and because he thought of man he made all terrestrial things. Through many ages and up through a succession of changes the earth was brought to a state which fitted it for his home. He adorned it with beauty, he filled it with treasures, and when all things had been prepared he said, "Let us make man." In making he reached the end for which other things were made.

The Bible teaches us also that he is God's child. The formula used at the time of his creation is peculiar. — " Let us make man in our image, after our likeness." The pattern for man was not found in earth, but in heaven — in the image of the Creator himself was he made. " So God created man in his own image, in the image of God created he him." Of nothing else, of all created things can this be said.

This likeness was two-fold. First, he was made like God in that a spiritual nature was given to him; and, secondly, he was like God in sinlessness. And, though he fell, he did not thereby wholly lose this likeness. He lost his purity. His sinlessness gave way to sinfulness. His spiritual nature, however remained. This fact is abundantly recognized in subsequent declarations of the Scriptures concerning him. For instance, when the law concerning homicide was given to Noah, saying, "Whoso sheddeth man's blood, by man shall his blood be shed." You remember the reason assigned was "for in the image of God made he man." There is a sacredness about human life because there is in man a likeness to God. This is the reason. But this reason would be of no force whatever — it could not be a reason at all — if in the fall the likeness to God was wholly lost. Then, too, we find this likeness still recognized by James, an apostle, when he reproves his brethren for a wrong use of the tongue, saying, "Therewith bless we God, even the Father; and therewith curse we men, which are made after the similitude of God." This he argues is inconsistent. It is as if the same fountain should send forth at the same time both sweet water and bitter. If we love God and bless God, we must love man and bless man; because he is made in the image of God. Or, again, Paul argues against idolatry from the nature of man. His argument rests upon the likeness between man and his Maker. "Forasmuch then as we are the offspring of God," he reasons, "we ought not to think that the Godhead is like unto gold, or silver, or stone, graven by art and man's device." The nature of the Father he argues from the nature of his child.

In the genealogy of Jesus, as given by Luke, the fatherhood of God to man is plainly stated. Beginning with Joseph he traces the line back, saying, "Who was the son of Heli, who was the son of Mathat, who was the son of Levi, who was the son of Melchi," and on back, and back, and back, until he concludes the long line by saying, " who was the son of Cainan, who was the son of Enos, who was the son of Seth, who was the son of Adam, who was the son of God." So that, as truly and as really as we are the sons of Adam, we are the sons of God; for the line does not end in Adam, but in God. And this, not by virtue of adoption, not because of grace, not because we have been the subjects of any special change, but simply in virtue of the fact that God is the Father of us by natural generation.

There is a school of religious philosophy extending from the days of Augustine to our own time which teaches practically that we are by nature the children of Satan. The likenesss, even at our birth, is strongly marked. We are totally depraved. There is no good in us. We are, from the beginning wholly prone to evil and wholly averse to good.

The modern application of the doctrine of evolution as an explanation of the origin of our species makes us, by nature, the children of the gorilla. Begining down at the lowest imaginable point there has been a slow evolution, reaching upward all the time, until we come to man as its highest development — its flower. I have a work on "Man's Place in Nature," written by an eminent teacher of this school. I confess I have not read it with special care, but from a cursory examination of it and from its profusion of pictures of monkeys and apes and gorillas and such like, I learn that it traces our genealogy downward to the gorilla, and not upward toward God. The whole question between the old theology, the teachings of modern science, and the doctrine of the Bible is this — are we, by nature, sons of Satan, sons of the gorilla, or sons of God?

But, you ask, are not Christians only sons of God? Is not this the teaching of the New Testament and the doctrine of the church? How then do you reconcile it with the idea of natural sonship? In this way. In many large families we find children divided into two classes, the obedient and the disobedient. So in God's great family. There are those who do not love him, they will not give heed to his counsels, they obey not his will. They go from his presence having no desire for his fellowship. They are wayward and prodigal children. "We have all gone astray." But some come back. He forgives them and clothes them and prepares for them a feast, as did the good father in one of Christ's parables. They are nearer and dearer to him, and are sometimes spoken of as if they only were his children. Yet those who wander in sin are his too. And his call is the loving entreaty of a father, calling back his wayward son.

There is a practical lesson in this: The obligation to obey God is universal. There seems to be a view of this matter, quite generally received, which is very erroneous and hurtful. Many appear to think the obligation to lead a religious life does not rest upon them unless they *assume* that obligation. Just as the commander of an army has no right to command me unless I voluntarily place myself under his authority, thus assuming the obligation to obey him. So the obligation to live a Christian life rests upon no one until he voluntarily assumes that obligation. This is the popular view. It is wholly wrong. There are natural obligations as well as assumed ones, and our obligations to serve God belongs to this class; yea, is chief among all obligations. The obligation of the child to obey its parents is not an assumed one, but arises from the relationship. So the obligation of each man and woman to love God, and obey him, and honor him in all things by their lives arises from the natural relationship which exists between each one and the All-Father. This obligation is increased by God's manifestations of love for us all, and the provisions of his grace. The obligation *already* rests upon you, O, brother man, to live for God, and lead day by day, a Christian life. It is not waiting to be assumed. You have no right or reason to say "If I professed to be a Christian, I would not do this or that." The simple profession does not make it your duty to refrain. It is your duty already. You are God's child and should obey him. Let this thought find a lodgement in your heart.

But the divine estimate of man is most clearly seen in God's gift of his Son to save. For God so loved the world — not the elect, not saints, not good people only — but God so loved the world that he gave his only-begotten

Son to save it. Yet even this passage has been perverted by presenting man as absolutely worthless, that the divine love may appear more lovely. But is not this heightening love at the sacrifice of judgment? To love that which is worthless and wholly unworthy of love is esteemed degrading in man; how can it be exalting in God? The very fact that he reaches down his arm to rescue us, shows he must regard man as worth saving.

I am walking along the street, a lady alights from her carriage; she pauses a moment, then quickly bows down and thrusts her hand into the melting snow and filth of the gutter and seems anxiously searching for something lost. At once I conclude it must be something exceedingly valuable to her. She has lost her diamonds — precious to her beyond their intrinsic merit by sacred memories. So when God thrusts down the arm of mercy into the moral filth of this world and searches in the places of iniquity — searches diligently and persistently for the lost — I conclude that to his heart they must be very dear. God so loved the world that he sent his Son to seek and to save the lost. Not, God was filled with wrath and the Son came to appease the Father and reconcile him to the world. Ah, no — not that; although that is the way it has been often represented. But I prefer it as it reads in the Book, *" God so loved the world."* Fallen and stained and blasted in character; rushing headlong toward ruin; sinful and sinning, yet God looked down from heaven, and with more than a mother's care he sought to save the lost.

You remember the parable of the prodigal son? Well, it seems to me it would be better to call it the parable of the good father. How tender was his goodness, how cordial was his welcome to his returning son! What could be more gracious? He does not inquire into the past, nor chide him for his sins; he does not suffer him to complete the speech, full of penitence and promise and humility, he intended to make. He does not give him a servant's place, as he had determined to ask — "Make me as one of thy hired servants." But a cordial embrace and a fatherly kiss; a robe and a ring and a feast; joyous music and merry dancings and the features that brighten the scene of that welcome. How gracious!

And yet this — full of grace and mercy as it is — this does not fully represent the grace and mercy of God toward us. Have you ever thought upon it? That father did not once send after his wandering boy; he did not ask him to return; he made no promise of forgiveness, should he come back. None of these things appear in that parable. Yet they all appear in the case of the universal Father. He sent prophet after prophet; he made promise after promise. Finally he sent his own Son, — his only-begotten and well-beloved. He came to call the children back to their Father, against whom they had sinned.

Nor is this all. He *died* to bring them back. His cross stands as the symbol of his ministry of reconciliation. It is God's appeal. It is love's demonstration. "For when we were yet without strength, in due time Christ died for the ungodly. For scarcely for a righteous man will one die; yet peradventure for a good man some would even dare to die. But God commendeth his love toward us, in that while we were yet sinners, Christ died for us." In the presence of the cross, radiant with the beams of love, while it trembles under the burden of its sufferings, I can no longer doubt the feeling of God's heart toward man. Crown of his terrestial creation; his child, though wayward and disobedient; upon him he pours of the fulness of his love and the riches of his grace, and seeks to win him back to filial obedience and loving fellowship.

But my presentation of the divine estimate of man would be fearfully imperfect were I not to add that God thinks him in great peril through sin. The great sacrifice of his Son shows this; his terrible warnings show it; the earnestness of his call shows it. Were I to rush to your house at night while you sleep, and vigorously ring your bell, and shout vociferously, and batter against the door as if I would break it down, to arouse you, you would suppose that danger, imminent danger threatened you. I cry fire! fire!! fire!!! until you are startled and rush for safety. So is the call of the gospel. It is God's call to the endangered. He knocks at the door; he rings every bell; he cries to you to flee for safety, and the alarm of fire sounds the knell of the world. O! thou crowned one of God, O! thou child of an everlasting, ever-loving Father, O! thou ransomed one of God, flee for safety and come home!

MUTUAL HELPFULNESS.

We then that are strong ought to bear the infirmities of the weak, and not to please ourselves. Rom. xv:1.

Bear ye one another's burdens, and so fulfil the law of Christ. Gal. vi: 2.

The importance which should be attached to these injunctions is indicated by the connection in which we find them. For they are not incidental or casual words of advice but deliberate and fundamental rules for Christian life. The first stands as a summary conclusion and practical application of the argument of the entire preceding chapter — the fourteenth chapter of Romans, — while the second is immediately followed by the statement, "and so fulfil the law of Christ." The first is a brief application of practical charity toward the weak; the second is a practical application of what Paul calls the law of Christ.

The law here referred to is the law of love. You may find it in the thirteenth chapter of St. John. "A new commandment I give unto you," said Christ, "that ye love one another; as I have loved you, that ye also love one another." It is called a *new* law, and *the law of Christ*, not because it is absolutely new, nor because it emenated from Christ originally, but because he lifted the law of love into greater prominence and made it serve a new purpose. He makes it *the* law of his kingdom and the badge of discipleship to him. "Love is the fulfilling of the law." That is, all the laws of my reign find their centre in this law — it inspires obedience to all laws. In another place he says, "If ye love me you will keep my commandments," and, conversely, it is true that if we do not love him we neither will nor can, in any worthy sense, keep his commandments. The world is to know that we are his disciples because they see in us a practical exemplification of this love of love. "By this," he says, "shall all men know that ye are my disciples, if ye have love one to another." Men are to know that we are his followers not by any peculiar forms of speech, as "thee" and "thou," "yea" and "nay;" nor by any peculiar cut of clothing, or style of hats and bonnets; not by sanctimonious, pharisaical faces, nor by church connection, and Sunday communion, but by the gentleness and helpfulness and beneficence of love. As the motive of his earth-life and ministry was love, so must this be the controlling principal in us. It is this which differentiates the Christian.

It is true that mutual burden-bearing and helpfulness may be found elsewhere. In commercial circles we sometimes find the strong bearing burdens for the weak — a man's creditors do not press him, men of capital may extend a helping hand to lift a business man over temporary difficulties — but these, as a rule, do not arise from disinterested love. They arise from business considerations. So also men band themselves together for mutual help through secret organizations, but the motives which control them in doing this is selfish. Many life insurance companies are organized upon the same basis. The thought is, I desire help and so I will bind myself to extend help. The principle is essentially different from that which underlies the injunction of the texts.

It is not until we come into the domestic circle that we find anything like the burden-bearing and helpfulness of which the apostle speaks. In the family, the strong bear the infirmities of the weak. Infancy and age are ministered to out of love. The infirm, the weak, the afflicted are nourished by the care of affection. The law of Christ is simply a broader application of the law of the household. As men and women do in the best homes, so let them do in the church and the world. Under the magic power of the gospel, and the example of Christ —

Love takes up the harp of life, and smiles on all its chords with
 might,
Smites the chord of self, that, trembling, glides in music out of sight.

Before speaking of the burdens we may bear for others it may be well to say there is one burden which each must bear for himself — no one can bear it for another — and that is the burden of personal responsibility. Paul mentions this in connection with each text. In Romans he says, "Who art thou that judgest another man's servant? To his own master he standeth or falleth." And in the same chapter he says again, "So then every one of us, must give account of himself to God." The emphasis belongs on the word *himself*. No one can account for us. Then in Galatians he says, "For every man shall bear his own burden," meaning the burden of personal responsibility. So this is not to be classed with the burdens we are taught to bear for the weak.

When he says that the strong ought to bear the infirmities of the weak, and not to please themselves, it seems clear that he refers to weakness of faith; for of that he had been writing. In that day there was a diversity of opinion and feeling concerning some matters of minor importance, owing to differences in early surroundings and training. Some thought it a great sin to eat certain meats, while others ate of these with perfect indifference. Some esteemed certain days as sacred, and thought they should be so observed, while others regarded all days alike, and so treated them. The first, Paul calls weak; the latter strong. They had so grown in the nature and matter of the Christian faith that such distinctions had vanished. The difference between these two clases very naturally tended to discussion and strife.

It was in view of all this that he wrote. He teaches the strong how they should bear themselves toward the weak, and the weak how they should bear themselves toward the strong. The law for each was the law of love. The fourteenth chapter of Romans is the thirteenth chapter of first Corinthians applied. The strong should not contemn the scruples of the weak, but in brotherly love accommodate themselves to these scruples in all matters of indifference. On the other hand, the weak should not be exacting, and endeavor to bind his brother under a yoke made of his scruples. There is liberty in Christ. The kingdom of God is not meat and drink, but righteousness, and peace, and joy in the Holy Spirit. Religion is not observances, but inward states and experiences, The unity of Christ's kingdom is a unity of spirit rather than uniformity in the details of life and worship. He who exacts absolute uniformity mistakes the nature of the heavenly kingdom, and is forgetful of the liberty allowed us in Christ. But we must not use this liberty so as to offend them or cause them to stumble. We that are strong ought to bear the infirmities of the weak and not to please ourselves.

There is room for this exercise of brotherly charity to-day. There are questions concerning matters of indifference now as there were in Paul's time. We may feel assured they are matters of indifference and yet we must not so bear ourselves as to hurt or hinder others. He that is weak in the faith is to be received, but not to doubtful disputations.

A man may differ from me in my interpretations of many passages of Scripture, but I am not to refuse to recognize him for that. Here comes a man, for instance, who says, "I do not understand the last verse in the twenty-fifth chapter of Matthew just as you do. I do not understand it to teach the endlessness of future punishment, you do. But, while I do not agree with you in your interpretation of this passage, I do love Christ with all my heart, and I am earnestly striving to walk in all the commandments and ordinances of the Lord blameless. Will you exclude me for the difference I have named?" I answer, no. For while I am certain that the doctrine of the endlessness of future punishment is taught in that passage, and elsewhere in the Word of God, yet that difference shall not mar the fraternity between us. Or another says, "I cannot agree with you in your interpretation of Acts ii: 38. I do not think that baptism in order to the remission of sins is taught either there or elsewhere in the Word of God, yet I believe with all my heart that Jesus is the Christ, the Son of the living God; I trust him and love him; I desire to be baptized in obedience to his command. Will you baptize me, not holding with you that baptism is in order to the remission of sins?" I answer, certainly. At the same time, it seems as clear to me as it could possibly have been made, that when Peter said to inquirers at Pentecost, "Repent, and be baptized every one of you in the name of Jesus Christ for the remission of sins," he teaches that baptism is for, or in order to, the remission of sins. Yet this man loves Christ and desires to serve him. I receive and baptize him.

There are also matters arising in the details of worship which call for charity. The lack of it has destroyed the peace and ruined the usefulness of many churches. The smallest questions are large enough to lead to division and disaster if men and women, without love, arrange themselves on opposite sides of them. The place where the choir should sit, the way the house should be warmed, whether there should be an organ or a baptistery, plans for work, method of receiving converts into the fellowship of the church, and a score of other questions will arise which might easily be settled where love rules, but where narrowness, and self-conceit and bitterness reign — they grow into tests of fellowship.

In the section of country in which I was reared the custom of receiving converts into the church was that each member should extend the hand during the singing of a hymn. I remember there came a new preacher to one of the churches who, in giving the hand of fellowship, simply asked the members to rise while he, in their behalf extended the hand. This was a departure — an innovation — a step towards apostasy! A good old man came to see my father and, had the new preacher been guilty of some gross immorality, it could not have created deeper concern! I knew a lady who would not attend the church of which she was a member simply because a baptistery had been put in. I have known many to act in the same way because an instrument of music was there. I once preached a sermon in a church where an organ had been recently introduced. Some remained out of the house, waiting to see whether it would be used on that occasion, before they would even enter the building!

Such cases may seem extreme and absurd to some of you, and yet many of these are earnest, godly men and women. You say they are weak in the faith, and fail to understand the liberty allowed us in such matters. What shall be done? Ridicule and contemn them? No. But with brotherly kindness we are to bear with them. If they are lovers of Jesus Christ, striving to serve him and to do good in the world we are not to allow differences to kindle into animosities. Ye that are strong ought to bear the infirmities of the weak and not to please yourselves. This is practical charity.

Then, too, we are to bear with their moral weaknesses. In Galatians Paul was speaking of these weaknesses, for he had just said, "If a man be overtaken in a fault, ye which are spiritual, restore such a one in the spirit of meekness; considering thyself, lest thou also be tempted. Spiritual power, the ability to resist temptation to evil, is much stronger in some than in others.

I believe in inherited moral weakness as I do in that physical and mental weaknesses may be inherited. We are familiar with inherited tendencies toward drunkenness and other forms of vice. Dr. Dugdale, of New York, has brought to public notice a striking illustration. He followed the lives of descent from one Margaret Jukes through six generations, including in all seven hundred and nine persons — thieves, prostitutes, murderers, and idiots. The whole line was morally corrupt. The Chinese so firmly believe depravity to be a taint of the blood, that a criminal's father and grandfather are sometimes required to perish with him.

Then, too, early surroundings and, later on, our business associations have much to do with the question of moral strength. You who have been so blessed as to have grown up in Christian homes, do you suppose God will judge the child of the alley and the den of the same standard as that by which you will be judged? According to strength, according to ability, according to opportunity must each be judged. You say that it would be unjust to require the child, physically weak, to bear the same burden that the robust can bear with ease. But why not apply the same reasoning when the weakness is moral instead of physical?

Men often form habits, before conversion, which become so really a part of themselves that grace cannot remove them at once, and supply the weakness which these habits have caused. Simon, of whom we read in the eighth chapter of Acts, was a remarkably successful magician. For a long time he had deceived the Samaritans. He seems to have been enterprising in the prosecution of his questionable calling, gathering from every source and regardless of expense, new stores of knowledge of the magician's arts. When he fell, it was through the weakness formed through this habit; for when he saw that through the laying on of the apostles' hands the Holy Spirit was given, he offered them money, saying, "Give me also this power, that on whomsoever I lay hands, he may receive the Holy Ghost." His practices had made him weak at that point.

But whatever may be the weakness, or from whatever cause it may come, it is to receive Christian consideration. Not that we are to look upon sin as a matter of indifference. No, no. We are to abhor evil. We should strive, however, to abhor it as God abhors; for while he abhors sin he loves the sinner. There are those who seem to think the abhorrence of evil can be shown in no other way than by detesting and shunning the evil-doer. So thought the Pharisees in Christ's day. So has the sect of the Pharisees thought from that day to this. But was not Christ's way of abhorring evil the truer, better way? He showed his abhorrence by loving the sinner and seeking to rescue him from its dominion. A man who says he abhors evil, goes down the street and he meets a *gamin*, a bundle of depravity, and gives him a kick. That's the way he shows his abhorrence. Another, coming after, sees the specimen of depravity and shuns him, saying, "I abhor that which is evil." By and by, here comes another who, seeing him, says, "I abhor that which is evil," and he takes the lad to his home and seeks to cure him of his evil. He shows a divine abhorrence of evil.

In church discipline we need the wisdom of a loving heart. Let us not erect absolute standards by which each is to be measured. Here comes a man, for instance, weak in some point of his moral constitution. He desires to follow Christ. He makes an honest effort. Soon he gives way, through weakness, to sin. He tries again and fails. What should we do? We should bear with him and encourage and help him. I believe that so long as men sincerely desire to live right and honestly endeavor to follow Christ we should do this. Do not say men should be cast out for doing certain things. That will not do, for men of genuine love for Christ, men who are struggling for a better life, may be overtaken by that very fault. Though the number of their failures be seventy times seven, we are to seek to restore them. The controlling idea should be their final salvation.

We often need the patience and perseverance of a mother's love. Her child is sick with some loathsome disease. She says, "I abhor this disease," and so she watches over her child day and night, using every means she can command for its recovery. She does not abandon hope, nor does she cease her vigilance. The child sinks very near the gates of death. Still she cares for it. She does not grow weary. Her ministries are constant. After weeks have passed by, her watchings and ministries are rewarded by returning health. Such love, such care, such patient ministry do we need sometimes in restoring men to spiritual health. We are to bear with them patiently, yet not with the patience of indifference, but with the patience of love.

There are also burdens of daily trials, of rasping, wearing cares, of afflictions which we should help others to bear. The cases which Christ will mention with appprobation in the final judgment will be those of help extended to the helpless. You have fed the hungry, given drink to the thirsty, clothed the naked, visited the sick and the imprisoned, and ministered to the children of want. There are always in the world men and women who seem to be pre-ordained failures. They come into life badly organized, lacking the elements of success. There are those who struggle on in the great march of life as the disabled soldier, unable to bear arms, unable even to keep place in the ranks. We are to help them.

There are those with whom the affairs of life never run smoothly. They inherit a deranged nervous system. Every thing that touches them rubs the wrong way. Even harmony grates as discord on their ears. Life is full of annoyances, of forebodings, of cares, of burdens. They cannot be at peace as other men are.

Blessed are they who have good nerves. Blessed are they who have been well born. Blessed are they who feel that there is harmony between themselves and their circumstances. Blessed are they who can discern music in the movements of events, for they are the elect of the earth. Blessed are they who know how to be patient and sympathetic and helpful, giving of their strength to supplement the weakness of others. Ye that are strong ought to bear the infirmities of the weak and not to please yourselves. Open your hearts in sympathy, extend your hand in benefactions, speak words of cheer, lose yourself for others, and your life shall be a hymn of praise and a holy benediction.

I would fain offer some suggestions to aid in the performance of this pleasant duty. Of course, we cannot literally take burdens from other's shoulders and place them on our own. But we can do that which answers the same purpose —

we can make them strong to bear these burdens. So, also, we are to bear ourselves in such a way that we will not place upon them burdens too great for their strength. There may be many things which you can do without injury to yourself, which they, essaying to do, would be crushed. Be considerate of their weakness.

Were I out on a holiday with these children and should we, in our ramblings, come to a swollen mountain brook, I might be able to cross it with ease. My stature and strength enable me to stand against the current. But I must not be forgetful of the weaker ones about me. Were I to cross, they might attempt it and be swept away. While we pray "Lead us not into temptation," let us be careful lest by our example we lead others into temptations too great for them.

Then, too, if we desire to obey the injunction of the texts, we should study men and burdens. We should know how to quickly detect these burdens, and then how to get hold upon them. Kindness of heart is a good instructor. Yet have I seen some who by their very awkwardness make the burdens heavier and more grievous to be borne. We need tact.

Let us not look for too great a field for the display of our brotherly help. Great afflictions bring many sympathizers; while daily troubles, and the accumulated burdens of petty sorrows and annoyances, have to be borne alone. Do not aim too high. Some one has beautifully said that one Niagara, with its mighty thunder and rush and roar, is enough for a whole continent. What we need are bright streams flowing through woodland and meadow and field, singing as they go, making their banks beautiful with verdure and flowers.

It is a part of our mission as Christians to make this world happier, by making it stronger in all virtue and all goodness. We are to shine as lights. We are to brighten homes and gladden hearts and inspire songs. We are to relieve the oppressed and bring liberty to those who are bound. We are to wipe tears from the face of sorrow. We are to bring the light of hope to those in the gloom of despair. We are to be eyes for the blind and feet for the lame. We are to be gentle and kind and compassionate and helpful to all. In brief, we are to reproduce the spirit of Christ in the midst of weakness and want. He went every whither doing good. He was not harsh in judgment wherever he saw weak natures in sin, yet struggling against their weakness. He was severe against pretense, against hypocrisy, against great professions without goodness, against religion that had not benevolence, against self-righteousness — against these he was terrible. His words sounded as the thunders of judgment, and smote as lightings of wrath.

But to the oppressed he was a deliverer, to the sin-burdened, a savior. He came to take upon himself the burdens we could not bear. "Behold the Lamb of God that beareth away the sin of the world." There is a burden too great for us to bear. It is the burden of sin. Lower, and yet lower, it will sink us. No one but Christ can take this burden and bear it for us. You remember that Bunyan's Pilgrim struggled in vain under this burden until he bowed at the foot of the cross. Then it rolled off. He arose free. So, O you sin-burdened I ask you to come to the cross and cast down your burden, there. Christ will give you liberty by bearing it for you.

SERVICE AND HONOR.

If any man serve me, let him follow me; and where I am, there shall also my servant be; if any man serve me, him will my Father honor. John xii: 26.

This saying of our Master contains two thoughts which it is my purpose to eleborate briefly this morning. The first is, that Christian living is service to Christ; and the second, that God, the Father, will honor the servants of his Son. May we, by a devout meditation upon these matters, be led to a clearer apprehension of our calling, and be encouraged by the blessed promise of divine honor, to greater fidelity as the servants of Christ.

1. The New Testament idea of religion is that of willing, cheerful, hearty service rendered daily to Christ. "If any man *serve* me." Some one has said that practical religion contains three elements — working, fighting and enduring; and that to work devoutly, to fight wisely, and to endure patiently is the sum of Christian duty. This is an excellent summary of the elements of practical religion. These may, however, be classed under one general head — service to Christ. For if we work devoutly, it is under the yoke and guidance of Christ. He is our Master and our Model. If we fight wisely, it is that we may please him who has called us to be soldiers. And if we endure patiently it must be because of our trust in Christ, our reliance on his promises, and the inspiration of his example as a patient silent sufferer.

Willing, cheerful, hearty, daily service to Christ is therefore a most complete generalization of practical religion.

A favorite conception of religion, especially among a certain class of religionists, is that it consists of particular forms of faith, and phases of feeling; of ecstatic emotions and Sunday observances. In some mysterious way, as they think, God breathes in upon the soul and this divine inflation is religion. The practical nature of service — daily service — if often overlooked.

James gives us a statement of his view of religion which is, in every way, thoroughly practical: "If any man among you seem to be religious, and brideleth not his tongue, but deceiveth his own heart, that man's religion is vain. Pure religion and undefiled before God and the Father is this: to visit the fatherless and widows in their affliction, and to keep himself unspotted from the world." Here are given three tests of the genuineness of every profession of religion; and they show that, according to his understanding, all true religion is very practical. First, pure religion is shown by the wise government of the tongue. The liar, the slanderer, the tale-bearer, the scandal-monger, the gossip, the complainer, — every one who does not bridle his tongue, whatever his profession may be, this apostle declares that his religion is vain. Horace thus describes a man: —

> "He said
> Or right or wrong, what came into his head."

There are some of this class yet, and they seem to pride themselves on their candor, and to rejoice in their liberty of speech! Their religion is vain, however, an apostle being judge. Then another mark of genuine religion is personal purity — keeping themselves unspotted from the world. Not in any pharisaical way, not by secluding themselves as hermits do, but by the power of a purifying faith within their heart. They are in the world, but not of it. In the midst of corruption they are undefiled, as the sunbeam shines into all manner of impurity, and itself remains pure. And a third mark of genuine religion is active charity — visiting the fatherless and widows in their affliction. He who in life manifests these elements of self-control, purity, and practical benevolence shows the genuineness of his religion, for in these things he follows Christ.

Nor are we to regard this practical life of service to Christ as simply one phase of his religion. It is true there is both doctrine and duty in religion; it is both a science and an art. But doctrine is only the guide to duty, and the art is nothing but the science applied. The aim of all teaching is right-living, and we do err whenever we so separate between practical religion and doctrinal religion as virtually to divorce them. The most profound problems of revelation, the deepest reasoning in inspired theology form the roots of holiness and goodness in life.

The strongest chain of close-linked reasoning to be found in the Bible is in Paul's letter to the church in Rome. In that letter he deals with the whole theory of human redemption and the profound problems involved. He sketches the picture of the moral degradation of man, shows the universality of sin and demonstrates the impossibility of justification by deeds of law. He contrasts Adam with Christ, and shows how by the atonement which Christ has made, God can still be just and yet the justifier of them that believe in Jesus. In his reasonings he descends into the deep things of God, and traces the marvels of his grace and wisdom in the solution of the problem of sin and redemption, chapter after chapter, until at the close of the eleventh chapter he emerges with the exclamation, "O the depth of the riches both of the wisdom and knowledge of God! how unsearchable are his judgments and his ways past finding out! * * *

For of him, and through him, and to him, are all things: to whom be glory forever. Amen."

But no sooner does he conclude his course of profound reasoning than he turns it all to practical account. It bears upon life. It is the root from which humility, and fraternity, and helpfulness, and industry, and patience, and benevolence, and obedience to civil rulers, and all Christian virtues spring, and by which they are nourished and made strong. The practical exhortations in the concluding chapters of this epistle find their reason and strength in the profound reasoning of its earlier chapters. The vital cord that joins the two parts is found in the word *therefore*, in the opening of the twelfth chapter — "I beseech you *therefore*"— in view of all the foregoing — "I beseech you therefore, brethren, by the mercies of God, that you present your bodies a living sacrifice, holy, acceptable unto God, which is your reasonable service."

Even doctrine — which now popularly means speculative theology or statements of faith concerning matters of controversy — even doctrine, in New Testament phraseology, means simply teaching, and that, as a rule, concerning daily duties. Paul, for instance, earnestly desired his sons, Timothy and Titus, to be sound in doctrine. His letters to them abound in such expressions as these, — "Take heed unto thyself and to the doctrine,"—" In all things showing thyself a pattern of good works; in doctrine showing uncorruptness, gravity, sincerity," — " Speak thou the things which become sound doctrine," — " Be instant in season, out of season; reprove, rebuke, exhort with all long-suffering and doctrine. For the time will come when they will not endure sound doctrine." But I need not multiply illustrations of his anxiety for the soundness of their doctrine. He was, certainly, deeply solicitous.

Yet when we examine into this — which to so many seems wholly removed from daily life — we find that by it Paul meant practical teaching concerning life and duty. For instance, instructions concerning the duty to provide honestly for those dependent upon us is sound doctrine; for he says: "These things give in charge that they may be blameless. But if any provide not for his own, and especially for those of his own house, he has denied the faith and is worse than an infidel." Doctrine — sound doctrine — was sound teaching concerning deportment, for he says: "But speak thou the things which become sound doctrine: that the aged men be sober, grave, temperate, sound in faith, in charity, in patience The aged women likewise, that they be in behavior as becometh holiness, not false accusers, not given to much wine, teachers of good things; that they teach the young women to be sober, to love their husbands, to love their children, to be discreet, chaste, keepers at home, obedient to their own husbands, that the word of God be not blasphemed. Young men likewise exhort to be sober-minded. * * * Exhort servants to be obedient to their own masters, and to please them well in all things; not answering again, not purloining, but showing all good fidelity; that they may adorn the doctrine of God our Savior in all things." All manner of personal impurity, and immorality, and vice he regarded as contrary to sound doctrine for, after mentioning a long and fearfully dark list of these things, he concludes by adding, "And if there be any other thing that is contrary to sound doctrine."

It is clear that doctrine was simply teaching, and this concerning the practical affairs of life. With this understanding of it, I can say I think we need more doctrinal preaching. Let us not think of making all men and women profound theologians, but let us strive the rather to teach them how to live. Let us endeavor to make them thoroughly orthodox in heart and life. According to the New Testament, religion is a very practical affair. It is the daily subjection of all our powers to the will of Christ. It is willing, cheerful, hearty service rendered to him.

But how can men engaged in business, and women cumbered with domestic duties give their lives in daily service to Christ? I suppose this question has already come to your mind. You think it easy for a minister of the gospel to do this, for he is in large measure free from business cares; but how can men and women who are not exempt from these things, but are compelled to give themselves to secular and domestic concerns, give their lives in daily service to Christ?

Many, supposing that it is impossible to serve Christ fully while engaged in secular callings, have abandoned their callings and secluded themselves that they might give undivided time and attention to spiritual concerns. They shut themselves in from the world. But is it needful to do this in order to serve Christ daily? Is this, after all, the best service we can render to him?

Paul teaches servants to serve Christ even in the service which seems rendered to an earthly master only. "Servants obey in all things your masters according to the flesh; not with eye-service, as men pleasers; but in singleness of heart, fearing God; and whatsoever ye do, do it heartily as to the Lord, and not unto men." The lowest service may be exalted, and sanctified, and may become a means of grace if only it be done *as to the Lord*. If, then, the service which was exacted of a slave can be performed, transfiguring it through lofty motive, that it becomes service to Christ, surely all service may be ennobled and transfigured. There is no position in which one can be placed, there no duties that can be made incumbent upon him, there are no tasks he can be required to take up, but that in them he may serve Christ.

> " We need not bid, for cloistered cell,
> Our neighbor and our work farewell:
> The trivial round, the common task,
> May furnish all we ought to ask —
> Room to deny ourselves, a road
> To bring us, daily, nearer God."

Let me suggest to you some rules which I have found helpful, and which I trust may prove profitable to you in your effort to make your every-day life a service to our blessed Lord.

First, of all, do away with the idea that religion is limited to certain services. The usual broad distinction between things sacred and things secular is erroneous and hurtful. Religion does not find its full application and field of activity within the limited range to which it is too often practically confined. It is not a duty, nor a certain *class* of duties, but it has to do with the whole range of life and should sanctify all duties. We should carry it into business, into society, into pleasure, into politics — everywhere and into all things. Let it reign over the marts of trade, let it control all activity, let it sanctify wealth, let it ennoble toil, let it purify social intercourse, let it brood as a loving presence over all the ways and works of men. Let it elevate all things secular until they become sacred. Religion does not belong to the church and to holy day only, but to every place and to every day.

In the second place, cultivate a sense of the perpetual presence of Christ. Too many seem to think of him as confined to sacred places, and that he is present with us only when we worship. Like Jacob, when resting in a desert place, he thought of the Lord as not there, but as in his home he had left, so are we. It was a surprise to him to find the Lord with him in that solitary place. "Surely the Lord is in this place; and I knew it not." Enoch walked with God; Moses endured as seeing him who is invisible. This is the explanation of their endurance, their power, their holiness. The sense of his presence will be sanctifying and sustaining. It will become an easy thing to serve him in our daily callings if we come to think of him as ever present.

In the third place, train yourself to carry a devotional spirit, a loving heart, an active conscience into all you do. It will aid you greatly if you will, now and then, all through the day lift up your heart in prayer. This, it seems to me, is what Paul means by praying always. We can train our hearts to cast loving, reverent glances toward our loving friend.

And last, of these rules to help us to serve Christ in our daily calling: Remember that for *all* thoughts, *all* words, *all* work we are at least to give account to him. Oh, how this will help us to do all thing as, not unto men only, but "as unto Christ." So may we all — so may we always serve Christ, and he has said: "If any man serve me him will my Father honor."

2. The second thought is that God, the Father, will honor the servants of his Son.

I have not yet attained to that exalted state in which it is thought to be unworthy of us to be influenced in our Christian living by the promises of reward. Nor do I mourn this fact very deeply. For so long as it is said of Moses that he had "respect unto the recompense of reward;" and of the patriarchs, that their desire for a better country which God had promised them led them through all their wandering; and of Christ himself that for the joy that was set before him he endured the cross — so long as these examples endure I need not feel ashamed to confess I am influenced, in a measure, by the promises which are given to a life of service. They are given as motives, as inspirations, as helps. By these exceeding great and precious promises we are to be made partakers of the divine nature. By patient continuance in well doing we are taught to seek for glory, honor and immortality. The promise of divinely-bestowed honors, therefore, should incite us to more faithful service.

I cannot venture an effort to picture what this promised honor will be. "Eye hath not seen, nor ear heard, neither have entered into the heart of man, the things which God has prepared for them that love him." I know that he honors the servants of his Son, even in this life, with special blessings; for it is not until we enter upon that service that we can claim the blessings of forgiveness, adoption and the indwelling of his Holy Spirit as ours. I know that he honors these servants with exalted titles. They are the elect, the salt of the earth, the light of the world. They are exalted to a royal priesthood. They are sons and daughters of the Lord Almighty. "Behold, what manner of love the Father hath bestowed upon us that we should be called the sons of God. * * * Behold, now are we the sons of God, and it doth not yet appear, what we shall be; but we know that, when he shall appear, we shall be like him; for we shall see him as he is." The glory which awaits the servants of Christ will not be made manifest until he shall appear in the clouds of heaven, clothed with the glory of his Father and attended by the angels. Paul says, "When Christ, who is our life shall appear, then shall ye also appear with him in glory."

There is coming unto every faithful servant of our Lord a time of exaltation. When countless hosts shall stand in one vast assembly before the throne of his glory they shall be crowned. "Well done, good and faithful servant; thou hast been faithful over a few things, I make thee ruler over many things. Enter thou into the joy of thy Lord." There is come a day of glorious transfiguration—of manifestation. The faithful toilers in places of obscurity, in fields of difficulty, in circumstances of discouragments shall come forth. The world knows them not and is not worthy of them. They shall come forth. It is the day of their coronation. The trumpets of angels usher in the glad day. The implements of toil, the raiment of servitude are laid aside. Crowns and robes and scepters are given. The palace of God resounds with notes of joy.

> "Nearest the throne, and first in song,
>   Man shall his hallelujahs raise;
> While wondering angels round him throng,
>   And swell the chorus of his praise."

Whose servants are you? Are you striving to serve Christ according to the measure of your ability and the field of your opportunity? Be encouraged. Be faithful. Let nothing cause you to grow weary of that service. The promise of our Master is sure. The Father will honor the servants of his Son.

Whose servants are you? Are you serving self; serving base passions; serving sin; serving Satan? Remember that the wages of sin is death, but that the gift of God is eternal life. Choose you, this day, whom you will serve. Christ calls you to his service, and through service to rest and glory. "Come unto me all ye that labor, and are heavy laden and I will give you rest. Take my yoke upon you and learn of me; for I am meek and lowly in heart; and ye shall find rest to your souls. For my yoke is easy, and my burden is light."

HERE AND HEREAFTER.

> Be not deceived; God is not mocked; for whatsoever a man soweth that shall he also reap. For he that soweth to his flesh shall of the flesh reap corruption; but he that soweth to the spirit shall of the spirit reap life everlasting. And let us not be weary in well doing; for in due season we shall reap, if we faint not. Gal. vi: 7-9.

The light of revelation falls on both sides of Jordan. For it reveals not only the land which lies beyond but interprets the present; and the present is interpreted, in great degree, through its revelation of the future. Recently unusual interest has been manifested in the nature of the connection between this life and that which is beyond the grave. It is not my purpose to engage in the present discussion, yet it seems to me an opportune time to study the main question involved.

It cannot be denied that the Scriptures uniformly teach that there is some connection between the present and the future — that the destiny of each individual is determined, in part at least, by his own conduct — that what each one is here indicates, if it does not absolutely decide, what he shall be hereafter. Descriptions of the general judgment imply this; Christ's parables of final reckoning rests upon it. All the motives for right living here, drawn from the great hereafter, find their appropriateness and force in the fact that there is a normal connection between our daily doings and our destiny.

The nature of this connection seems to me to be more clearly set forth in the figure of the text than elsewhere, for nowhere in the word of God do we find an attempt made to set it forth formally.

Let me then, as briefly as possible, present some items which seem to me to lie enwrapped in this figure. For the sake of clearness and to aid memory I will number them.

1. The use of this figure seems to teach that the entire present stands to the limitless future as seedtime stands to harvest. This is the time for seed-casting, that the time of grain-gathering; this is spring-time, that an eternal harvest-time, we sow here, we reap hereafter.

2. Throughout this life each one must sow. The husbandman may neglect or refuse to sow, but we cannot. Unless we can stop the flight of time we cannot cease to sow. In the hour-glass placed in our hands the sands are falling seeds. They ceaselessly fall. Not until the sands of life cease falling can we cease sowing.

3. Amid the diversified employments of men there are two, and only two, kinds of sowing possible — to the flesh and to the spirit. Just as, according to the broad generalization of the Scriptures, there are two kingdoms in this world, and only two — the kingdom of darkness and the kingdom of light; two ways through the world, and only two — the broad way and the narrow; two natures in man, and only two — the carnal and the spiritual; so only two kinds of sowing are possible — to the flesh and to the spirit.

4. We are free to sow to either. If not, then are we to be held responsible for consequences while causes are placed beyond our reach. We are under the despotism of fate — blind, cruel, heartless — and the justice of moral judgment is a myth. Accountability is but accounting for one's ability, and if ability be denied us the ground of our accountability is destroyed.

5. In our depravity it is easier to sow to the flesh than it

is to sow to the spirit. This is abundantly shown by the history of our race and our own observation. It is confirmed by our own experience. It is naturally easier to do wrong than it is to do right; to go with the current than to go against it; to go down than to ascend.

6. Each must, unless forgiven, reap the full harvest of his own sowing. As to the kind of sowing we will do there is room for choice, but there choice ceases. The harvest that each must reap grows and ripens under changeless and universal law. As but two kinds of sowing are possible, so but two kinds of harvest are to be gathered. Only two sides to the throne of judgment, two groups before that throne, two sentences from the lips of the Judge, two places in the eternity beyond, two harvests to be gathered there!

7. After the seed has gone from our hands it is irrecoverable. Without a figure — the past is irrevocable and irreversable. The past is absolutely changeless. We cannot obliterate it. Deeds are eternal in their nature. Whatever you and I have done, whether good or evil, it stands forever true that we have done these things. No power can annihilate a fact. Sins are deeds and so, strictly and literally speaking, sins cannot be washed away. Divine grace may do that which will be practically the same, leaving us before the throne of justice as if we had never sinned. But it is true, from the nature of things, *we* cannot do even this. Within ourselves, we are hopelessly bound by our records. There is no thraldom like the thraldom of evil deeds.

8. Finally, the time of sowing will soon be over with all here this evening, and each must then enter upon the eternal harvest of his sowing. "Be not deceived; God is not mocked; for whatsoever a man soweth that shall he reap. For he that soweth to his flesh shall of the flesh reap corrup-

tion, but he that soweth to the spirit shall of the spirit reap life everlasting."

These thoughts lie at the basis of the Christian conception of this life. According to the divine purpose the present life is to find its completion in a life yet to come. There is to be a divine evolution. God gives the seeds, the germs, to be developed according to a divine plan. These purposes concerning us are to be *realized* in each individual. He who *realizes* the divine *ideal* achieves the highest destiny possible. A failure to realize the divine ideal works ruin. If one lives out of his carnal nature, and for it, the inevitable result is a harvest of corruption; but if he lives out of his spiritual nature, and for it, he must reap life everlasting. These alternatives are expressed in the text by sowing to the flesh and sowing to the spirit.

This revelation of the bond by which our daily life is bound to that eternal one enhances the value of the present beyond all expression. The Bible revelation of the life beyond is not so given as to put this life to shame, as some are claiming. The glories of the future state might have been so revealed as to paralyze all effort and all desire in the present, through the intensity of desire for that future. But, instead of this, our future is so disclosed to us as to give dignity to our every-day life. The present is vitally joined to the future. Whatsoever we sow we shall reap. Through this revelation there is given to us an inspiration to right living. It quickens beneficence; it strengthens all goodness. It gives courage under difficulties and dangers. What I do and endure here decides what my harvest shall be hereafter.

Even when we limit our thoughts to the boundaries of time we esteem those deeds great which in the years beyond their doing are fruitful in results. When Robert Raikes, in

1781, gathered neglected children from the streets of Gloucester, and had them instructed on the Lord's-day perhaps few thought it a work of special importance. But now, when almost a century has passed, the Christian world looks back upon it as one of the events in religious history worthy of special celebration. Sunday-school workers are already preparing for a grand centennial. When Luther raised a protest against the sale of indulgences by posting on the doors of the Schlosskirche at Wittenburg, the last day of October, 1517, his ninety-five Latin theses, I suppose it was generally regarded simply as a bold yet rash act of a brave religious fanatic. Yet out of this came the great reformation of the sixteenth century. The event is important because of its effect on religious liberty and civilization. So in science, in politics, in art, in society, everywhere, we esteem those events great which project themselves into the future.

What, then, can give more importance to the events of an ordinary life than the doctrine that our sowing here decides our reaping hereafter? Daily deeds decide destiny. The thoughts we think, the purposes we cherish, the words we speak, the things we do unite to form the harvest we must reap. Our lives here decide our state hereafter. Whatsoever a man soweth *that* shall he reap, and not something else or different. The Christian conception of life exalts it by making it the seed time of eternity.

No wonder then that with such warmth Paul exhorts us against deception on this point. All deception is to be dreaded, but as the matter increases in importance so our dread should increase. Should deception result in temporary discomfort you would avoid it; should it result in injury to your health you would vigilantly guard against it; but should it be such as to threaten your life you would dread it with feelings of terror. What, then, when it involves destiny?

Whence the danger of deception concerning a matter which seems so manifest?

In the first place, we are in danger through our natural unwillingness to believe this truth. As we look back over our lives we find them very unworthy and sinful. We shrink back from the thought of reaping the normal results of all this. We prefer to think that however we may live here it will, after all, be well with us hereafter.

The will exerts a wonderful influence over our belief. We find it easy to believe that which is pleasant to our feelings, but difficult to receive as true that which is painful. When we are convinced of the truth set forth in the text we are convinced against our will. I know the theory of faith is this: A proposition is submitted and evidence is presented in its support. When this evidence is examined and found to sustain the proposition the proposition is embraced as true. This is the theory, and as a theory it does very well, but as a matter of fact it is not a representation of the ground of popular faith. Popular faith is largely shaped by the bent of the popular will. The masses choose their faith through their feelings. There are many in our churches who have little better ground for much that forms the substance of their faith than the fact their affections were in some way won to the church with which they are identified.

Another cause of deception concerning the truth set forth in the text is the fact that so long a time elapses between the sowing and the reaping. A man who starts in the world to live a moral, upright life, dealing honestly, judging charitably, keeping pure in character, seems to fail in almost every undertaking. Another starting at the same time, careless in regard to morals, devoid of honorable principle and unjust in his dealings, seems to meet with success in all his undertakings. Such cases are about us, and they lead us to question whether sowing decides the reaping or whether, after all, it is not a matter of chance. The wicked flourish; the righteous seem afflicted. Sin is exalted, goodness is cast down.

To this difficulty I answer: First, temporal prosperity is not the normal reward of moral goodness. Whatsoever a man soweth *that* shall he reap, and not something else in kind. Secondly, this is not the time for the full harvest. This is sowing time; the time for reaping is yet to come. And, third, if this life is a probation the full reward of our doings must be postponed to a state beyond this. Were rewards to follow close-linked to the things we do, probation would be entirely out the question. If I thrust my hand into the fire, or cast myself from a precipice the suffering follows without delay. Not so the consequences of sin. They are mercifully rolled back to allow us opportunity to reform. This life is a probation, and this is an essential feature of the probation.

Still another danger of deception is found in the conclusions we deduce from imperfect and one-sided views of the divine character. God is many-sided. If we stand over on one side of the divine character and look upon what is there manifest, and fail to make note of other features, our conception of that character must be imperfect. For instance, we stand here and looking, say "God is mercy, goodness, gentleness, patience, forgiveness and all the gentler virtues. This is God." And then from these alone we reason to the conclusion that he cannot allow any to perish, and that he is too merciful to allow any to suffer. Were we to reason in this way we would but follow a way already popular. Why blind our eyes to the fact that justice and judgment are elements in that character? For he is sternly, inflexibly just. Judgment belongeth to him. He cannot look upon sin with allowance. Let us not suffer ourselves to be deceived by reasoning from imperfect premises.

The last source of deception I shall mention is the declarations of false teachers. The masses follow guides. A few do the thinking for the many. A bold denial of any truth has as much influence with many as a demonstration can have. When, therefore, men teach the ultimate happiness and glory of all regardless of their lives here (and so practically deny the truth of the text) their teaching is received as true. Or, even where intimations are made that destiny is not decided when this life closes, these intimations are received with delight. Not that God has authorized such intimations or given to these teachers a new message; not that they bring to light teachings of the Bible which have escaped the notice of others. No, no. The teaching is *theirs*, but owing to their position as religious guides it is received as of God. Beecher's "Background of Mystery" and Canon Farrar's "Eternal Hope" seems to me to belong to this class. Others are bolder, even affirming ultimate salvation for all, regardless of life and character.

But, whatever the source of deception may be — whether from unwillingness to believe a truth so unwelcome, or from the long delay between sowing and reaping, or from conclusions drawn from imperfect conceptions of the divine character, or from declarations of religious teachers — whatever may be the things which tend to deceive us concerning a matter so important, over against them all I place the apostolic exhortation, "Be not deceived; God is not mocked; for whatsoever a man soweth that shall he reap."

This principle I believe as firmly when applied to morals as I believe it when applied to sowing and reaping in the literal sense. I believe we must sow, and that we must reap, and that the harvest we must reap will in each case be determined by the character of our sowing. I desire to present some reasons for this belief.

Were you to close the Bible you have not shut out all evidence for such a faith. Nature demonstrates it.

If you give me an arc of a circle I can from that describe the entire circle. This is mathematics. There is a circle which embraces the universe. There is a circle of law. All things are under law, from the atom to the planets, from the insect of a day to the angels of God. The universal reign of law is a well established fact. Whatever is essentially true of law here is true of law everywhere. A treatise on the law of light, if true here must be true concerning light on the planet Mars. Now one essential feature of law is that its violation brings its penalty. A law without penalty is practically no law. If it be an essential feature of law that its violation brings penalty then it is true everywhere. We know it is true here. This is an arc in the circle of law. I sweep the circle and find it must be true hereafter. This is of the nature of a demonstration.

Our own observation and experience teach us the same. Remember, we see no results in their fullness here. The harvest is growing. But, just as I can walk through fields before the grain has developed, and say "this is wheat," or "this is barley," or "this is oats," even though the grain has not made its appearance, so can we, before the time of the eternal harvest, tell what that harvest will be. As we look at the moral aspects of our race we see that vice and sins and all forms of moral evil tend toward degradation, and that goodness and righteousness and all virtues tend toward elevation. Extend these lines infinitely and we have infinite degradation on one hand and infinite elevation on the other.

Open the Bible and we find this truth confirmed, beyond all question, by numerous and plain declarations. Character tends toward permanency. When we pass beyond the limits of this life he that is unholy must be unholy still and he that is righteous must be righteous still. We must reap as we have sown.

A truth so important as this, lying at the basis of life, has many practical lessons. I close by pointing out a few.

First, in planning life, look far ahead. Every life should have its plan. It is unworthy of us to live, day by day, the the sport of circumstances. Nor should we live simply for to-morrow or the near-lying future. The ultimate aim of our lives should be found in the far distant future. In selecting our associates, in choosing our profession, in adopting any course of life we should never fail to ask, what effect will this have upon our destiny?

Again, it brings encouragement to those who feel they are living right at a losing rate. This is the application Paul makes of the text: "Let us not grow weary in well doing; for in due season we shall reap if we faint not." All sowing seems to be a loss of labor, time, and seed. The farmer who takes the grain and with liberal hand casts it over the field seems to have lost it. Only one thought can induce him to do this, and that is he shall reap by and by. You have been striving to live right; to do good. It may be you are growing weary and discouraged. Think of the harvest, of the certainty of reaping, and renew your courage.

And, finally, you who have been living only for this world, sowing to the flesh, can you look to the coming harvest with any feeling of joy or even of satisfaction? "He that soweth to the flesh shall of the flesh reap corruption." Are you willing to reap such a harvest? If not, there is only one alternative. Through the sufferings and sacrifice of Christ,

God has provided forgiveness. Wonderful provision of still more wonderful grace! "For he hath made him to be sin for us, who knew no sin; that we might be made the righteousness of God in him." "The blood of Jesus Christ his Son cleanseth us from all sin." "There is therefore now no condemnation to them who are in Christ Jesus." Only in him can we find pardon, peace and salvation.

IDLERS INTERVIEWED.

And about the eleventh hour he went out, and found others standing idle, and saith unto them, "Why stand ye here all the day idle?" Mat. xx: 6.

In reading this parable of the laborers in the vineyard have you never observed how strikingly Christ brings out the Master's great desire to secure laborers? First, he pictures him as going *early in the morning* to hire them. That looks as if he were very much in earnest about it. Then as going out frequently, at short intervals. during the day, — early in the morning, first; then, at the third hour; then again, at at the sixth hour; still, again, at the ninth hour; and, finally at the eleventh hour. That looks as if he felt he *must* have a good supply. This earnest desire is shown, still further, by the fact that he continued these efforts until near the close of the day; for, when he went at the eleventh hour, only one hour of the day remained, And, finally, the urgency of the demand for laborers is shown by the fact that, in each case, as soon as he employed them he sent them into the vineyard to work. He did not engage them to go the first of the next week, or to begin next morning, but *at once,* "go ye into my vineyard." If the "householder," in this parable, is designed to represent Christ, our Master — as undoubtly he is — then we are to learn from it something of Christ's great desire to secure laborers for his vineyard.

I ask your attention also to the very reasonable excuse these men in the market-place offered when he said: "Why stand ye here all the day idle?" They promptly replied: "Because no man hath hired us." They seem to have been in search of employment. They were in the right place to find it; for the market-places then were different from what they are now. They were places of general resort. All classes could be found there, so that it became the best place for those to go who desired to secure employment. A recent traveller in the East remarks having noticed, every morning before the sun was up, that a numerous body of peasants were collected at the market-place with spades in hand, waiting to be hired for the day to work in the surrounding fields. He speaks also of passing the same place late in the day, and seeing some still standing there idle. They had failed to find employment. No man had hired them. It was the place whither those who desired to find laborers would go, as is shown by the conduct of the householder, mentioned in this parable. The excuse — no man hath hired us — was, therefore, a very reasonable one, when given by those who stood in the market-place.

Had the master gone to his vineyard, after sending these men there, he would have found many of them still idle; or else that vineyard was very different, in this, from the spiritual vineyard which it is supposed to represent. For in the spiritual vineyard there are often more idlers than workers. There is a very small percentage of active Christian workers in the world. In almost every church the labor is performed by a select few. The many do nothing. They are idlers. Nor can *they* say they stand all the day idle " because no man hath hired " them. They have been engaged to work, and they were sent into the vineyard for just that purpose.

And this fact, that our churches have so many idlers in them, is a more serious matter than you may be disposed to think at first. The work is suffering, the fruit is wasting, the idlers become demoralized, others are discouraged, and sacred obligation is ignored. I desire, therefore, to speak to you very candidly about this matter. Many in this church are doing nothing. Why is it? Why stand ye here all the day idle? I desire to interview you. I do not come in the spirit of complaint or censure, but I come with a feeling of brotherly interest — of deep, loving concern. I desire to deal fairly and candidly with you; to frankly hear and meet your excuses. If there are difficulties in your way I trust I may aid in removing them. I desire to enlist your services for our common Lord. You have entered his vineyard — you have been in it, it may be for many years, yet you are doing nothing. I come to *you* with the question " Why stand ye here idle all the day? " Will you please give some reason.

" Well, I didn't know I was expected to work," you say. " Many were in the vineyard when I entered, who were doing nothing, I had noticed that in every church there were two classes — workers and idlers — and it seemed to be wholly a matter of taste and personal inclination as to which class any one would join. Besides, when I was invited to enter, if the matter of working was mentioned at all it certainly was not made prominent. To be candid, I came in because I thought there was danger outside, and also because I thought I would receive more attention within."

That is candid. Not many will state the reason which induced them to enter the church as plainly and frankly as you have. No doubt many are in the church because they thought they would receive more attention within its fellowship. They have come in to be helped. Others are in because it seemed to be the only place of safety. They did not think as they entered that they became the servants of Christ.

Let me, therefore, say to you plainly that the call authorized by Christ *is a call to work.* If those who induced you to enter the vineyard did not make this prominent they failed to do their duty as his messengers. No one has any right to extend a call that has not in it this feature. From first to last it is, "Go into my vineyard and work." You have entered; but if you are not willing to work you are in the wrong place. Our Master does not send men into his vineyard to idle. If you are unwilling to work, if you cannot be induced to do something for the Master then get out. The church will be better by your leaving. But if you are willing to give yourself in practical service to Christ, then quickly find something you can do, and do it. No time to be lost. Lay hold upon that which is nearest to you and do it so faithfully that the Master will open before you fields of larger usefulness.

Another says, "I see nothing to do. I have looked around — I offered to teach in the Sunday school, but every class seemed to be supplied; I once thought of preaching, but there seems to be more preachers now than are properly supported. I see no opening."

Don't wait for an opening. Don't be discouraged if you do not at once, and without anxiety or search, find a place. Those who succeed in any calling in life are not the ones who wait for openings. If you do not see an opening *go to work and make one.* With so much to be done, with fields white already to the harvest, and with laborers few, it seems strange there is nothing for you to do. Study this field, then study yourself, and among the many things to be done select some which *you* can do. But, if you are not qualified, go to work and qualify yourself. In what other field can men and women work successfully without thought and training? Why then should you suppose that you can succeed in serving Christ in good works without thoughtful training? Skill must be acquired. Efficiency must be gained through repeated effort.

Go to work. The successful business men in this city, are not, as a general rule, those who inherited fortunes. They began as poor young men. They did not wait for some easy place, some flattering opening. They took hold upon some work and by fidelity, by diligence, by perseverance, they rose to their present position. God does not call idlers to great fields. Elisha, Saul, David, Peter, James, John, Matthew, and many, many others whom he called to great works, were already busy in the fields where they were.

A loving heart will greatly aid you in finding your place. I remember the case of a girl who was reared in a family wealthy and worldly. She was sent away from home to a boarding-school, and there met with some who were thoroughly Christian in heart and life — they became her companions. Gradually she was won from worldliness to Christ. She gave her heart to him and consecrated her life to his service. After her graduation she returned to her home, and although her parents did not approve of what she had done, they supposed that her case would be like that of many others — that her religion would end in simple profession. But she had lovingly consecrated her life to the service of Christ, and she could not be content until she found something to do. The first Sunday after she returned home she went to the Sunday School and asked if she could be of any service there. She was informed that all places were filled. She felt she *must* have some one to whom she could impart a knowledge of the way of life and salvation. So the next day she went upon the street, and this question was in her mind all the time — what can I do? By and by a rude boy of the street came near running against her and she stopped him and began talking with him. With much persuasion she secured a promise that he would come to the Sunday school on the following Lord's day. This encouraged her, and so she continued her efforts in that direction until a large class had been gathered of the neglected and abandoned boys of the street. What more Christlike! Yet the good she did them was not the only fruit borne of this spirit of consecration. The entire school took on new life. Other classes grew, and eternity alone can reveal the full harvest of that persistent effort of love.

Many of us are blind to our opportunities, because our hearts are too cold.

Another is asked, "Why stand *you* here all the day idle?" and the answer is, "I am tired and discouraged. I have been at work, and found real joy in it while it prospered. But now it seems at a stand still. I see no fruits — no prospect of success, and so I am discouraged."

But, what is that to you? You are only a servant. The question of fruitage belongs to the Master. In the day of reckoning he will not say, "Well, done good and *successful* servant," but "Well done good and *faithful* servant," If you are only faithful, if you really do the best your circumstances allow, you may leave results with the Master. I know it is natural, and I believe it right for us to feel deep solicitude for the success of the work in which we are engaged; but I am sure it is wrong for us to cease to serve Christ simply because our work does not seem to prosper.

It was to meet just such a tendency as this that Paul wrote, "Let us not be weary in well doing; for in due season we shall reap, if we faint not." Those who sow seem to be losing their grain and wasting their time. They must patiently wait to see the results of their labors. You may be mistaken, my brother, as to actual results of your efforts. Remember that time only can fully show what you have done. Right living cannot be barren of results, and many deeds which have seemed to us to be wholly lost we may some day find have been hidden away in another's heart and working out good in another's life.

> "I shot an arrow into the air,
> It fell to earth, I knew not where;
> For, so swift it flew, the sight
> Could not follow it in its flight.
>
> I breathed a song into the air,
> It fell on earth I knew not where;
> For who has sight so keen and strong,
> That it can follow the flight of song?
>
> Long, long afterward in an oak,
> I found the arrow, still unbroke:
> And the song, from beginning to end,
> I found again in the heart of a friend."

Dr. Judson labored diligently for six years in Burmah before he baptized a convert. At the end of three years, he was asked what evidence he had of ultimate success. He replied, "As much as there is a God who will fulfil all his promises." Hundreds of churches and thousands of converts already answer his faith. In Western Africa, it was fourteen years before one convert was received into the church; in East Africa, ten; in New Zealand it was nine years before there was one baptism, two more before the second. Yet it is a remarkable fact that where the faith of the church has been peculiarly tried by these discouragements, the success has been most rich and abundant afterward. Let us not be discouraged because we cannot both sow and reap in the same season. Let us not grow weary of well doing. Be thou faithful.

"Why stand ye here all the day idle?" And the answer comes from another group, "We do not work because others will not. They will not help. A few of us kept on after they quit, but what is the use? We cannot do everything. If others would help — if all would only take hold as they ought we would gladly do our best."

Well, that *is* discouraging; but you will not have to answer for them, neither will you be held to account for more than you can do. Every one of us must give account of *himself* to God, and all are to be judged according to the measure of our ability.

Then, too, your fidelity will appear only the more conspicuous in the midst of such discouragements, and it will surely meet with appropriate recognition. There was, at one time, quite a flourishing little Presbyterian church in a certain town in Illinois. From different causes it went down, until finally the Synod decided to formally disband it and sell the house. For this purpose they sent a committee to the place. In vain they searched for members, officers or trustees. At last some one told the committee of an old lady who had been a member from the beginning. They called to see her and stated their mission, — but she most positively refused to be disbanded! They insisted; she persisted. Finally they decided to send a preacher there. The cause was revived and the church became more flourishing than ever before. As the darkness of the night brings out the stars, so the gloom of her surroundings makes her devotion shine out with greater splendor. It is not much to our credit to be faithful and diligent in work only when everything favors such a life, and the tide of events bears us in that direction. Though others idle and even abandon the field, continue diligent, do the work faithfully which the Master has given *you* to do, and verily thou shalt be duly rewarded.

"I'm not doing anything," answers another, "because when I tried, and did my best, I was rewarded by adverse criticism. Some didn't like the *way* in which I did my part; while others said I pushed myself forward and made myself too prominent. So I quit."

I beg you to remember, my brother, that you are not alone in being the subject of adverse criticism. Paul, the most eminent of Christ's servants, was in the same category. Christ, himself, was met at every stage of his work with adverse, even bitter, criticism. Do not expect every body to be pleased with your work. Be sure you have your heart in your work, that you are moved by proper motives, that you are really serving Christ and not working toward selfish ends and you may well ignore all these adverse criticisms. Your Master has said: "Woe unto you when all men shall speak well of you."

But, now and then, these criticisms may be made really helpful. Let us not be too ready to suppose that there is no just ground for them. Give them candid consideration, and you may be able to improve by them. It is said that Mr. Spurgeon keeps a scrap-book in which he puts every adverse criticism he can find concerning himself and his work and uses them as correctives and as an antidote to pride. He says he finds them helpful. So may we. But even if we cannot extract counsel or help from them, let us learn not to chafe under them; and, above all, suffer them not to turn you from the service to which you have been called. We are exhorted by an apostle to work " not as men pleasers, but in singleness of heart, fearing God; and whatsoever ye do, do it heartily, as to the Lord, and not unto men; knowing that of the Lord ye shall receive the reward of the inheritance: for we serve the Lord Christ."

A word also to you, O you carping critics. "Who art thou that judgest another man's servant? to his own master he standeth or falleth." You have not been chosen to sit on the judgment seat. Your place is in the vineyard. If you understand better than your brother-laborer just how the work should be done, show your superior knowledge by superior work. It is, however, no mark of superior wisdom to be a fault-finder. It is more frequently a sign of a bad spirit. As a rule men and women find in this world what they are looking for. The vulture finds carrion, for its tastes lead it to seek for carrion; but the bee finds honey, for its tastes lead it to seek for honey. So you are telling a bad story on yourself whenever you open your lips in evil speech and adverse criticism. Stop it, for your own sake; stop it, for the sake of others; stop it, for the sake of the cause of Christ. Stop it, and go to work,

And *you*, my brother, standing off there with arms folded, why do you stand idle?

"Well, were I to speak candidly, and to give you the real reason, I would be compelled to say that I shrink from such work because I am not what I ought to be. I feel unworthy. I found pleasure for awhile, after entering the vineyard, in the work I was doing, but in an evil moment I was led astray and I feel covered with shame. I would go to work again, but I feel that those who engage in such work should be of clean record. That is the only reason I am idle."

A candid confession; and I am sure you do not speak for for yourself alone, others feel just as you; for there is a conviction, almost instruction, that those who are engaged in the Lord's service should be of clean hands and pure hearts. Coupled with this feeling is often found the consciousness of sin. I sympathize with you, my brother.

What should you do? Strive to reform your character. Humbly and penitently confess your fault, and seek forgiveness. Do not allow past sins to drive you from the field. If you have wronged any one, strive by every means at your command to make restitution. Peter denied his Master, in a way and under circumstances which made his apostasy a very grievous one. But he did not abandon the work, nor forsake his Lord. He wept bitterly, and at the first opportunity gave himself to Christ more truly and humbly again. On the day of Pentecost he did not say, "I'll not have anything to say, for I denied my Lord." Nor did his co-laborers advice him to remain in the background and keep silent. But he came to the front and with new power and fervor advocated the claims of his glorious and gracious Lord. And in all his after life, we can see his chastened spirit, as it speaks in brotherly counsel and admonition to others.

Nothing can so help to restore your spiritual health as faithful labor. It will give tone to your spiritual nature and add strength to your character. It will be a safe-guard against temptation. Your idleness exposed you to the attacks of Satan. For your own sake, then as well as for the good of the cause of Christ, repent of your sins, confess them humbly before God, make restitution, and *go to work*. And may the Master abundantly bless you in your labors.

"As for myself," says another, "I am not trying to do anything, because what I can do is so little, it is hardly worth doing."

Two passages, from the lips of Christ, it seems to me, were spoken for the special benefit of such as you. The first, as an encouragement. It is the commendation which he pronounced upon the poor widow who gave into the treasury only two mites. But it was all she could give, for it was all she had. "Verily, I say unto you, this poor widow has cast more in, than all they which have cast into the treasury. For all they did cast in of their abundance; but she of her want did cast in all that she had, even all her living." Are not these words of Christ full of encouragement unto you, O ye who feel you can do but little? Our Master has regard for our weakness and the measure of our ability,

The other case to which I refer furnished a solemn warning. It is the case of the man who had only one talent and he "digged in the earth and hid his lord's money." He could not do as much as the others, and so did nothing. But remember his fate when the master returned to reckon with his servants. While he pronounced an equal blessing upon the others, because they had shown themselves equal in fidelity, he said concerning this one, "Take, therefore, the talent from him * * * and cast ye the unprofitable servant into outer darkness; there shall be wailing and gnashing of teeth." This is a fearful warning to us to whom our Lord has committed only one talent. Let us use what has been committed to our trust with all fidelity, although the results which attend our efforts may not seem so fruitful as others.

I cannot, however, deal with excuses longer. This morning it may be I have not touched upon your excuse. If you are not at work for Christ, why not? Out with your reason! What is it? Are you willing to present that before Christ at his coming? Have you no desire to serve him who has ransomed you by his own blood? It seems to me the strongest desire of every believing heart would be to serve him. Conscious of sin, yet rejoicing in his saving grace, prostrate at his feet we lie and ask, "Lord, what wilt thou have me to do?"

I will detain you only long enough to name some reasons why we should at once enter upon active service.

1. First, the field is suffering for it. The master went out early and often because he saw the need for laborers. The case was urgent. He taught his disciples to pray for more laborers.

2. You need it for your own good. Idleness is very demoralizing. It may be you are not enjoying your religion. Work will help you. It will bring you into fellowship with the best Christians, and, more than that, it will bring you into fellowship with Christ.

3. The master has a *right* to expect it of us. We are not our own. By every title of ownership we belong to him. Our time, our talents, our means, our energies, our influence every thing we have and are, belongs to Christ. He, therefore, has a right to our service.

4. There is coming a day of reckoning. The Master will return. We know not when. But when he comes will he find us doing that which he has left us to do? In his parables he represents some as sleeping, some drunken, some at work when he returns. How will he find *you*? Often ask yourself, suppose he should come now —— ? Yet he sees and knows your conduct and your heart all the time.

If you can do nothing more you can pray for those who are at work, and speak encouraging words to them. Like Aaron and Hur you can hold up weary hands. And even though you may be able to do many other things, do not fail to do this. Pray for more workers; pray for those already in the field; speak encouraging words to them.

And now, I pray you, go forth gladly to toil. Go forth with the inspiration of love. Go forth with a song. Go forth carrying with you the thought of the divine presence. Go forth willing to work anywhere and at any thing that will glorify our Lord. We want no idlers here. We want this church to be known not as "The Church of the Heavenly Rest," but as "The Church of Heavenly Work." Whatever man may think of the orthodoxy of our creed let us by the abundance of our good works convince them of the orthodoxy of your lives. And may the Lord of the harvest abundantly bless us in our labors. Amen.

THE DISTINCTIVE PECULIARITIES OF THE DISCIPLES.

But we desire to hear of thee what thou thinkest; for as concerning this sect, we know that everywhere it is spoken against. Acts xxviii: 22.

This congregation, whose history I briefly sketched this morning,* stands connected with one of the most remarkable movements that has occurred since the great apostasy. The rapidity of its growth alone is enough to arrest the attention of every thoughtful observer. The reformation, which was begun in England, by the Wesleys, with such vivifying results more than a century ago, and which has made its power so felt in this land, is remarkable for the rapidity with which its ranks increased. But statistics will show that rapid as was the growth of that movement, the reformation which was inaugurated in this country in the early part of this century, has been more rapid. For although the famous declaration and address written by Thomas Campbell (then a Presbyterian minister recently come from Scotland), was not published until 1809, and although that stands as the first distinct proposal and call for this reformatory movement, yet we already stand in the front ranks in numerical strength in the United States, according to its latest official census returns; and, in other

---

* This sermon was preached at the Semi-Centennial Celebration of the Seventh Street Christian Church, Richmond, Virginia, March 5, 1882. The morning sermon gave a history of the congregation from its organization by Thomas Campbell, in 1882.

lands, as England and Australia, there are to be found many devoted to the same plea and movement. These facts I mention, not in the spirit of party pride, but to indicate that the movement is worthy of your thoughtful attention.

I propose to speak with the utmost candor to-night of the distinctive peculiarities of this brotherhood of Christians known to the world as the Disciples of Christ. For we have peculiarities. If we had none, or if those we have were not matters of deep conviction with us, there could be found no adequate apology for our existence as a separate and distinct people. I cheerfully recognize the right of all to know just what these peculiarities are, and why we hold them. And, although these points involve matters of controversy, I will not speak to you in that spirit. I shun controversy. Especially do I shun the *spirit* of controversy. I am aware also of the natural tendency to unduly exalt, in politics, in science, in society, in religion, in everything where men think and differ, those points over which they differ and around which controversy has raged. With us all our peculiarities are our pets. Knowing this weakness of human nature, I stand on guard against it. Before taking up the special points to be considered to-night, I desire most cheerfully and emphatically to recognize a fact too often forgotten when speaking of religious differences; the fact that in many things — yea in most things — yea, more, in the best things of our common faith and holy religion — all professing Christians are in substantial agreement.

Were you to ask of me one word which would most exactly present the central purpose of the peculiar plea presented by the Disciples, I would give you the deeply significant and and comprehensive word *restoration*. For it was their purpose, as they declared in the beginning, and as, without variation they have continued to declare to the present, to restore to the world in faith, in spirit, and in practice, the religion of Christ and his apostles, as found on the pages of the New Testament Scriptures. The originators of this movement did not propose to themselves as their distinct work the reformation of any existing religious body, or the recasting of any existing religious creed. They proposed to themselves, and to all who might choose to associate themselves with them in this work, a task no less than restoration. They clearly saw, and from the beginning distinctly recognized, that in order to do this, they must ignore and pass back back beyond all ecclesiastical councils, with their creeds and confessions, their speculations and controversies, since the days of the apostles, and take up the work just as these inspired men left it. In the study of any movement it is of great importance to understand its purpose; and this I present as *the* purpose of the movement whose peculiarities we are to consider to-night. Our aim is certainly right, and the work proposed is needed. Whatever peculiarities we have arise from an honest effort to realize that aim. We may have erred in some of the details. The Bible *alone* must decide that. I do not stand here to claim that we have practically, and in all its details, accomplished the end proposed. We are only working toward it.

With these preliminaries, I now proceed to a more detailed statement of distinctive peculiarities, asking for them only a candid consideration in the light of the New Testament Scriptures.

I. *We are peculiar in our plea for Christian union.*

Open your New Testament and your will find that the church there is a unit. One flock, one body, one spiritual temple, one household, are some of the figures under which we therein find it presented. It was of one mind, and of one heart. But if we look abroad over the Christian world, do we find this true to-day? Leaving out of view for the present, the larger factions into which it is divided — the Greek, the Papal, and the Protestant — and fixing our eyes upon the last named only, what do we behold? A house divided against itself; a kingdom made weak by internal discord and division. Turning again to the book, we hear the Savior, in the very shadow of the cross, praying for all who may believe on him, through the apostolic word, that they be one; we find all divisions deeply deplored; schismatics are sharply censured; not even a Paul, an Apollos, or a Cephas, allowed to be the leader of a party; and sectism branded as a sin so great as to prevent the world's believing in the divine mission of our Savior. Others may say division is unwise, but in the light of this we say *it is sinful*. And whatever apologies may be made for the present divided state of the religious world, it must be evident to every one that the restoration for which we plead cannot be complete until it can be said again, as Paul said in his day, "There is one body, and one spirit, even as ye are called in one hope of your calling; one Lord, one faith, one baptism, one God and father of all, who is above all, and through all, and in you all."*

As we study the historic development of this movement, we find its protest against divisions, and its plea for Christian union was its first strongly marked feature. The declaration and address of 1809 was an arraignment of sectism, depicting its evil consequences and its sinful nature, and an earnest call upon ministers and churches to labor for the union of Christians as they were united in the beginning. "After considering the divisions in various lights," says Dr.

---

* Ephesians, iv: 4–5.

Richardson, in his Memoirs of A. Campbell,† "as hindering the dispensation of the Lord's Supper; spiritual intercourse among Christians; ministerial labors, and the effective exercise of church discipline, as well as tending to promote infidelity, an appeal is made to gospel ministers to become leaders in the endeavor to remedy these evils; and especially is this urged upon those in the United States, as a country happily exempted from the baneful influence of a civil establishment of any particular form of Christianity, and from under the influence of an anti-Christian hierarchy." This movement did not arise from controversy about any particular views of baptism, spiritual influence, or kindred questions mooted at a later date, in the progress of the work. Let this statement be considered emphatic, since the popular idea seems to be that out of such controversy we arose, and that our plea finds its roots in these questions. *The central aim was restoration; the first feature sought to be restored was the union of Christians as in the beginning.*

During the past fifty years a great change has come over the churches and their pulpits on this question of union. Then it was seldom advocated, and was exceedingly unpopular. Now it is one of the most popular of pulpit themes. The change that has taken place has greatly toned down our appearance of peculiarity on this one point. Others now advocate union. Many, recognizing the force of increasing popular feeling against divisions, are striving to show that in the midst of all strife, or rather underlying all existing divisions, there exists an essential unity. These different religious bodies, they tell us, are only so many divisions of one grand army. Here is the light infantry, here the heavy artillery, here the cavalry,

---

† **Memoirs of A. Campbell**, Vol. I., p. 253.

here the navy; but all are fighting under one commander, and follow one flag. Now, most cheerfully conceding all the unity in doctrine, and in spirit, and in practice, which exists among these hundreds of separate bodies, let us pause to inquire whether the parts of this beautiful figure actually set forth the facts in the case. In the grand army the proper authority has so ordered the division of it, and given not only the sanction of authority to such division, but also defines the duties of each. The right of each division to be what it is, and to do what it does, can be and must be traced up to the head of the entire army. The law that constitutes it an army at all, constitutes it just the army it is. Can this essential point be claimed by the denominations of Christianity to-day? Where has the Great Head of the Church authorized such a division of his body, and in what place do we find him defining the the duties of each? Or again, does the mutual support and helpfulness which exists among the armed forces of a nation, find any parallel among these denominational divisions of the church? The cavalry, the infantry, the artillery, the navy exist as separate parts of the force, that it may render more effective service by the support each may render to the others. But, when we speak in harmony with the facts concerning the church, we are compelled to confess with grief and shame, that, instead of mutual support, much of its strength is worse than wasted in fratricidal strife. Rivalry, contention, excommunication, and anathema, tell the sad story. The figure may be beautiful and rhetorical, but it lacks the important feature of fidelity to facts. I have heard it said again, that it is better for the church to stand like the frowning cliffs of the riven rock than to lie like the dead sand of indifference on the barren beach. But, must we confess that our choice is limited to these two conditions? Has it come to pass that the church can live only by rending strife, or lie down in indifference, indolence and death? This is a poor apology for division; that a delusive presentation of a hidden union. These voices are but the dying echoes of the opposition to union which were heard all over the land years ago.

The fact is, the idea of union is becoming more popular as the years pass by. Yet while this is true, the plea for union, which the Disciples present, is still peculiar. They oppose division not simply as unwise and impolitic, but as *positively sinful*, and to be repented of and forsaken as any other sin. They plead not simply for an underlying and hidden unity, but for an open and manifest union, such a unity and union that the world may see it and believe, concerning Christ, that God sent him into the world.* They do not call for a confederation of sects, but labor for the total abolition of sectism. On this point we desire to see produced what is advocated in apostolic teaching. There should be no divisions among us.† This first point is our first peculiarity, historically considered, and is, logically considered, the prominent feature of our plea.

II. *We are peculiar in reference to human names for the children of God and the body of Christ.*

We reject all human names. Our reasons for opposing human names are such as these: —

1. Because they perpetuate party spirit. It is frequently asked, "What's in a name?" I answer, There is in every name what its surroundings and attendant events have put into that name. A time was when there was nothing in the name *Napoleon*, but the daring and sanguinary life he lived who wore that name, the victories that crowned his military exploits, as kings became uncrowned and nations

---

* John xvii: 21. † I. Cor. i:10.

cowered at his feet, has made that name to signifiy military genius; nothing in the name *Howard*, until John Howard, released, from prison in France, and made high sheriff of Bedford, entered upon his work of prison reforms, and continued to prosecute this work of humanity and benevolence, spending more than thirty thousand pounds from his own purse, and traveling over fifty thousand miles through fatigue and danger, made that name the synonym of unselfish benevolence; nothing in the name *Washington*, until by fortitude and bravery, born of devotion to his country, in just cause, our own countrymen made it mean to all the world Christian patriotism. So it is in reference to party names. There is in them what attendant circumstances and events have placed there. They all have been born of strife and christtened with wormwood and gall. The church divides. Party spirit runs high and becomes regnant. A new name is chosen for a new party, and party spirit lies embalmed in that name.

It is almost impossible to adequately describe the hidden potency of these names; they have a sway over human nature which we are slow to acknowledge. Let any one enter a church that wears a different name, and announce himself by his denominational name, and if recognition be accorded him it will be formal rather than fraternal. There are pulpits from which I am practically excluded, but into which I would be cordially invited *with the very message I now deliver*, if only I would assume their party name. There are churches from whose communion table I am excluded, but to which I would receive a fraternal welcome should I simply assume their denominational name. These are facts. I give them as samples of many more. They show something of what there is in a name, and how party names perpetuate party spirit.

2. We reject them simply because it is impossible to find a human name which all Christians would consent to wear. That is, you cannot unite all the children of God under an existing denominational name. Take the most honored of these names — names worn by some of the most saintly of earth — as Methodist, Baptist, Presbyterian, Episcopal, Lutheran — names like these, and can you suppose for one moment, that all Christians could be induced to unite under any one of them? Moreover, would it be right if they could? *Yet union is right, and division is sinful.* If we labor for restoration, we must labor for union; if we labor wisely for union, we must, so far as name is concerned take only that which all can consent to wear without wounding of conscience; if we take only that which all can consent to wear without wounding of conscience, we must take only what inspiration sanctions; if we take only that which inspiration sanctions, we must reject all human names for the children of God and of the body of Christ.

3. We reject them because we hold it quite enough to be simply a Christian. But if we are only a Christian, why do you need more than that name to tell what you are? If you are a Christian, and something besides, then whatever that is you are besides, for that you need some name besides. If you aim to be a modern modified Christian, rather than such as were made under inspired teaching, you should have some name to fitly set forth that fact to the world. But, if you aim to be simply a Christian, then you need no other title than some one found in the book to set forth that fact. *We hold it is quite enough to be simply a Christian.* We use all revealed truth, all ordinances, all means of grace to make men such, and to develop them in Christian character. We do not desire them to be other than this, and we reject all human names.

4. We reject them as dishonoring to Christ. His is the worthy name by which they they were called in the beginning.* For him the whole family in heaven and in earth is named.† To us he is all in all. He has washed us in his blood, and we have been espoused‡ to him. The church is his bride, the Lamb's wife.§ Christ is called the bridegroom.‖ The wife should wear the name of her husband, and it would be held by the world as dishonoring him, should she wear the name of one of his servants, however faithful that servant might be to him, or that of a friend, how devoted soever his friendship may be. In the church at Corinth they were sharply rebuked for saying, "I am of Paul; and I of Apollos; and I of Cephas."¶ Although two of these were chosen apostles, and the other an eloquent man and mighty in the Scriptures.** "Is Christ divided? was Paul crucified for you? or were you baptized into the name of Paul?"†† are the questions with which he expresses his reprehension of such a course, and his amazement. Take the names of any in later times, eminent for their devotion and services, and with equal justice may these questions be propounded to the churches wearing their names. It is no reflection upon them or their worth to refuse to be called by their names, but to wear them is a dishonor to Christ, although not so intended.

For this reason we have refused with an earnestness and persistency which are a perplexity to some, to wear the name of Campbell. Our refusal to be called Campbellites is grounded on principle. We cannot consistently consent — we *will not* consent — to wear the name of any man. To do so would be to sacrifice a fundamental principle. It would

---

* James ii: 7. † Eph. iii: 14–15. ‡ 2 Cor. xi: 2
§ Rev. xxi: 9. ‖ Mark ii: 19–20. ¶ 1 Cor. i: 12.
** Acts xviii: 24. †† Cor. i: 13.

be a practical abandonment of the work upon which we have entered. "But," it is objected, "your exclusive appropriation of the name Christian implies that, in your opinion, there are no Christians in the world except yourselves." In this objection there would be force if we really aimed at an *exclusive* appropriation of this name. But this exclusiveness is not in our claim. We distinctly teach there are most excellent Christians who are not enrolled with us. Were this not true, pray why should we plead for the union of Christians? *We* are united, and, if we did not believe there are Christians in the world outside of our ranks, our plea would be senseless and absurd. The point in which we are peculiar is simply this — *we persistently reject all human names.* We rejoice that there are so many devout Christians in the world, and we call upon them to abandon all party names, and be content to be known by those names only which we find in the New Testament.

III. *We are peculiar in our rejection of human creeds and books of discipline, for the faith and government of the church.*

The claim of Protestantism is, that it takes only the Bible as its rule of faith and practice. As has been tersely and strongly put, "the Bible, the whole Bible, and nothing but the Bible, is the religion of Protestants." And yet the parties into which Protestantism is divided practically nullify this high claim by adding creeds of their own construction. We reject all man-made creeds, and for such reasons as the following: —

1. Because we believe the Bible *alone* is sufficient. We hold the sacred Scriptures as given of God to meet all the purposes of a guide to our faith, a rule for our life, and law for the government and discipline of the church. As Paul has said, "All Scripture is given by inspiration of God, and

is profitable for doctrine, for reproof, for correction, for instruction in righteousness; that the man of God may be perfect, thoroughly furnished unto all good works."* What more can we ask than is here claimed for the Scriptures? They are profitable for doctrine; this covers the whole ground of truth needed to make us wise unto salvation. They are profitable for reproof; that is, they are sufficient to silence heresy. They are profitable for correction; no other book of discipline is needed. They are profitable for instruction in righteousness; in them may be found all that we need for development in righteousness and personal holiness. This, remember, is God's own estimate of his word, and his description of its purposes and use. We say it is enough. We, hence, reject all other books of faith and discipline.

Moreover, we claim that to prepare and issue any other book, as binding on the faith and practice of the children of God, is a *very grave* mistake. It not only implies that the Scriptures *alone* do *not* thoroughly furnish the man of God for the important matters specified, but the man-made creed is a step toward apostasy. As another has illustrated — "Compare this with a well known feature in the Roman apostasy. The Bible declares there is one mediator, between God and man, and that there is salvation in none other; that his blood cleanseth us from sin. What, in this cardinal point, is the very gist of Roman apostasy? Denying Christ? No. Denying that he is the Mediator? No. What then? She adds other mediators — the virgin and the saints. This is recognized by all Protestants as the very essence of her apostasy on this point. But, men and brethren, I submit to you whether the case in hand be not precisely parallel. God declares that the man of God who sincerely re-

---

* 2 Tim. iii: 16–17.

ceives and adopts the Bible, is *perfect* for certain specified purposes. But the creed-makers declare that the man of God who sincerely receives and adopts the Bible and *this creed* is perfect for the same specified purposes." Rome adds mediators to the one Mediator appointed of God; creed-makers add creeds to the one Book given of God. We reject not only the added mediators, but added creeds. The Bible alone is sufficient.

2. We reject them because they make speculations and opinions matters of faith. Every creed has risen out of controversy. Its chief purpose has been to define the position, on these controverted points, of those who subscribe to it. Almost any one of the many creeds now in existence would serve as an illustration of this point. They are full of speculative, philosophical, metaphysical untaught questions. They undertake to define exactly what we are to believe about the many questions which cluster around the doctrine of the Trinity, the fall of man, free will, divine decrees, irresistible grace, miraculous regeneration, etc., etc. Fine-spun, hair-splitting distinctions are foisted into articles of faith. Do you ever read any of these creeds? You will find what I say is the simple truth. Take the Athanasian as an illustration. I will read you only the first paragraph: —

"Whosoever will be saved, before all things it is necessary that he hold the catholic faith," *(not the Roman Catholic)*; "which faith except every one do keep whole and undefiled, without doubt he shall perish everlastingly. And the catholic faith is this: That we worship one God in Trinity, and Trinity in Unity; neither confounding the persons, nor dividing the substance. For there is one person of the Father, another of the Son, and another of the Holy Ghost; but the Godhead of the Father, and of the Son, and of the Holy Ghost is all one; the glory equal, the majesty co-eternal. Such as the Father is, such is the Son, and such is the Holy Ghost; the Father uncreate, the Son uncreate, the Holy Ghost uncreate; the Father incomprehensible, the Son incomprehensible, the Holy Ghost incomprehensible; the Father eternal, the Son eternal, the Holy Ghost eternal; and yet they are not three eternals, but one eternal; as also there are not three incomprehensibles, nor three uncreated, but one uncreated, and one incomprehensible. So likewise the Father is Almighty, the Son Almighty, and the Holy Ghost Almighty; yet they are not three Almighties, but one Almighty. So the Father is God, the Son is God, and the Holy Ghost is God; yet there are not three Gods, but one God. So likewise the Father is Lord, the Son is Lord, and the Holy Ghost is Lord; yet there are not three Lords, but one Lord. For like as we are compelled by the Christian verity to acknowledge every Person by himself to be God and Lord, so we are forbidden by the catholic religion to say there be three Gods, or three Lords."

I might read more of this which is gravely set forth as essential to the faith that saves; but, should I continue to the end, I fear you would feel so bewildered as to need a directory to show you the way out of church. I give you this as a sample. Every question about which men have differed, every fine distinction of which schoolmen have dreamed and disputed, every point of controversy that has risen and agitated the body of Christ, has been lifted into an article of faith. The natural tendency of controversy is to magnify into undue proportion the points involved. But, every man-made creed of Christendom has either risen directly or indirectly out of a religious controversy. It is, therefore, but the outgrowth of a natural law that they foist speculation and matters of opinion into articles of faith.

There are other reasons which I cannot take the time to

elaborate; such as these: No man, no body of men, *has the right* to say what faith is essential. That prerogative belongs to God only. Again, creeds of man's composition *are useless*. For if they contain more than is in the Bible, they contain too much; if they contain less than is in the Bible, they contain too little; if they contain only what is in the Bible, they are wholly useless. And, finally, time has demonstrated that instead of their being bonds of union they *are schismatical* in their tendency. We seek to avoid speculations on untaught questions. We hold that they gender strife. The silence of the Bible is to be respected as much as its revelations. "Infinite wisdom was required as much to determine of what men should be ignorant as what men should know. Indeed, since, in regard to all matters connected with the unseen spiritual world, man is dependent upon Divine revelation, the limits of that revelation must necessarily mark out also the domain of human ignorance, as the shores of a continent become the boundaries of a trackless and unfathomed ocean." Out of this view there have arisen among us such maxims as these: "Where the Bible speaks, we will speak; where the Bible is silent, we will be silent," and "Bible names for Bible things, and Bible thoughts in Bible terms."

IV. *We are somewhat peculiar in our division of the Bible, and the exclusive authority we ascribe to the New Testament.*

That you may understand our position on this entire question, I submit these points: 1. We hold and teach, as others, the *inspiration* of the entire Bible. We believe that in olden times "Holy men of God spake as they were moved by the Holy Spirit." 2. We hold the New Testament *only* as a *book of authority* to us. "God, who at sundry times, and in divers manners, spake unto the fathers by the prophets, hath, in these last days, spoken unto us by his

Son."* 3. We hold that the Old Testament was a book of authority to the Jews, but that with the establishment of the new covenant, of which Christ is Mediator, the old covenant closed and the *authority* of its book gave way to the authority of the Scriptures of the new covenant.† 4. We believe that the Old Testament is necessary for *our understanding* of the New, and that it contains, for us, many examples of faith and godliness, and lessons in personal holiness. In the declaration and address of 1809 may be found this proposition, submitted along with others, looking toward restoration and union.

"That although the Scriptures of the Old and the New Testaments are inseparably connected, making together but one perfect and entire revelation of the Divine will for the edification and salvation of the church, and, therefore, in that respect cannot be separated; yet, as to what directly and properly belongs to their immediate object, the New Testament is as perfect a constitution for the worship, government and discipline of the New Testament church, and as perfect a rule for the particular duties of its members, as the Old Testament was for the worship, discipline and government of the Old Testament church and the particular duties of its members."

Very early in our movement the broad distinction between the law and the gospel, as held and taught by the Disciples, attracted attention and aroused hostility. For a while the Campbells were connected with the Redstone Baptist Association. At the meeting of this Association in 1816, Alexander Campbell preached his famous sermon on *The Law and the Gospel*, from Romans viii: 3, which created such a

---

* Heb. i: 1-2.

† Heb. viii: 6-13; II Cor. iii: 6-11; Rom. viii: 2-3; vi: 14; Gal. iii: 24.

stir among the members of the Association that the Campbells were compelled to withdraw for the sake of peace. With us Christianity is not a modified form of Judaism; the gospel is not an appendix to the law; no precept of the old covenant *as* such is binding upon us. If a precept in that covenant is binding upon us, it is because it has been re-enacted and promulgated in the New. With many precepts this is true — they are found in both. But the authority which binds them upon us is found in the New. Just as many of our present civil laws were laws for the colonies when under the British crown. But these laws are now binding upon the American citizen, because they have been re-enacted and promulgated in our new Constitution, and form a part of the American law. The old law, described as "the handwriting of ordinances," Christ nailed to the cross.* The "ministration of death, written and engraven in stones," and given to the Jews by Moses, their mediator, Paul declares has been done away.† We do not send sinners to Sinai now to hear the thunderings of that law. We do not direct them to the Psalms of David, or to the utterances of the Jewish prophets to find peace. The New Testament alone is our guide to the inquiring sinner, and our law to the believing saint. The gospel testimony is given to produce saving faith;‡ the Acts of Apostles shows how men and women were made Christians under the preaching of inspired men; the epistles give directions in practical life, for individual Christians, and instructions to churches as such, while the book of Revelation is a highly symbolic description of things which were shortly to come to pass.

We are not under law, but under grace.§ The law was

---

* Col. ii:14.   † II. Cor. iii:7–11.   ‡ John xx:30–31.
§ Rom. vi:14.

for a nation only; the gospel is for the world. The law was never of authority to any but a Jew, either by birth or by purchase. It was never given to us. It was provisional and preparatory. When the new covenant was given the old one was removed. The new found its formal beginning and its first authoritative announcement on the ever-memorable Pentecost which followed Christ's ascension. From that point we go forward to find the question of salvation from sin through the merits of his blood answered. We do not send sinners to a dead covenant to find life. With us the New Testament only is a *book of authority*, and we follow this fundamental fact to its legitmate conclusions.

V. *We are peculiar in the position we give to the Messiahship and the divine Sonship of Jesus.*

With all who are known as evangelical, we hold that Jesus of Nazareth is the Messiah long promised by Jewish prophets, and that he is the only begotten Son of God. But with us this is not *an* article of faith, standing on a plane with others, but it is *the* article of faith in the Christian system. In the records of the work of apostles and evangelists we find it treated as *the problem* of the gospel. They turned all testimony to the support of the proposition — Jesus is the Christ, the Son of the Living God. John recorded his wonderful words, and preserved an account of the miraculous signs he wrought that this might be demonstrated.* The belief of this is saving faith, according to his statement. Upon this Christ built his church.† As every system centres in some fact or doctrine, as every organization among men must have some cornerstone in common thought and faith, so in the system revealed in the New Testament and the church built by Christ and called his own.

---

* John, xx: 30-31.   † Matt. xvi: 15-18.

It was this which in the beginning men were required to believe and to confess before they were baptized.* Properly speaking, this constitutes *the* Christian confession of faith. We lift it above all other things, it is pre-eminent above all other teaching. We sweep away all speculations, and place the fact of the Messiahship and the divine Sonship of Jesus in their stead, as the one thing to be believed. As the definition of the circle in geometry embraces within itself every proposition afterward deduced and demonstrated in the further prosecution of that study, so there lies enwrapped in this brief proposition all revealed truth. Our after-growth in knowledge is but an enlargement of our conception of this pregnant proposition. The emphasis we place upon it, the position we assign it, the use we make of it, constitute one of our peculiarities.

VI. *In reference to spiritual influence in conversation, we are peculiar.*

To correct a popular mistake, I desire to state, with with all possible clearness, that we believe in the existence, the personality, the divinity of the Holy Spirit. We believe that he is the author of our conversion. We teach that he is the abiding comforter, and that he dwells in Christians. But we repudiate all theories of direct spiritual influence exerted, independent of the word of God, upon sinners, to make them Christians. Others teach the absolute need of the direct agency, and work to enable the sinner to believe, to repent, and to obey the commandments of God. We reject this, and with it all theories of human depravity which render it necessary. We hold that no special divine influence, super-added to the word to energize it, is either needed or promised. We believe that the Word faithfully preached

---

* Acts, viii: 36–38.

produces faith, and that where it fails to do so, the fault is in man, in the quality and condition of the soil, not in the lack of energy or spiritual force in the seed. Paul says faith comes by hearing the Word of God.* When Paul and his companions entered the synagogue in Inconium, they so spake the Word of the Lord that a great multitude of both Jews and Greeks believed.† If it be impossible for man to believe unless there be exerted over him some subtle influence to make him believe, where is there ground for any moral quality in faith, or any just ground of condemnation for not believing? Yet our Savior says, "He that believeth not shall be damned."‡ Nor does any man need some subtle power, independent of that which dwells in God's Word, to enable him to repent and turn. God calls him to turn. Then he has the power. He demands repentance. Then man can repent. The revelation of the fearful consequences of sin, the marvellous goodness of God, the pathetic pleadings of the cross, are to lead men to repentance and reformation of life. He needs no magic power to enable him to bow down in humble, filial obedience. The call of God runs upon the supposition, from first to last, that man can heed the call and be saved. He treats man as a rational, responsible, free, moral agent. The word he sends to us is the word of the Spirit. He is the great revealer. He works on sinners, so far as we know, only through the word. Christ, in speaking of the coming of the spirit, says distinctly, " Whom the world cannot receive."§ We, therefore, in rejecting these theories, of necessity reject the anxious seat, with all that belongs to the anxious seat system. We teach men that they are able to hear, to believe, to repent, to obey, and so, to be saved. Perhaps no point, of all that is peculiar to us, has given greater offence than

---

* Rom. x:17.   † Acts, xiv:1.   ‡ Mark, xvi:16.   § John, xiv:17.

this. And, yet, it is a necessary result of our fundamental principle, and is in perfect accord with apostolic practice in preaching. Where do you find an apostle teaching men of this inability? Where do you find them inviting them to come forward to be prayed for, that they may be converted? Where do we find an inspired preacher closing a meeting with many seeking? These are modern things. They spring from modern theories of man's necessity. Worse still, these theories are often mischievous in their consequences. The word is the seed of the kingdom; it converts the soul; it imparts life; it is God's power to save.* We reject all theories which make his word a dead letter, and that teach sinners to expect and await some special spiritual quickening power apart from it.

VII. *We are peculiar in our teachings concerning the* DESIGN *of Christian baptism.*

But, perhaps, not *so* peculiar as many suppose. There seems to be an idea quite common that the one great and overshadowing peculiarity of the Disciples lies just here. I suppose I would not exaggerate were I to say that if the masses outside of our membership were asked to state the peculiarities of the Disciples, a majority would state that their first and chief peculiarity is concerning the *design* of baptism. Yet, in doing so, they would do us an injustice. For, neither in point of time, nor in degree of importance, is this chief. Our peculiarity concerning this ordinance is the out-growth and an after-development of our central and fundamental peculiarity, which, as already stated, is restoration.

To correct a common but gross misconception, let me say, *we do not believe in what is popularly understood by the phrase*

---

* Rom. 1:16.

"*baptismal regeneration.*" We attach no mystic, magic virtue to the baptismal waters, or to the act of obedience in this ordinance. We do not teach a water salvation. So far from this, we teach, with a clearness and constancy, which it seems should have made such a mistake impossible, that unless this ordinance is, in each case, preceded by a heartfelt faith, and a genuine repentance, it is not worthy the name of Christian baptism. Or, as Mr. Campbell put it in his debate with Dr. Rice, "I have said a thousand times, that if a person were to be immersed twice seven times in the Jordan for the remission of sins, or for the reception of the Holy Spirit, it would avail nothing more than the wetting the face of a babe, *unless his heart is changed by the Word and Spirit of God.*"*

Our peculiarity is this: We teach that, according to the Scriptures, baptism is for the remission of sins. Or, to elaborate the statement, we teach that baptism is one of three divinely-appointed conditions upon which God promises to forgive an alien's sins. You will do us a favor by remembering this statement, and thinking it carefully over, item by item. You will see that we do not place baptism by itself. Faith and repentance go with it and before it. You will see that it is not held as a *cause* of forgiveness, but a *condition*. It has no *essential* connection with pardon, but stands related to it only by virtue of a divine appointment. We do not say God cannot forgive without it. We speak only of what is promised. It is not a condition upon which hangs the promise of pardon to any but to aliens The Christian finds forgiveness through repentance, confession and prayer.

Is it, then, a divinely-appointed condition which God promises the forgiveness of the alien's sins? This is clearly

---

* Campbell and Rice Debate, p. 544.

a question of fact. To the law and to the testimony for some of the reasons for our teaching. I can give only a few passages to answer the question, Has God placed baptism before the promise of present salvation or forgiveness?

"And he said unto them, Go ye into all the world and preach the gospel to every creature. He that believeth and is baptized shall be saved; but he that believeth not shall be damned." Mark xvi: 15-16.

On what two things does salvation here depend? Is baptism one of them?

"Then Peter said unto them, Repent and be baptized every one of you in the name of Jesus Christ for the remission of sins, and ye shall receive the gift of the Holy Ghost." Acts ii: 33.

What two things did Peter command his audience to do? Did he command them to do these two things *for* remission of sins? Is baptism one of the things commanded?

"And now why tarriest thou? Arise, and be baptized, and wash away thy sins, calling on the name of the Lord." Acts xxii: 16.

What did Ananias command Paul to do? Did he command him to wash away his sins? In what act?

"For as many of you as have been baptized into Christ have put on Christ." Gal. iii: 27.

How does Paul here say we enter into Christ, or put on Christ? Is there promise of forgiveness outside of Christ? I give these passages only to indicate the tendency of the testimony of the Scriptures, and to show something of the ground of our teaching on this point.

VIII. *In reference to the subjects of baptism, or the persons who are scripturally qualified for baptism, we are peculiar.*

For, while we are in general accord with all Baptist bodies in practising believer's baptism only, we differ from them in this: We do not demand the narration of an experience; we do not require them to spend a season in seeking; we do not require them to say they believe they are already forgiven; we do not require them to come before the church to be voted upon. None of these things were required in New Testament times, and we do not require them now. As then, so now, heartfelt faith in Christ, with a genuine repentance of sin, is enough. As an indication that Christ publicly confessed, was, and therefore still is, sufficient, we find that in the great commission it reads, faith first, then baptism; in the cases recorded, as occurring under inspired preaching like Paul to the jailer,* and Philip to the eunuch,† it was heartfelt faith in Christ, confessed, and then baptism without delay, and then rejoicing.

If it be objected that this makes access to this ordinance too easy by not hedging it in with sufficient restrictions, our answer is: first, perhaps it is not so easy as you suppose. We require a heartfelt faith and a genuine repentance. Secondly, what right have we to hedge it in by restriction which our Lord, who gave it, has not seen fit to place around it? If it be said that the simple confession required is not enough to keep out heretics and false teachers who may desire to come in, we answer it was not enough to do that in apostolic times, for Paul says false brethren had come into the Galatian churches in his time,‡ and yet *they* did not endeavor to prevent this by the imposition of more stringent conditions, but continued to practice this simple confession of faith. Should it be objected further, that hypocrites can make this confession and so come in, we reply, so can hypocrites give in most glowing experiences, or meet the requirements of the most rigid conditions you

---

* Acts xvi: 30-34. † Acts viii: 35-39. ‡ Gal. ii: 4.

may see fit to impose, provided they are determined to deceive. Would it not be well to reflect also that in your zeal to keep out all these of whom you have spoken, there is danger of imposing conditions which would be stumbling stones and hindrances in the way of some honest souls whom the Lord would receive? I think we have kept quite as clear of these objectionable characters as others, and it is certainly well not to be wise above what is written.

IX. I come now to consider the last point in our peculiarities. *In at least two things, concerning the Lord's Supper, we are peculiar.*

1. In its weekly observance. We teach that the Lord's Supper should be observed each Lord's Day. The Christians in the beginning certainly met on the first day of each week. We learn that one purpose — if not *the* purpose of their meeting — was to break bread.* This was a part of their regular worship on the first day. The day which was set apart to commemorate the resurrection of our Savior, found also spread in the midst of the Disciples the table on which were the memorials of his sacrificial death. It should be so now. While in this we are not in accord with any religious body known to me, we are in perfect accord, in theory if not in practice, with such great reformers and leaders as Calvin and Wesley, and a host of others.

2. Our position on the question of close communion is peculiar. We hold that the Supper is simply and only a *memorial* feast. We emphasize and exalt the *memorial* idea to the exclusion of every other which has, in the course of time, attached itself to this observance. "*Do this in memory of me.*" This is the full explanation of the divine im-

---

* Acts xx: 7.

port of this simple and sacred observance. We eat, and drink, and worship as we remember our suffering Savior. We do not partake of the emblems to signify our indorsation of others who may choose to partake at the same time. Paul says, "Let a man examine himself, and so let him eat of that bread and drink of that cup, for he that eateth and drinketh unworthily, eateth and drinketh damnation to himself."* Fix clearly in your mind the idea that it is *simply* a memorial feast, and you will be prepared to understand me when I say that the Disciples are neither open-communionists nor close-communionists. In this view it is no more reasonable to speak of *open* or *close*, in connection with the Lord's Supper, than it would be in connection with singing, prayer, or the contribution. These are acts of worship in which Christians unite, but who thinks of raising such questions about them?

And, now, that you have listened patiently to this statement of our peculiarities, presented, I humbly trust, in none other than a Christian spirit, I take the liberty of asking you, in the same spirit, what you think of them. "Not exactly the points that current reports present," do you reply? Well, that may be; but I do not think I overstep the bounds of modesty in claiming that what I say on these matters is worthy of more weight with you than that which Madame Rumor may present. I have enjoyed the best possible opportunities of knowing exactly what the Disciples believe and teach. I was born among the Disciples; my venerable father is a preacher among them of nearly fifty years standing; I have been brought up on their literature, and I attended their largest school; I know their leading

---

* I. Cor. xi: 28–29.

men throughout this entire land. I now candidly present this as their views upon the points involved. "Well," says another, "the points in which you are peculiar are neither so numerous, nor are they so great as I expected to hear." I am glad of that. I do sincerely regret that there exists any necessity for our being peculiar on any point. I love to think of those things in which we all agree, rather than of those in which we differ. I rejoice that the changes which have taken place in the religious world during the last half century have caused these points to appear less peculiar than formerly they did. For one, I rejoice in the general drift of religious thought. I hope for a better day. But, in the meantime, could you advise us to relinquish our position and abandon our work? Is not our aim worthy of zealous endeavor? Would it not be better for a divided religious world to go back to the unity of the beginning, casting aside all creeds but the Bible and all names but Christ's? Is it not true that the New Testament alone is the book of authority for the Church of Christ and for its members? Would it not be better to sweep speculations and dogmas away by giving to the doctrine of the Messiahship and divine Sonship of Jesus the place it occupied at first? Would it not be a gain to truth, at least, if we would attach to the ordinances of Baptism and the Lord's Supper the significance which their Author gave them? And, would not we come nearer to primitive preaching and practice if, instead of teaching men to look for strange sights and sounds, and mysterious and inexplicable spiritual influences, we should exalt the word of the Lord as the faith-giving and converting and saving power of God?

But, if you are not able to agree with me in these matters, I sincerely trust you may cheerfully and heartily agree with me to exercise that Christian charity which will not allow our differences to kindle into animosity; that you will join with me in praying for the peace and prosperity of all them that love our Lord Jesus in sincerity; and, that we will renew our prayerful study of the sacred volume, hoping for the time when we may see eye to eye, and face to face. The Lord hasten that day. Amen.

www.ingramcontent.com/pod-product-compliance
Lightning Source LLC
Chambersburg PA
CBHW021150230426
43667CB00006B/337